The Standard Book of Dog Breeding

A New Look

By Dr. Alvin Grossman

Doral Publishing

Wilsonville, Oregon
1992

Published by Doral Publishing, 10451 Palmeras Dr., Sun City, AZ 85373
Printed in the United States of America.
Copyedited by Luana Luther
Book design by Mary Jung
Sketches by Tim Bakke
Typesetting by Pioneer Graphics, Wilsonville, OR 97070

Third Printing

Library of Congress Card Number: 91-70232
ISBN: 0-944875-18-1

Grossman, Alvin.
   The standard book of dog breeding : a new
   look / Alvin Grossman. -- Wilsonville, Or. :
Doral Pub., c1992.

   p. ; cm.

   Includes bibliographical references and
index.
   ISBN 0-944875-18-1

   1. Dogs--Breeding.   2. Dogs--Genetics.
I. Title.
SF427.2.G   636.7'082 20
                             91-70232

DEDICATION

To my grandchildren Matthew, Kimberley and Brett

Dr. Alvin Grossman.

Other books by Alvin Grossman

- Breeding Better Cocker Spaniels
- The American Cocker Spaniel
- The Standard Book of Dog Breeding
- The Great American Dog Show Game
- Winning with Pure Bred Dogs - Design for Success (with Beverly Grossman)
- Data Processing for Educators (with Robert Howe)

Videos:

- The Life in the Dog Show Game Series

Contents

Ch. Salilyn's Condor.

First Things First

The world of purebred dogs is truly a fascinating one. It can become all inclusive, which for many becomes an entirely new way of life, or one can invest only a part of oneself and still enjoy and participate in many of the activities offered. Like anything else in this world, one gets out of it what one puts into it. Breeding and showing can be extremely satisfying, fascinating, and full of joy, but can also be extremely cruel, frustrating, and heart-breaking. Most breeders experience both the joys and the heartbreaks.

The prospect of engaging in some phase of breeding or exhibiting appeals to some types of people more than to others. Usually there is an appeal to those who are competitive and creative in nature. Breeding is a creative art whereby the breeder fashions his ideal concept based upon a mental image of perfection. It is not uncommon to find that most successful breeders are also artistic to some degree and have the ability to perceive space/depth relationships. Exhibiting dogs is a competitive sport which often serves as the motivation for constant improvement of the breed.

Most available literature advises the budding novice to obtain the very best bitch he or she can afford and proceed from that point with a sound, well-thought-out breeding program. On the surface this appears to be excellent advice, but a closer look reveals many obstacles.

First is the question of what constitutes a *good* bitch. Second, there is the problem of where the novice might find this good bitch. Third, on the assumption the good bitch is found, it is not likely she would be available to a novice breeder, money being no object. In addition, how can a novice breeder possibly be expected to follow through with a sound, well-thought-out breeding program at this stage of his development as a breeder?

By advising *everyone* to start with that good bitch, the assumption is made that everyone wants to be and is cut out to be a breeder. A person's probability of success as a breeder can almost be predicted in advance. There are certain abilities that enable some people to achieve a greater degree of success than others. For example, those who have an innate "eye for a dog" have a much easier time understanding the various abstract concepts of breeding such as *balance*. Other individuals, by employing great tenacity and persistence, have taught themselves to acquire an "eye for a dog." Still others never achieve this ability and do not become successful breeders—yet they may and often do excel in many other areas involving dogs.

The importance of having an "eye for a dog" cannot be overstated. As mentioned previously, the breeder attempts to fashion his ideal which is based upon his personal mental concept. If that mental concept lacks clarity, is not well defined and balanced, then the breeder cannot possibly translate it into reality. There are some extremely knowledgeable breeders who have never attained this faculty and whereas they can "talk a great dog," they are not able to produce an outstanding specimen.

Obviously, some people are just not cut out to be breeders and have been forced to assume the role because it is the expected thing to do. Any person who finds the prospect of becoming involved with dogs a fascinating one would do well to examine his talents, abilities, interests, and expectations before committing himself to a specific course of action.

There is a great turn-over among breeders, with the average kennel life lasting but five years. How and in what manner an individual begins participating in the world of breeding and showing and from whom and in what manner he acquires his basic knowledge are very important and will contribute strongly to that person's eventual success or failure. This in turn will be reflected on the breed as a whole, which makes an in-depth discussion of this matter desirable.

It is amazing how many people expect to be able to purchase good dogs from breeders who have not proven themselves to be successful in producing good dogs. One reason is that it doesn't take much—perhaps a few blue ribbons and some puppy match trophies—to convince the average beginner that he is dealing with the greatest and most successful of breeders. While it is possible that these breeders could have good stock, they are usually not in a position to sell their best products to others because they are striving for their own place in the sun. Therefore, a good rule of thumb for the beginner is to buy from a successful and well-established breeder. Any breeder's reputation should be judged by objective criteria—what he has actually accomplished during his career as a breeder. Have his dogs finished with good show records and in good competition or did they finish in poor competition taking a long time to do so? Does he sell his good dogs to others or does he keep them for himself? Are his dogs and their bloodlines in demand? Are they producing (in terms of quality) lines? Do others breed to his dogs? The answers to all these questions should be easy to obtain and easy to check. A breeder should not be judged on the size or scope of his operations or on information volunteered by himself or hearsay related by others.

It is not truly possible to separate the breeder from the exhibitor, although it is possible to separate the exhibitor from the breeder. The only objective criteria for success or failure as a breeder lies within the show ring. While many breeders might feel their main interest is primarily concerned with the various aspects of breeding, they must nevertheless display their prowess with some regularity within the show ring, which provides the only opportunity of displaying their progress to the world. To neglect this phase would be to invite lack of progress in their breeding program, and any breeding program which does not progress has very little to offer.

It is very important to the eventual success of a beginner for him to form a good relationship with a successful and knowledgeable breeder. Breeding is an art which requires much thought, study, understanding, and perception. The beginner should be encouraged to ask questions, sift the facts out of much advice and many opinions that are offered, develop his eye, constantly add to his experience, etc. The novice is not gifted with these insights over night and must acquire them from others who have previously gone the route. Breeders, more than anyone else, realize these facts, and they instantly back off from the beginner with the know-it-all attitude. On the other hand, no true breeder can resist helping the sincere novice who really wants to learn.

The first step toward engaging in a breeding/exhibiting program is to purchase a good dog or bitch. Some novices will be offered better opportunities than will others. If a novice is serious about a show career for his about-to-be-purchased puppy and will engage the services of a professional handler, he will be offered a better quality puppy. A novice may assure a breeder that he will show a puppy to the best of his own ability and will find it difficult to understand the breeder's reluctance to let the puppy go under these circumstances. If the beginner will allow the breeder to guide him with respect to the puppy's upbringing to some extent, and for the first breeding in the case of a bitch, he will often be offered a better quality puppy.

The novice should be aware of the fact that whereas he may be able to buy a fairly good bitch, his chances of having a great or an outstanding bitch are practically nil. In any breeding program the importance of a good bitch is paramount. A good bitch is one which not only is endowed with the necessary physical traits enabling her to be a winner of some note in the show ring, but also backs up her physical attributes with a heritage enabling her to reproduce these traits. To this must be added physical and mental stability as well. Most breeders would not consider selling a bitch of this quality to a novice, for they would want some guarantee that the bitch would be shown and bred to advantage. It is bitches such as these that found entire kennels and bloodlines and it takes but one.

It should be apparent that the bitch that is available to the novice must be a lesser bitch. How much lesser depends on from whom she is purchased, how much she is purchased for, and how much the novice has to offer in return. This bitch ideally is one which, if properly bred, will produce better than herself with her offspring upgraded in one generation.

Purchase prices differ somewhat from one part of the country to another. There should be some similarity in price, depending upon quality, within any one general area. A young puppy should be less expensive than an older puppy, and an unpointed and/or unproven bitch should be less expensive than a pointed, finished, or proven bitch. While a young puppy can be obtained at less expense, the buyer should understand that by obtaining one so young he is taking many risks. If the puppy matures with the quality indicated by its early promise, then the buyer has purchased a good individual at relatively low cost. On the other hand, should some serious fault appear that was not indicated at the early age (such as the second teeth coming in bad), then the novice is encumbered with a faulty specimen on which he has wasted time, effort, and money, to say nothing of his own emotional involvement and his stymied breeding program. All these factors should be taken into account when contemplating the purchase of a young puppy. It becomes quite obvious that a larger sum spent in the beginning often proves to be the cheapest in the long run. Ideally, the best time to buy a puppy for the purposes of showing or breeding is about eight months of age. By then the puppy should look pretty close to the way it is going to look at maturity, will have gone through most of the various ungainly stages, and will still be young enough to adjust to a new home with little or no difficulty and still be enjoyed as a puppy.

It is much easier to buy a better quality male puppy than a bitch puppy. Many breeders won't keep males unless one comes along that is of "Specials quality" or is vital to their breeding program. While there isn't an overabundance of "Specials quality" males, there are many good males which are capable of having good show careers and which, for lack of takers, end up in pet homes. Therefore, many breeders are delighted to sell their above average males at reasonable prices to those interested in showing—in many cases whether they be shown professionally or not. There are some circumstances when a novice would be further ahead with a male of this caliber than he would be with a lesser bitch. If the enjoyment of showing a dog is of more interest than the prospect of becoming a breeder, a good quality male would add to that participation and enjoyment, whereas a lesser quality bitch, which would have to be bred in order to upgrade her potential, would be a detriment.

Sometimes the opportunity to lease a bitch is offered. Bitches offered for lease are usually older, although not necessarily so, for sometimes bitches that are pointed, proven, or even finished are offered for lease. Usually in such cases they are offered for lease so that the breeder may make room for younger stock but still control the destiny of the bitch offered for lease. A typical lease agreement provides that the lessor selects the stud dog to which the bitch is to be bred and receives part of the litter in return. When the obligation has been met, the bitch usually becomes the property of the lessee. The lessee usually pays any fees or costs involved not only with regard to the breeding but also with respect to raising the litter. There are many, many different types of arrangements. Too often if these arrangements are not set down in writing they can result in hard feelings on both sides. A lease arrangement can provide a beginning breeder with the opportunity of obtaining the type and quality of bitch not usually obtainable by a novice. On the other hand, a beginning breeder can also be tied up in an unrealistic lease arrangement from which he will not benefit in the slightest and will be saddled with an undesirable bitch as well. Therefore, be cautious before committing yourself in a lease arrangement, and any such arrangement should be put in writing for the protection of all concerned.

The typical beginning breeder finds himself with (1) what was originally a pet dog, (2) an improved dog that is still not good enough to show or breed, and (3) a first really promising dog. Some people never progress beyond that improved dog that is still not good enough to show or breed, but they do show it (and when it doesn't win, they cry "foul"), or they breed it (and when it doesn't produce, they also cry "foul")! Eventually they drop by the wayside, bitter and disillusioned.

The acquisition of dogs should entail the responsibility of caring for them properly. They should be kept clean, trimmed, brushed, and well taken care of at all times. If these standards cannot be maintained, the number of dogs should be reduced to the point where these standards can be maintained.

Of course it is impossible to keep an unlimited number of dogs and still maintain a home within a residential neighborhood. In addition to one's own sanity, there are the county or city zoning laws to be observed. Therefore, when that first good litter of puppies comes along, the novice is often forced to choose between retaining one or more of the puppies or his original and older pets. For many there is no choice—they either decide breeding is not for them, retain their older dogs, and sell the puppies, or they make the effort to find good homes for their pets and continue on with their good breeding stock. For many people this choice is an agonizing one—a choice not lightly made. It is often this situation that decides whether a future breeder is born or is lost to the fancy.

There is much to be said for a housing situation which necessitates strict selection of stock. The breeder does not become overwhelmed with maintenance and his stock is uniformly of high quality. While these restrictions must result in a limited breeding program as compared to a more experimental and expanded type of breeding program, they, nevertheless, do not have any real effect on the eventual success or failure of a breeder. There are many outstanding and successful breeders operating with as few as half a dozen animals with one (or less) litter per year as there are outstanding and successful breeders with unlimited facilities, many dogs, and multiple litters per year.

Most people find that when they commit themselves to pursuing the fascinations of breeding, their lives change quite drastically. Non-doggy friends are gradually replaced by doggy friends, and one's values and goals often become altered as well. Non-doggy friends don't appreciate broken dates because a litter of puppies is on the way, nor do they appreciate that litter being raised in the kitchen. Doggy friends don't turn up their noses at a bit of dog hair, nor do they become uncomfortable in the presence of a playful puppy. Therefore, it is advisable for anyone embarking upon this venture to embark gradually and slowly lest he find out it doesn't suit him or vice versa. If such is the case, he then can reverse his direction with a minimum amount of difficulty.

Everyone should set some type of goal for himself with a time limit—a flexible time limit to take unavoidable delays into account. From the time a person becomes really interested in breeding good dogs and sets out to do so, to the time when positive results can be expected, should not take forever. If some positive results cannot be seen within the first few years, such as breeding one's first winner, then something is wrong. The foundation bitch is wrong, the advice followed is wrong, the stud dog selected is wrong, etc., and a careful reappraisal is in order.

Most breeders encounter some difficulties along the way. Those who have become successful obviously didn't stumble over the various roadblocks in their way—or if they did, they had the capacity to pick themselves up and continue toward their goals.

The St. Bernard.

Getting Down to Basics

The evolution of a breeder is marked by various stages of development. There is the first stage where interest and desire are born; the second stage is where this interest and desire are implemented by the acquisition of quality breeding stock; the third stage takes place when breeding plans are formulated to improve upon the original stock; and the fourth stage is launched when the breeder can first exercise his own selection in evaluating the results of his breeding program. This chapter will deal with this last stage along with some highlights of the more important, though often overlooked, general principles of breeding.

Most beginning breeders feel twinges of self-doubt when it comes to choosing the best puppy or puppies from their early litters. Many articles have been written telling how to select the best puppy in a litter but most are merely a re-phrasing or re-wording of the breed Standard. In other words, one is told to pick the puppy with the best of this and the best of that, but saying or reading it and actually *doing* it are two different things. The beginning breeder usually makes every effort to learn about each and every little trait so that his selections will be the correct ones.

As a breeder, you know that your breed is classified as a Sporting Dog, a Hound, a Terrier, etc. Many owners dismiss the possibility of using their dogs for the purpose for which they were originally bred. Primarily, such owners are just not interested, but even if they were, they undoubtedly would say, "Look at what it would do to the coat!" and not give the matter further thought. However, in order to appreciate your breed you need to know that every breed came into being for a specific purpose. This is what the authors of the breed Standards had in mind when writing the Standards. While breeders may not wish to follow through in this direction, they should, nevertheless, keep in mind the basic purpose for which the breed was created, *else what is the point?*

There are various reasons for the many existing breeding programs of today which run the gamut from an idealistic "improvement of the breed" to blatant desire to "breed a winner." Be that as it may, even those interested in breeding nothing more than dogs that can win in the show ring would find that they would be able to breed a better quality dog if they were able to understand some of the implications behind the Standard. Memorizing the Standard will not help breed a better dog, but understanding what it is attempting to convey will. All breeders would do well to view the dog in terms of what it was originally and what it was expected to do. By keeping these very basic principles in mind, it becomes quite clear why certain traits are emphasized more than others. It is definitely not meant to say that the glamour should be discarded or even overlooked—on the contrary, the glamour is *part* of any breed, but it should be superimposed upon a basically sound, well-balanced dog.

Far too many breeders seem overly concerned with the individual parts of the dog. Many breeders subconsciously feel that when they know, to their own satisfaction, what a good head is, what a good front is, what constitutes good neck and shoulders, what a well-angulated rear looks like, etc., that there is nothing more for them to learn. Their learning all but stops and they continually evaluate their dogs and those belonging to others as an assemblage of the various "parts." The concept of relating the various parts of the dog to each other and viewing this relationship as a *whole*, rather than as a series of individual good or bad traits, is the *key* that so many breeders never grasp. It is not possible to overemphasize the necessity of understanding this point, for this is the concept of *balance* and is so very basic, and so very necessary, to successful breeding.

Understanding the concept of balance makes it easy to understand that balance is the fundamental principle on which selection and breeding plans should be based. Any one part of the dog's anatomy being in proportion to any other part of the dog's anatomy is the clue to the concept of balance. The result is *the dog as a whole is more important than any one of its individual parts.*

It is balance that breed Standards are all about. Yet there are breeders who inadvertently perpetuate faulty breeding programs because they are not able to understand or accept this. If they are told their dog is steep shouldered and its excellent rear quarters are therefore ineffective, they will argue that most dogs have steep shoulders, which, to a point, is true. However, they do not take *degree* into account and it is the degree that is important. When dealing with a dog's shoulder placement, one needs to be aware of the small but major difference between "excessively" steep and "acceptably" steep. What would have been an excellent rear on a balanced dog with the proper shoulder placement becomes an over-angulated rear for the steep shouldered dog and as a result must eventually cause serious problems. What these breeders cannot seem to appreciate is the fact that they have created an artificial and extremely faulty dog. In its own way, a dog such as this is just as faulty as the dog with a very bad head, a very long back, a very poor front, a very weak rear, etc. The inherent danger in such a dog is that it doesn't *look* faulty—rather, it often looks quite spectacular. When shown under incompetent judges, a dog such as this *can* and often does win, thus making it even more of a menace to the breed as a whole, especially should it be a male promoted at stud.

Another popular misconception about what is good and what is bad pertains to neck and shoulders. Many breeders feel that "outstanding neck and shoulders" are only those that blend so smoothly and perfectly that it is difficult to tell where one ends and the other begins. Breeders who are concerned with this trait usually won't settle for anything less. The result is that by having lost sight of the "whole dog," they invariably end up with lightly boned, shelly specimens which are "poor doers." It is true that they usually obtain the very smoothest shoulders possible, but then they wonder why their dogs lack bone, substance, and size. These breeders would be ever so much further ahead if they would allow themselves to think in terms of the *whole dog* and *learn* that it is the angle of the shoulder that is vitally important and that the smoothness is "secondary."

While it is absolutely necessary to know about the various traits of your breed and appreciate them for what they are, it is *more* important to *put them all together first* and view the results as a whole. If they don't add up, they are basically worthless regardless of how outstanding any one of them may be by itself. In addition, it is just not possible to set down a list of the various characteristics to take heed of, and have them apply to each and every individual in the same way. There are differences among many of the bloodlines in a breed with respect to the growth of puppies, and the consequent development of their many and various traits. What might be considered as vital in one line need not be of great importance in another. For example, "heavy shouldered" puppies need not be of great concern in lines where this is a *known* phase of development. This *is* a *known* phase of development in certain lines, and it is also *known* to pass at an approximate age. The same holds true for "low-on-leg" puppies and "plained-out-headed" puppies, to name a few specifics. When these traits occur, and are the rule rather than the exception, they do not and should not loom as formidable threats. However, should these same developmental characteristics appear spontaneously in lines not noted for their appearance, they then must be regarded in an entirely different light.

Just about every trait a puppy possesses is subject to change. Beautiful, plush, puppy heads can turn into plain, poor adult heads—a long neck with smooth shoulders can turn into a short neck with heavy shoulders—a short backed puppy can become a long backed adult—a well angulated rear can straighten, etc. While these develop-

mental changes are not particularly rare, it is extremely rare that characteristics which are originally faulty and undesirable correct themselves and become desirable. It is for this reason that the outstanding young puppy has a far greater chance of achieving maturity as a good specimen than the so-so puppy has of maturing into an outstanding adult. Breeders who keep a mediocre puppy with the hope that maturity will bring about desired changes are merely kidding themselves.

It is because knowledge of the various developmental changes takes time to acquire that the experienced breeder has a big edge over the beginner. Through experience a breeder learns many of the various idiosyncrasies that pertain to the line in which he is breeding. If he has been associated with one line over a long period of time, it becomes quite easy for him to exercise his own selection with assurance and self-confidence in his choices. He knows what developmental changes to expect in his stock and at what times to expect them. It is fairly easy for him to predict the potential of his young stock as it is for him to select them originally. When faced with a puppy from an entirely different line, a breeder's evaluation must be concerned only with the puppy as it presently appears rather than its future potential. What pertains to one bloodline with respect to growth and development often does not apply to another.

When evaluating a litter of puppies, it is only natural and desirable to pick each one up and attempt to stand it in a show stance so that the puppy's various traits can be seen, admired, faulted, and compared. This is also done to acquaint the puppy with the ritual of "stacking" and to afford the opportunity of giving the puppy necessary handling and individual attention. While all these practices are both necessary and worthwhile, it is a common mistake not to go beyond them. The stacked position is not natural to the dog when carried to the extreme, and too many breeders carry it to the extreme. A dog that is built properly will stack almost naturally. However, a dog that is not constructed properly can also be made to create the desired effect by pulling it off the grooming stand by its tail, swinging its front legs out from under it, and tugging on its tail so that it will crouch and lean forward. By starting early with a young puppy and applying enough force and repetition, *any* dog can be manipulated so as to assume the desired look in a stack and therefore satisfy the image in the breeder's mind. So, what does this prove? It doesn't really change the dog's conformation, but it does tend to create an entirely false conception of the dog not only on the part of the viewer at ringside but all too often on the part of the breeder and/or owner as well. Thus the breeder may come to believe that he has something other than what he really does have. Obviously, such self-deception does nothing toward creating a better specimen. When a dog such as this is owner-shown, the owner never does have the opportunity to view his dog out of the stacked position and in motion. Sometimes the breeder really has no idea that his dog, which has been cranked so beautifully into an artificial pose, loses every bit of its manufactured outline as soon as it is left to its own devices.

Therefore, the astute breeder will not delude himself by judging and evaluating his dogs *only* in a posed position. He will pay as much or more attention to how his dogs look on the ground and how the dogs handle themselves without benefit of being stacked. The dog which *sets itself up properly* under natural conditions, which has a good top line, which has rear quarters that are let down properly and are well under it, which has a front that is straight, and which carries its head proudly and high is the dog which has what it takes and is the one deserving the most consideration.

There is an intangible quality possessed by some dogs and not by others. Some call this intangible quality "heart," others call it "spirit," and still others might call it "showmanship." Whatever it is called, it is that extra something that makes one dog stand out from another, even though they be of equal conformation. There are dogs which look absolutely breathtaking when viewed on a table; put the same dog down on the ground and it is lost amidst a group. Then there is another dog, which, when viewed on a table, could use a bit more of this or a bit less of that. This dog, however, when on the ground is a standout and calls all sorts of attention to itself. This is the dog which really makes the most of what it has, which really does great things for itself and has the ability to communicate this extra something to others. This inner quality is more than showmanship, for showmanship is something that can be acquired through good training. This inner glow is almost a form of communication that takes place between the dog and the viewer, whether it be the breeder, judge, or spectator. It comes through in the form of "look at me; I'm the greatest!" It is the same quality that every top winner of every breed possesses. Without this inner quality, the most perfectly put together dog is "just another dog."

Too many breeders have a type prejudice—not a preference but a real and deep-seated prejudice. To have a type preference is only natural, necessary, and desirable in formulating one's mental concept of the ideal specimen of the breed. A type prejudice can short-circuit a successful breeding program.

When breeders have a definite prejudice in favor of one certain type of dog (and against all other types of dog) and will only breed to those dogs fitting that exact pattern with bitches of similar type and consequently retaining puppies of like type, the eventual result must be dogs of such *extreme* type that they are all but worthless. There are times in every breeding program when dogs and bitches must be utilized which do not fit exactly into the breeder's type preference. By keeping open minds, breeders should be able to take advantage of the many good traits different types of dogs have to offer, and therefore they will utilize the good traits of good dogs.

It should be noted in the foregoing that the breeder has not been advised to pick the puppy with the best head, the most outstanding neck and shoulders, the shortest back, etc. These things go without saying. Proficiency in breeding and selection will come only with experience and most breeders will come to the realization that most things will not be strictly black or white but will be made up of many shades of gray. They will also find it will be of great help if they are flexible in their approach to breeding. In breeding purebred dogs, so many times things do not turn out the way they were originally planned, and in such cases if the breeder can see another way, he is often further ahead. It is for all these reasons that this chapter has taken a general approach to the subject, in the hope of laying a basic foundation for effective breeding.

The West Highland White Terrier.

Beginning a Breeding Program

The consistent breeding of show quality dogs should be considered an art. To some breeders this comes naturally with little effort, others have to learn this art, and still others will never achieve success in this most vital and important area of purebred dogs.

To some breeders, "having an eye for a dog" is second nature. Breeders lacking this natural talent can become self-taught provided they have the intelligence and motivation to discern between the good and poor examples set before them.

To be sure, the consistent breeding of show quality specimens depends on other important factors besides the natural or acquired talents of the breeder. The breeding stock, itself, is of prime importance and should be the very best the breeder can obtain. Many breeders still operate under the illusion that second best will produce as well as the choice specimen—pedigrees being equal. This will hold true in isolated instances, of course, but it will not hold true consistently.

Another most important element contributing to the success or failure of any given breeding program is that of chance or luck. Everything else being equal, sex distribution, puppy mortality, timing, transmission of the best hereditary factors (or the poorest), etc., all depend to a great extent on chance or luck.

There is no short cut to breed improvement—no miraculous or secret formula which can put Mother Nature out of business, so to speak, and place the breeder in full control. There are, however, many do's and don'ts which could be used as a formula of sorts to minimize the chances of failure and to encourage the chances of success. These do's and don'ts are axioms of almost every breed, yet there are breeders who ignore and bypass them. There are others who take what they have to teach seriously and from these ranks come the serious and successful breeders.

The first step in any animal breeding program is to decide what is ideal. Until a breeder knows what kind of specimen he wants, he is stopped cold and can neither select the best nor discard the worst. This is where the breeder's capabilities and talents come into play, for this is the basis of selective breeding, which is the backbone of any successful breeding program.

There is more to breeding top quality dogs than breeding any given bitch to any given dog, raising the resulting litter of puppies and hoping for the best. *Quality begets quality* and a good foundation bitch is of prime importance. One can take the results of breeding a poor quality bitch to an outstanding sire and upgrade by continually breeding in turn to other outstanding sires. Eventually, quality may be attained. However, a breeder will be much further ahead in terms of time, money, effort, reputation, and success if he begins breeding properly with a *quality* bitch. Therefore, the most important thing to a beginning breeder is the acquisition of a *good* foundation bitch. This bitch should be as free as possible from any major faults that would be considered difficult to breed out in more than one generation. Certain traits are more important than other traits, and a basic understanding of these will be of major help in making a good start.

There was a time when several bitches were considered vital to any breeding program. However, due to rising costs, the diminishing availability of land, and stricter enforcement of zoning codes, this has been proven quite unnecessary. Today, big kennels are more the exception than the general rule—thus, necessity has helped breeders realize that *one* really *good* bitch is all that is needed to begin any breeding program.

A good foundation bitch should be "line bred." This means there should be some degree of relationship in the pedigree between the sire and the dam. Perhaps the sire and the dam have the same sire or the same dam or the same grandsire or the same granddam. This is important, for it ensures, to the extent possible, that the bitch's own traits are relatively well fixed and what is visible to the eye (phenotype) should be indicative—to a point—of the inheritance (genotype) behind the bitch. In other words, a line bred bitch has a better chance of producing those traits she exhibits because there is a concentration of a specific bloodline embodying those traits behind her. In comparison, a bitch which is a product of an "outcross" brings with her no assurance that she can produce anything resembling herself. An outcross signifies no degree of relationship between sire and dam in any given pedigree. There are times when outcrossing is most desirable in any breeding program, but it requires an experienced breeder to deal effectively with the results. A foundation bitch with a background that is a hodgepodge is usually worthless from a breeding standpoint regardless of how attractive the bitch may be or how ably she can compete in the show ring.

The proper way to select that good specimen entails laying a basic foundation so the beginner has some idea (and can convey that idea) as to what he really wants. If the beginning breeder would do a bit of homework before starting out to obtain that good foundation bitch, many mistakes could be avoided.

The vernacular of the world of dog breeding can be very confusing. Bloodlines, pedigrees, registered names, call names, etc., all sound like so much "Greek" to the uninitiated. Add to this the dog show jargon and the terminology used to describe various parts of the dog, and it is easy to understand how confusing this can sound to the beginning breeder. Therefore, he should familiarize himself with the various bloodlines so that when a breeder rattles off a pedigree to him, it has some meaning. He should also familiarize himself with some of the more common terms that are used in talking about dogs, such as "stifles," "hocks," "stop," "layback," etc. It would also be of great help to have some idea of which bloodlines are producing bloodlines and which are not. In this way he can distinguish, to some extent, between some breeders' facts and fancies. It is a good idea to visit as many local breeders as possible, look at their dogs, and ask as many questions as deemed necessary. (A word to the wise: if an appointment is arranged in advance so the breeder has the time to spend and the opportunity to have his dogs presented at their best, the novice will be more than welcome.) He should attend some dog shows in his local area, noting which entries attract him—then ask himself why—as compared to those entries which do not attract him. He should compare his choices with the judge's choices and see if they coincide. The beginning breeder should join a local breed or all-breed club. Most offer educational programs that are quite valuable, whereas others are primarily socially oriented and so serve to introduce the new breeder to the other breeders within the community.

When the beginning breeder makes a good purchase, it is usually because some breeder has offered him a good specimen—not because the beginner has shown great acumen in his selection. Another means of putting the odds in the beginner's favor is for him to enlist the help of a professional handler who has had much experience with the breed, or another trusted breeder who has nothing for sale himself. If possible, it is best to be able to see one's prospective purchase in the flesh before buying. This is not always possible, for the quality, sex, or color desired may not be available locally. The breed magazines offer the best source of showing what is available on a nationwide basis. When contacting a breeder at a distance, make sure the one or ones selected are those who have a reputation for *quality* dogs. Try to be specific in describing what is desired with respect to color, sex, age, whether or not a show career is in the offing, etc. Ask for pictures and pedigrees of what is available *if* seriously interested—however, make sure they are returned! Remember too that distance lends enchantment, so be cautious in your selection.

So, it has been established that the bitch to be purchased should be of the bloodline desired, which, hopefully, will be a producing bloodline. She should be line bred and of show stock. Any fault in the front assembly of the bitch such as short neck, heavy shoulders, wide front, steep (excessively) shoulders, etc., is a fault that is difficult to breed out and one that should be avoided if at all possible. A good, straight front with proper neck and shoulders should be a prime requirement when looking for that good bitch. Heads can be improved upon in one generation, top line can be improved in one generation, coat can be improved (or lost completely) in one generation, and general type can be improved in one generation. Size can be altered one way or the other within one generation. Bad tail sets are difficult to improve upon as well as bad bites and slipped stifles, so all should be avoided. Disposition is all important, for disposition is passed on to the bitch's offspring through her environmental association with them, as well as being inherited. Bone, substance, and general stamina are also important factors to be considered. It is wiser to select a bitch with an air of all-over class and perhaps a few minor faults than one who has relatively few faults but who is plain and ordinary. When colors are considered, it is preferable to sacrifice markings for soundness and type. Being flexible as to choice of color is to the beginning breeder's advantage. There are times when a really nice opportunity is passed by because the bitch offered or available is the "wrong" color.

Ideally, the foundation bitch should be show quality, and whereas she might not possess the ability to finish her championship, she should, nevertheless, be able to do some winning or come very close. This is suggested primarily to serve as some criterion against which quality can be measured. Some breeders believe that it matters little what a bitch looks like if the breeding behind her is of extremely high quality. This is a fallacy. Even the best bred litters contain a percentage of pet-quality puppies which will not produce as their better quality litter mates will, even though their heritage is identical.

When a foundation bitch is purchased from an established breeder with a good reputation for winning and producing dogs, the puppies will be more in demand than will puppies from a bitch which comes from a nondescript background, even though both bitches are equal in quality and pedigree. If the bitch is capable of finishing and does finish, the puppies not only will be more in demand (which should be taken into account when deciding for or against a show career) but also will command better prices.

Whatever faults the bitch possesses often become magnified in the beginner's mind. However, whatever faults and good qualities the bitch has serve the purpose of teaching the novice about those particular traits, and in that way he begins to learn about each and every trait of the bitch. Whatever faults the foundation bitch has should be scrupulously avoided when the time comes to choose the stud and to select the puppies for retention in a breeding program. Through experience breeding becomes recognized as a series of trade offs. When one problem or fault is eliminated, another may take its place. The successful breeder is one who eliminates the major and serious problems in exchange for the minor and less serious ones.

In keeping with the above, the first step in breeding is to know your bitch. Knowledge of any given bitch is more readily acquired when the immediate ancestors are available for scrutiny. When the bitch is selected with little or no background information, knowledge of the hereditary make-up is very difficult to acquire and often impossible to learn until the bitch has produced several litters. The best possible mating for the first bitch is often made after trial and error. It is easier for the breeder to select a stud for the bitch's daughter, and still easier to breed the granddaughter properly, for by this time the astute breeder has many facts to rely upon which aid his selection.

Only when a breeder really knows his bitch is he ready to proceed with the best actual choice of a stud. Rushing to breed to the big winner of the day for no other *reason* than that it is the big winner, is not likely to bring the best litter the bitch can produce. It is as important, if not more so, to look at what a dog sires as well as at the dog himself. To be sure, the dog is certainly important in that he should possess the qualities that the bitch in question lacks and the qualities the breeder wishes to incorporate in his breeding program. If a specific trait is desired, it is far better to breed to a stud possessing this trait than to choose one which does not possess it but which *could* throw it. Confirmation of non-visible traits can be determined only by test breeding. The possession of a specific trait does not guarantee that a dog has the ability to pass it on. However, a specimen possessing a particular trait has a better chance of passing it on than does the dog which does not show it visibly.

Each breeding should be carried out with the plan that the litter-to-be will have in it a dog better than in any previous litter—not a dog "just as good."

All breeders have the tendency to overlook undesirable features or even faults, if those features or faults are accompanied by some admirable quality. As an example, a breeder might repeat a breeding that gave him a beautiful head and a weak front instead of looking for something that will give him an equally fine head with added soundness and balance in front. The mistake of the average breeder is to become absorbed in one trait, such as head, neck and shoulders, rear quarters, etc., and to strive to obtain such a characteristic to his satisfaction at the expense of the others.

More and more breeders are becoming increasingly

aware of the necessity of acquiring knowledge of the basic laws of genetics. If you wish to understand why individuals related by descent resemble each other, why variation may be expected to occur, and how to predict with a fair degree of accuracy the results of a planned mating, the study of genetics is essential. It can also be of tremendous help in the elimination of an undesirable trait and the preservation of a desirable one.

Until the basic principles of breeding are understood, along with the knowledge of the various physical traits of your breed, separately and as a whole, it is not possible to make a really good, well-thought-out breeding. Many times when a good breeding *is* made, it is made primarily on the basis of luck. "Chance" is probably a better word for it, but, whatever, it plays its part with respect to sex, color, and general health of the litter (providing all the necessary cautions have been observed).

One of the very best sources of material for the beginning breeder is the old breed magazines. In these magazines collectively is a great wealth of material on almost every subject pertaining to dogs. Lucky is the beginning breeder who is able to borrow the old breed magazines from an old-time breeder and go through them thoroughly.

When choosing a stud dog for the first litter, most novices tend to consider (1) the big winning dog of the moment, or (2) the dog belonging to a breeder-friend. In some cases either choice could be the right one, but the beginner should be aware of the fact that either choice could also be the wrong one. Being a current top winner or having been a top winner in the past does guarantee that the dog is probably free from any major faults (regardless of what his competition might say) or else he would not be or have been a top winner. There have been instances when dogs not Specialed were very cleverly advertised to the point where they became much in demand as sires and, as a result, passed on some very undesirable traits to their descendants. A top winner does offer some guarantee of his own soundness, but his ability to win is no guarantee of his ability to produce. A *much better* criterion and one that is difficult to dispute is the dog with the producing record— if he was a top show winner, so much the better. Any dog which has a producing record offers undisputable evidence of his prowess as a sire. In addition to his own traits, the traits of his various offspring should also be noted. If these traits are what is needed, then one can ask for nothing more in the way of criteria in choosing a sire.

When planning to breed a line bred bitch, the breeder must decide whether or not he wants to continue within the basic line. If he is generally satisfied with the type and quality the line is producing or if he wishes to intensify some of the traits the line is noted for, he should continue with the line breeding. Chances are, it is a safe bet to line breed for that first litter. As an example, if the bitch's head needs to be improved upon (even though her line is noted for producing beautiful heads), she should be bred to a dog from her line that has the beautiful head himself. When grading the resulting puppies, the breeder should also evaluate the results of the line breeding. Do the puppies resemble their parents and others from their line? Do they show improvement where improvement was sought, or has there been a regression in quality? Line breeding, especially close line breeding, cannot be continued indefinitely without experiencing some eventual deterioration of size, vigor, and perhaps quality.

There are times when the breeder might feel it is time for an outcross because he needs more size, bone, and substance, and he is afraid that additional line breeding will further reduce what he already feels his bitch lacks. The breeder might then select an unrelated line that is noted for the trait his bitch and her line lack, making sure the dog selected possesses this trait. When an outcross is considered, the stud should be line bred himself so as to ensure his ability to reproduce his desired traits.

The role a pedigree should play in planning a breeding is primarily that of assisting the breeder in determining whether this dog or that dog represents good line breeding or a good outcross. Some people tend to get carried away by what looks beautiful to them on paper and they build entire breeding programs on nothing but pedigree. Building a breeding program on pedigree alone is a questionable tactic. However, with time and experience, a pedigree becomes much more meaningful. When a breeder has the opportunity to see most of the dogs in a four generation pedigree, the names then bring to mind a mental picture of how the dogs actually looked. When a breeder reaches this stage, he can *use* a pedigree *most* effectively in planning a breeding.

After taking pedigree into consideration for what it is worth, the *most* important aspect in planning a breeding is to select a dog that complements the bitch. In other words, he should possess those traits that she needs, and he should have proven his ability to pass them on. If she needs more rear angulation and more coat, he should be very well angulated and carry an extremely heavy coat. To go one step further, the majority of his offspring should also be very well angulated and carry very heavy coats. Since the male cannot be the perfect dog any more than the bitch, he should at least be adequate in those points where she does not especially need help or where she excels.

To summarize briefly, it has been determined that any given bitch is to be either line bred or outcrossed and the proper stud dog which complements her has been selected. The breeding has been made, the puppies arrive, are tenderly watched over, and begin to grow up. Hopefully, it is, indeed, a good breeding, and the results yield several good prospects, all carrying the dam's good

traits and showing great improvement in the areas where she needed help. But, what if it doesn't turn out this way? What if the breeding results in general disappointment with none of the puppies showing much improvement? The breeder might well ask how this can possibly happen when all the proper aspects were taken into consideration in planning this breeding.

This brings up the concept of "dominance." Test breeding is the only *true* way of determining whether a dog or bitch is especially dominant. Here again line breeding comes into play, for the closely line bred dog or bitch has a *much* better chance of being dominant by virtue of a concentrated bloodline than the dog or bitch that is not line bred. When selecting a stud to complement a bitch, it is important to take into serious consideration the qualities of his parents as well. For example, suppose a stud is sought to improve the bitch in head. Obviously, a dog with a beautiful head is chosen, but it is also important that his parents had beautiful heads as well. Then, the stud can be considered to be "homozygous" for this trait (this is an oversimplification for the purposes of clarification, for there are innumerable inherited characteristics that go into the make-up of any one trait such as head). If the dog selected does not have parents with beautiful heads or only one parent has a beautiful head, he is said to be "heterozygous" for this characteristic and his chances of producing it are diminished. Dominant dogs and bitches are homozygous for more of their traits, while less dominant dogs and bitches are primarily heterozygous in their genetic make-up.

The great majority of dogs and bitches are probably dominant for some of their traits and not especially dominant for others. It is up to the breeder to attempt to match up the proper combination of dominant traits, which is why the dog and bitch should complement each other—that being the *best practical* way of attempting to come up with the right combinations. There are some dogs and bitches that are completely non-dominant in their genetic make-up when bred to a dominant partner, so good things result provided that partner is of top quality. In this fashion a number of dogs and bitches have "produced" when, in reality, they did everything but produce. When a non-dominant bitch is bred to a non-dominant stud, the resulting litter is bound to be a disappointment. When a dominant bitch is bred to a dominant stud, it is also possible that the resulting litter will be a failure. This explains why some "dream breedings" result in puppies which do not come near either parent in their quality.

There are some dominant sires which, in turn, pass on the ability to their sons which also, in turn, pass on their producing ability to their sons, etc. Likewise, there are dominant bitches which pass on their producing ability to their daughters, granddaughters, great-granddaughters, etc. Thus some lines are noted for their outstanding producing sires and/or bitches. Such a line is a *true* "producing bloodline."

Much discussion between breeders has centered on the subject of which parent contributes the most, the sire or the dam. Theoretically and in fact, they each contribute 50% of their genetic heritage or an equal amount; but by so doing, their respective factors of dominance and recessiveness are brought into play. Thus, in reality, there is not an equal contribution, for if there were there would be no outstanding producers.

The producing bitch is a very special entity unto herself. Those fortunate enough to own or to have owned one will surely attest to this. When one of the distaff side has produced three or more champion offspring, she is singled out for recognition, and well she might be! Whereas the stud dog's production is unlimited, depending only upon his popularity, this is not true in the case of the bitch. Many stud dogs, in achieving a producing record, have sired hundreds and hundreds of puppies. The average bitch will produce between twenty and thirty offspring in her lifetime, which must drastically limit her chances of producing champions in any number. Taking this limitation into account, it becomes quite obvious that those bitches which produce quality in any amount must possess an attribute different from the average. To state it simply, that attribute is dominance.

The producing bitch may or may not throw the qualities she herself possesses. Her puppies will, however, bear a resemblance to one another and to subsequent puppies she will produce, regardless of the sire. Whether closely line bred or outcrossed, whether bred to a sire of note or to a comparative unknown, the consistency of quality and type will be apparent in the offspring of the producing bitch.

There is no foolproof way in which to determine in advance those bitches destined to become "producers." The odds will have it, though, that their dams were producers and their granddams and even their great-

granddams. Chances are they will come from a line noted for the producing ability of its bitches.

Occasionally a bitch will come along with little or no producing heritage close behind her, yet she will be a standout in producing ability. It can only be assumed that such a specimen inherited a genetic make-up "different" from that of her immediate ancestors, or else the potential was always there but remained untapped until some enterprising breeder parlayed it to advantage. There are known instances when specific bitches will produce only with one particular dog and not with others. In such cases the desired results are achieved through an ideal "blending" rather than by the virtue of dominance. It might be well to mention the fact that some bitches are extremely negative. Such a bitch bred to a prepotent stud will necessarily produce as a result of the stud's dominance.

The availability of a true producing bitch is necessarily limited. Whereas all are free to breed to the outstanding sires of the breed, few have access to the producing bitches. Their offspring can and should command top prices and demand always exceeds supply. Their bitch puppies, especially, are highly valued, for it is primarily through them that continuity is achieved.

The producing bitch imparts something extra, something special to her offspring. Though all but impossible to define, this something extra is determined genetically as well as are the more obvious physical traits which are handed down. She is a good mother, conscientious but not fanatical, calm, and possessing an even temperament.

Lucky, indeed, is the breeder who possesses a producing bitch, for she can and often does found a dynasty spanning many generations of outstanding specimens. It is not difficult to name those breeders or kennels which have enjoyed or which are now enjoying sustained success in breeding. If there is a short cut to success, it is through a producing bitch.

The Parti-Color Cocker Spaniel.

The Past Foretells the Future

There is more to breeding top quality dogs than breeding any given bitch to any given dog, raising the resultant litter and hoping for the best. We need to know more, much more.

In this chapter we will range backward in time to give a historical perspective to our discussion, explore the work of Gregor Mendel, and try to make practical applications from what we have learned.

The breeding of dogs is an extremely ancient art. As much as it may jolt the sensibilities of "modern" breeders, the main groups of dogs were created long before Christ appeared. According to Anthony Smith, writing in the *Human Pedigree*, they already existed when written history was making its first appearance, and when their various canine shapes and sizes were being made recognizable on stone and pottery. Modern breeders have actually added little since the end of the Stone Age. Smith notes there are several points of interest in dog evolution. Although all dogs belong to the canine species, there has been tremendous variation in dogs. There are, as we well know, prick ears, floppy ears, curly tails, long tails, straight coat, curly coat, etc.

As for weight, Chihuahuas can be confronted by Mastiffs forty times their size. The bulk of this differentiation has been caused by man, deliberately and for different purposes. Man has controlled their random mating and has demonstrated the extraordinary variability inherent in the species (for it is just one species). Natural selection tends normally to enforce a greater uniformity among individuals, but, given artificial selection or the artificial world of life with man, this variability can express itself.

In a sense, the history of the dog is an accelerated version of man's evolution. When early men banded together to form communities, they brought their dogs with them. Since that time both have experienced the cultural and environmental shocks that have marked man's "progress." From living in the open to heated dwellings, from natural foods to cans and frozen foods, all those things that mark modern civilization have affected both the dog and its master. Dogs, however, have passed through thousands of generations, because of their quicker breeding cycles, while man has gone through only hundreds.

We have learned that genetic change occurs fastest when people are isolated and have only occasional contact with one another. Some ten thousand years ago that was exactly the condition that prevailed. As man wandered to trade or make war with his closest neighbors, his dog was permitted a degree of genetic involvement with the neighboring dog groups. It is a well documented fact that the various tribes of American Indians each had their own "type" of dog. These types were not much different from each other, but as distances between tribes increased, the differences became more and more pronounced.

Then came a rush when the earth's inhabitants became extremely mobile and began to wander further away from home base to explore the world. Dogs were sold or captured and/or mated along the way. Today we know many dogs' names from the geographical area from whence they came.

Mankind's movements became more frenetic when the Age of Discovery began. As boatloads leapfrogged among the continents, many people took dogs with them and they brought dogs back. There was wide-scale interbreeding. New breeds were formed, many times at the expense of the native varieties.

The *Canidae* family derived more recently from primitive and ancestral predators. Among the *Canidae* were the wolves, a species that exhibited cooperative behavior when attacking its prey. The wolf competed with man for the available food supply. It is commonly believed that modern dogs derived only from the various races of the wolf species and that the association of wolf and man leading to dog occurred again and again: American Indians were accustomed to taking wolf cubs frequently, either to amend their dog stock or to start it afresh. Probably this process of turning wolves into dogs was spurred on by the considerable growth of forest when the ice retreated, and when man's extreme inability to smell out his prey in tangled hiding places became a terrible disadvantage.

Anyway, the dog was the first domestic animal. He could be tamed, if caught early enough or reared in human company. He could hunt and herd animals. He could protect and give warning. We can imagine how every tribe must have wanted this new aid to living, and good bitches must have been tremendously in demand.

Early man noted that a good forest dog was not necessarily suitable for the open plains, or for herding semi-domestic stocks, or for guarding the encampments. All indications lead us to believe there had to be a selective breeding for specific purposes. This is thought to have made much of its advance between twenty thousand and ten thousand years ago. Skeletal remains of recognizably different breeds of dogs have been recovered from archaeological sites of that age, notably in more northerly regions, and by the time the Stone Age began there were

The Bouvier des Flandres.

hunting dogs, sheep dogs, and even the "toy" dogs of the Maltese type. Egyptologists tell us that among the early Egyptians there were at least five major types: the Basenji, the Greyhound, the Maltese, the Mastiff, and a sort of Chow.

It is important to appreciate that the changes, however striking, were not basic. They were more of degree—of proportion.

Stone Age man lived in different environments, and his dog requirements therefore differed from place to place. Dog requirements have changed in more recent times also, and the breeders have had to adapt the supply. Because of the violence in modern society, the guard dogs have evolved in temperament and attack capability. In the ancient Aztec world, dogs were bred for eating, for their hair (as wool), as well as for their role as beasts of burden. John Marvin, in his writings on Terriers, tells us that the whiteness of the English Terriers was a requirement for greater conspicuousness within the undergrowth.

Muzzle-loading guns called for patient and stationary dogs, and so Pointers were used. With the advent of the faster breech-loading piece, the Pointer gave way to a Setter type. Therefore, history would seem to indicate that Setters were deliberately bred from Spaniel stock to sit, or "set," when the quarry was detected, and then to move forward when the faster gun was ready. Different dogs for different and evolving tasks have characterized mankind's history.

It is apparent from all we have learned that there is great diversity in the dog world. There are two major reasons. First, natural selection for the dog has been relaxed for a long, long time. Second, artificial selection—of the dog by man—has deliberately preserved some unwelcome canine mutations merely to increase that diversity. Does it follow, then, that the dog has suffered genetically? We know that natural selection is impartial and favors no species in particular, but has its lack of influence caused some lack and unfitness in the dog?

The answer seems to be that the dog does not seem to be genetically weak. Evidence from naturalists indicates that the current breeds are largely more fertile than their wolf ancestors. Burns and Fraser tell us that wolves mature at about two years of age and produce four or five cubs per annual litter. The dog is, on an average, sexually mature before the age of one and can produce two litters a year. By this criteria man has not harmed the dog.

Nor has man harmed it in the range of capabilities. As with humans, variety is the keynote, and today's dogs have brought all the old wolf characteristics. Terriers, to quote Scott and Fuller in their book on dog behavior, "are more aggressive than their wolf forebears; the Hound breeds less so. Greyhounds are faster than wolves; short-legged dogs, like the Dachschund, less so. The good scent dogs are better trackers than wolves, while Terriers are poorer. Sheep dogs can herd more effectively; other breeds would not know where to begin. Many game dogs are, reasonably enough, more interested than wolves in game and share man's enthusiasm for birds."

Let us now make a transition to a more modern time and see how man began his efforts to breed better animals.

For centuries mankind has observed that the parents of one species produce offspring of the same species. This is not surprising. Rather, it would be astounding if dogs gave birth to offspring with the characteristics of, say, deer! Through the years, men also have observed that animals tend to be like their sires and dams in appearance and general characteristics.

Characteristics such as height and coat color are known as "inherited" traits. They are traits which an offspring "inherits" or receives from his parents. Every living thing has an inheritance, or heredity. Inherited traits are passed along from generation to generation. As a result of heredity, each generation thus is linked to older generations and to past generations. A Doberman may resemble his parents with respect to height and the black and tan pattern. His grandsire or great-grandsire also may have possessed the same identifying features.

A whole science known as genetics has grown up around the study of heredity. Specifically, the science of genetics is the study of how the reproduction process determines

The Smooth Dachshund.

The Wirehaired Dachshund.

17

The Basset Hound.

the characteristics of an offspring and of how these characteristics are distributed.

In 1636, Sir Thomas Browne wrote: "It is the common wonder of all men, how among so many millions of faces, there should be none alike." Individuality is still a wonder, and the questions it provokes are relevant to matters far removed from physiognomy: dogs are as distinguishable to the breeder, as fruit flies are to the geneticist. The basis for individuality is variation. If men or dogs or fruit flies can be recognized as individuals, then it follows that their populations exhibit variation. Variation is the material of science, and variation among members of the species is the material of genetics.

Genetics is the past, the present, and each generation's permanent contribution to the future. The past reaches back to the very beginning, to the first particle of organic matter capable of self-replication, and all biology has an equally ancient ancestry.

Smith recounts, "The nineteenth-century monk Gregor Mendel, living at Brno in Czechoslovakia, who did more than anyone else to found genetics, knew nothing of the actual mechanism involved. Similarly, Charles Darwin, who did more than anyone else to put evolution in its place, knew nothing about the European monk. It is extraordinary that these two men, both assembling their respective and related jigsaws, were so successful when so many key elements were missing; the evolutionist having no facts of the laws of genetics and the geneticist without any details of the actual process. The similarity ends with the effects of their respective publications. *The Origin of Species*, published in 1859, was received vehemently, either for or against. Gregor Mendel's *Crucial Findings*, published six years later in the proceeding of the Brno Society for the Study of Natural Sciences, were greeted with some anxiety by his religious colleagues and silence from the scientific community. By the time Darwin had gotten up courage and published *The Descent of Man*, Mendel was still quite unknown. There was not even a single rebuke (or any applause) when the new Abbot of Brno quietly destroyed all Mendel's papers after his death. Mendel, for a former Abbot, had not just been ahead of his time, but too far ahead of it for appropriate recognition.

"Basically, Mendel's work had proved that traits can be passed from one generation to the next, both with mathematical precision and in separate packets. Before his time it had been assumed that inheritance was always a matter of blending, as if colored water was added to plain water with the result inevitably and inextricably being colored water of a weaker hue. Mendel foresaw genes, the differing units of inheritance (that are named incidentally, after the Greek for race). Genes remain distinct entities. They do not blend, like that of colored water. They can produce, to continue the analogy, either plain water, or colored water or a mixture between the two. Moreover, assuming no other genes are involved to complicate the story, they continue to create these three kinds of product in generation after generation. The packets remain distinct.

"The mathematics also has a pleasing simplicity, at least in the early stages. The human blue-eye/brown-eye situation is a good and elementary example. There are genes for brown and genes for blue, and everybody receives one of each from each parent. To receive two browns is to be brown-eyed. To receive two blue is to be blue-eyed. To receive one of each is also to be brown-eyed because the brown has the effect of masking the relative transparency of the blue. Therefore, if a population of blue-eyed people (who inevitably possess two blue genes)

The Irish Water Spaniel.

is mated with a population of brown-eyed people (who happen to possess a similar double of brown genes) their offspring will be 75% brown-eyed and 25% blue-eyed. Fifty percent of the off-spring will be mixed, having one blue and brown gene, and will therefore be able to pass on either a blue or a brown to their off-spring. In general, no one knows, without looking at his ancestors, whether his brown eyes are a mixed or a straight inheritance, whether brown-blue or brown-brown. With the recessive nature of blue eyes, so-called because they can be masked by the dominant gene, their existence is bound to indicate a double inheritance of blue-blue."

The clarity of Mendel's vision certainly helped science, but discovery of his work thirty-five years after it had been originally published, and the subsequent excitement, spread his name and his basic ideas far afield. It was assumed that all of inheritance was equally clear cut, with the ratio of three to one, or his equally famous ratio of nine to three to three to one (involving two characteristics) explaining all of our genetic fortunes. So they do, in a sense, but the real situation is much, much more complex. Only a few aspects of inheritance are controlled by a single pair of genes. Only a few more are controlled by two pairs. A feature like height, for example, may be organized by twenty or so pairs. Each pair is working in a Mendelian manner, but the effect of them all working together is a bewilderment. The mathematics still have the same precision but only for mathematicians, not for the rest of us. As for a feature like intelligence, with the brain differentiated to fill a tremendous range of different tasks, its inheritance cannot be thought of in a simple ratio of any kind.

There are literally thousands and thousands of paired genes within each animal, but no one knows the exact number. There are enough of them, and enough possible variations, to ensure that each specimen is unique. Never in history has there been a single specimen like the one that you have before you now. Never in all of future history will there be one just like it again. Your special dog is a combination that is entirely individual and yet his/her genes are common to the population he/she lives in. There is nothing unique about them—unless you are the owner of a recent mutation—and unless you could somehow select and extract the right genes from the population around you, it would be possible to create a replica of that specimen. However, it is impossible, and even its offspring, because of sexual reproduction, can spring from that animal's loins with only fifty percent of what that specimen could give them.

In *Human Heredity*, Smith points out that "In 1900 Mendel's work was discovered virtually simultaneously by three people in three different countries: Hugo de Vries in Holland, Karl Correns in Germany, and E. Tschermak in Austria. There was suddenly much talk of genes, and then of genetics when the British biologist William Bateson coined the word in the first years of this century. But what was the gene, this discrete packet of inheritance? Where was it? Attention focused on the chromosomes. No one knew much about these long strands in each cell nucleus, save that they accepted staining well—hence their name of colored bodies—and were later split length-wise during the process of cell division. Perhaps the genes were arranged along them—a statement first made in 1903—and could somehow split in two to give each daughter cell an equal share of the gene material. Thereafter this same material of inheritance would have to refurbish itself so that it could split again at the next division. And the next. And the next."

An American scientist, T. H. Morgan, working with the fruit fly, made a series of outstanding discoveries that led to the next steps along the discovery continuum. The fly has four large, exceptionally clear chromosomes. Morgan, by judicious breeding, and by working with readily identifiable characteristics, was able to plot the positions along the chromosomes of the genes that controlled these features. However, the physical nature of the genes eluded him and other researchers of the time. That is, all except a Swiss biochemist, Friedrich Miescher, who had discovered the substance deoxyribonucleic acid, hereafter known as DNA, that forms part of each cell nucleus. During the decade of the forties, DNA received its due—and thereby displaced all the notions that various proteins were carrying the genetic information. By taking some DNA from dead bacteria and injecting it into living bacteria of a different kind, the researcher Oswald Avery and others were able to give the new bacteria some of the properties of the original bacteria from which the substance had been taken. Through their experiments in the strange world of bacteria and bacteria eaters, the fact was confirmed: DNA was assuredly the stuff that genes were made of.

Before going further, let us take a closer look at Mendel's work. Mendel was not the first investigator who attempted to study heredity by hybridizing plants. He was, however, the first to achieve some consistent results. We can recognize some of the reasons for his success by examining Mendel's description of his work. His object was to find "the statistical relations of the various hybrid (offspring of two different varieties) offspring." He anticipated that there would be a mathematical regularity in the results. He brought to his task a knowledge of statistics as well as an understanding of the nature of the plants he chose as experimental organisms.

Mendel also was familiar with the microscope, and used it. He was aware of the process of fertilization which occurred in flowering plants following pollination. He knew that both the pollen grain and the egg nucleus made some contribution to the characteristics of the offspring, even though this contribution was not always evident. He recognized that the environment also contributed to the expression of hereditary traits. He designed his experiments so that he could rule out environment as a factor in the heredity of the characteristics he intended to observe.

For purposes of his experiment he selected the garden pea, a plant with a number of sharply defined differences, both easy to see and constant in these differentiating characters.

One race of peas was tall, growing to a height of six feet or more, while a contrasting race produced plants less than eighteen inches. Some pea plants produced purple flowers, while others had white flowers. There were also varieties of the pea that formed green seeds, while the contrasting trait was yellow. In all, Mendel was able to obtain peas in which seven pairs of inherited, contrasting traits were found, and these he determined to study.

Mendel decided to concentrate his attention on the inheritance of one characteristic at a time. By ignoring the simultaneous inheritance of other traits which might distract him, he avoided the confusion of some earlier workers.

Mendel began his experiments with several hypotheses. He was convinced that inheritance was factorial—that is, the result of the action of "unit characters." He also believed that the individual character elements were separated in the production of offspring. He hoped "to predict the number of different types that would result from the random fertilization of two kinds of 'egg cells' by two kinds of pollen grains."

He crossed pea plants that produced round, smooth seeds with plants that produced wrinkled seeds. Before he began hybridizing these two strains of peas he tested each strain for purity of type.

His first cross was between plants that produced only round seeds (pure round) and plants that formed only wrinkled seeds (pure wrinkled). He planted all the seeds formed by the parent generation plants in the same kind of soil. He tried to ensure each plant equal water, access to sunlight, and all other conditions he could control.

The hybridized flowers produced a total of 253 seeds. Each seed formed was round. There were *no* wrinkled seeds, even though each was formed by the combination of pollen grains and ovules, one of which came from a plant that produced wrinkled seeds.

Mendel then proceeded to plant all 253 round, hybrid seeds in separate plots. Each seed grew into a pea plant with many flowers. All the flowers were permitted to self-pollinate. Each flower formed a pod with seeds. A total of 7,324 seeds was produced by the hybrid plants. There were 5,474 round seeds and 1,850 were wrinkled. This is very close to a 3:1 ratio.

Mendel then decided to see whether the other traits were inherited in the same fashion. He separately hybridized pea plants that showed six other pairs of contrasting traits. He experimented with a single pair of traits, repeating the procedure he had used in his first experiment. Some of the crosses he made were between peas pure for yellow seed production and plants pure for the production of green seeds, tall pea plants and short or dwarf plants, and plants with purple flowers and those with white flowers.

In all of the crosses, one of the two contrasting characteristics appeared in all of the first generation hybrids. Thus the green x yellow cross produced plants in which all the seeds were yellow. All the hybrids of the tall x dwarf cross were as tall as the original tall parents, and all of the purple and white hybrids were plants with purple flowers. There was no evidence that each hybrid was produced by a cross in which one of the parents had a trait that did not appear in the hybrid: green seed-color, dwarfishness, or white flowers.

The first generation hybrids were allowed to self-pollinate. Each gave rise to thousands of plants for each of the crosses. In every one, the hidden characteristics (green seeds, dwarfishness, or white flowers), which apparently had disappeared, were again evident in some of the crosses, and the proportion of the two types of plants was remarkably close to the 3:1 ratio that Mendel had found in his round x wrinkled cross.

Gregor Mendel was both lucky and perceptive. He was lucky that all seven pairs of contrasting traits behaved in the same basic way when hybridized. He was perceptive in his analysis and conclusions which served as a unifying model—an orderly and simple way of explaining how things happened. His results are as valid today as they were when Mendel published them.

Mendel reasoned that every living thing that reproduced sexually, including his garden peas, inherits its traits equally from both its parents. He identified the hereditary mechanism as distinct units or "factors" which retain their constancy and identity through countless generations. Today the term gene is used in the place of Mendel's term, "factors."

Piggybacking now upon Mendel's work and that of later scientists, let us look at how we can take this knowledge and become better breeders.

We now know that each dog contains a pair of genes for each trait that it inherits, in each of its cells. One of the genes is contributed by the sire and the other by the dam. When, let's say, a dominant black Cocker Spaniel is bred to a buff one, all the first generation offspring will be black. Each parent contributed one gene for color to each hybrid offspring. One parent, obviously one that produces black color, contributed a "factor" for black color while the other parent passed along a "factor" for buff coat color. Why, then, were all the hybrid F_1 (first generation) offspring black?

Obviously the ability for black to overshadow buff is *dominant* over the tendency to produce buff color, which we can call *recessive*. The recessive characteristic was the hidden or masked one that did not appear in the hybrid offspring. A dog can show a recessive trait only when both factors (genes) are recessive in one individual. The dominant trait will appear when one or both genes present are dominant ones.

To clarify matters a bit, let's see what happens when our all-black hybrid specimen is crossed with another just like it. Every hybrid can pass on to each of its offspring either the black or buff characteristics. Therefore, the transmission of one or the other factor has a 50/50 chance. Remember, these are hybrid specimens which have a black (dominant) gene and a buff (recessive) gene. Let's

symbolize them B-Dominant, b-Recessive. Since the combination is random, the ways in which these can be combined in a hybrid x hybrid cross are shown in Figure 1. As shown, it is possible to predict not only the possible combinations of factors, but also the probability for each of the combinations.

Chance plays a part in both the biological and physical worlds. By chance we mean events that happen at random. Mendel was aware of this and knew something of the laws of probability. He used these in explaining his results. These laws say that we should be wary of interpreting the occurrence of a single random event. However, they go on to postulate that if large numbers of occurrences of the same event take place at random, there is a kind of order in the result in spite of the uncertainty of the occurrence of a single event.

For example, if we toss a coin with two faces (I'll match you for coffee), we cannot predict with certainty whether a head or a tail will fall face up. It is certain that it will be a head or a tail (now you see how the black/buff combination comes in). In the language of probability mathematics, the chance that an event will occur is written as a fraction. The chance that a tossed coin will fall with the head side up is ½. The chance that a tail will show face up is also ½. The chance that a head or tail will appear is ½ and ½ or 1. In probability, 1 expresses certainty that an event will occur while 0 represents certainty that an event will not or cannot occur. If the first of a series of coin tosses (breeding of hybrid Bb x Bb) is a head, does this mean the next toss will be a tail? The answer is no, since each toss of the coin is unaffected by any of the previous tosses. This is the nature of random events; they are not influenced by prior events. In any toss of a coin, the second, the tenth, or the hundredth toss, the probability of a tail appearing face up is ½. Theoretically, then, in 1000 tosses of a coin, there should be close to 500 heads and 500 tails. The actual results come closer and closer to the theoretical, as the number of events is larger and larger.

As noted above, both parents in the hybrid x hybrid cross carried one gene for black coat color and one gene for buff coat color. Each parent contributes only one of its two genes to each of its offspring: A gene for black coat color or a gene for buff coat color. Thus the probability of one or the other gene being contributed is ½.

Since each new individual receives one gene from each of its parents, the probability of any two genes combining is the product of their individual probabilities, that is

$$\tfrac{1}{2} \times \tfrac{1}{2} = \tfrac{1}{4}$$

or one chance in four. All the possibilities are shown in Figure 2.

At this point it is best to introduce some terms that are commonly used today. The pair of genes that determine the expression of the characteristics of the individual are called "alleles." Thus the colors black and buff are alleles

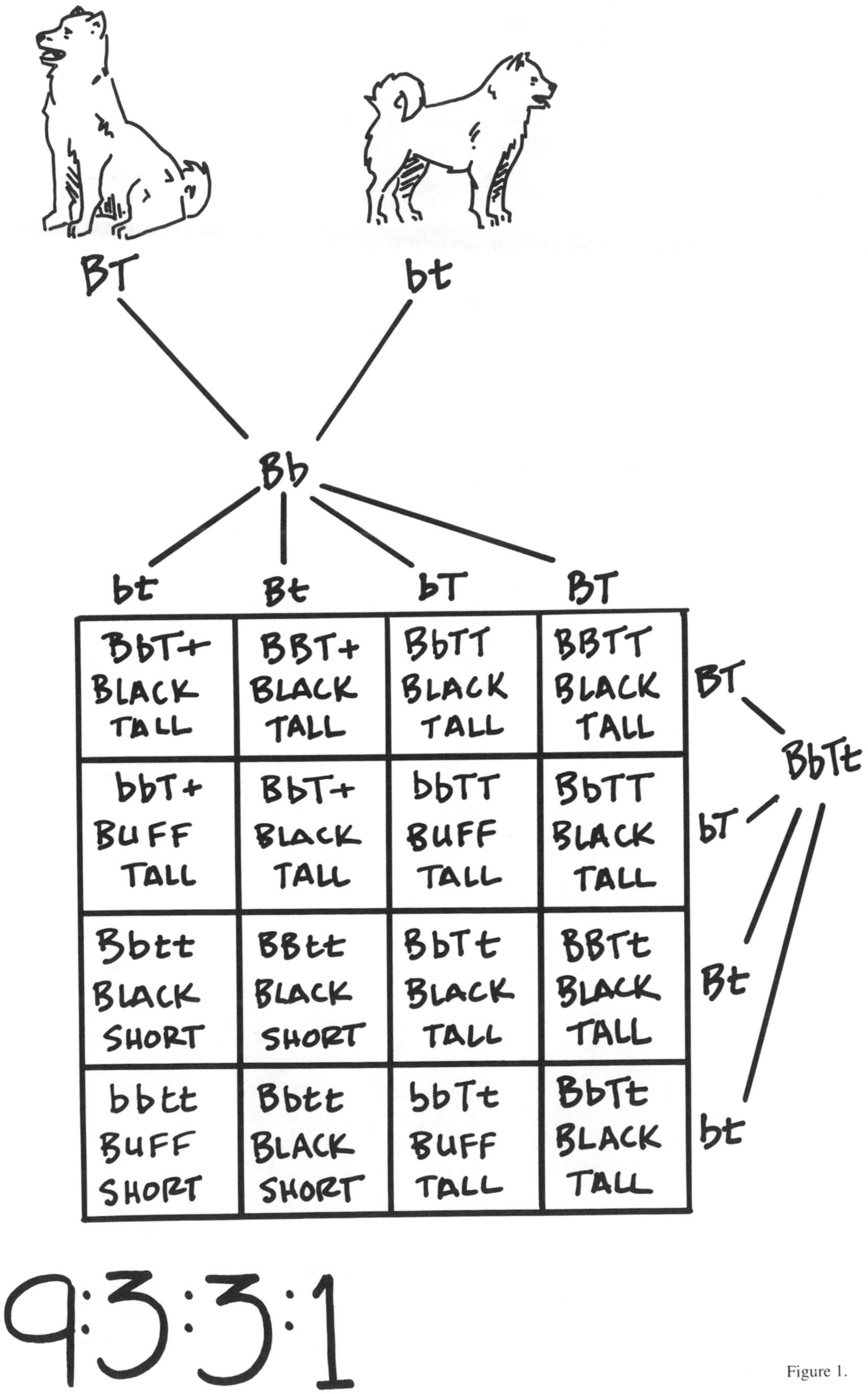
BT
bt
Bb
bt
Bt
bT
BT
BbTt
BLACK
TALL
BBTt
BLACK
TALL
BbTT
BLACK
TALL
BBTT
BLACK
TALL
BT
BbTt
bbTt
BUFF
TALL
BbTt
BLACK
TALL
bbTT
BUFF
TALL
BbTT
BLACK
TALL
bT
Bbtt
BLACK
SHORT
BBtt
BLACK
SHORT
BbTt
BLACK
TALL
BBTt
BLACK
TALL
Bt
bbtt
BUFF
SHORT
Bbtt
BLACK
SHORT
bbTt
BUFF
TALL
BbTt
BLACK
TALL
bt
9:3:3:1

Figure 1.

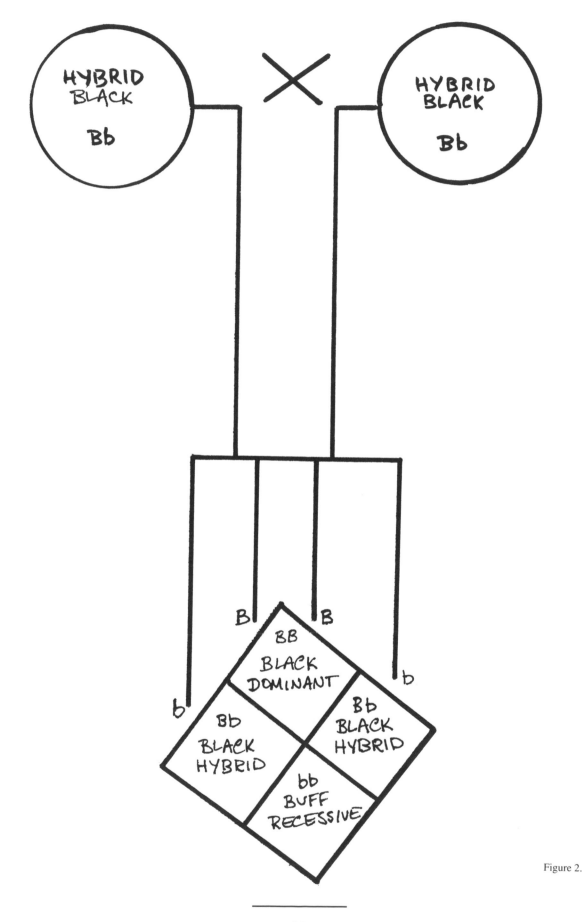

Figure 2.

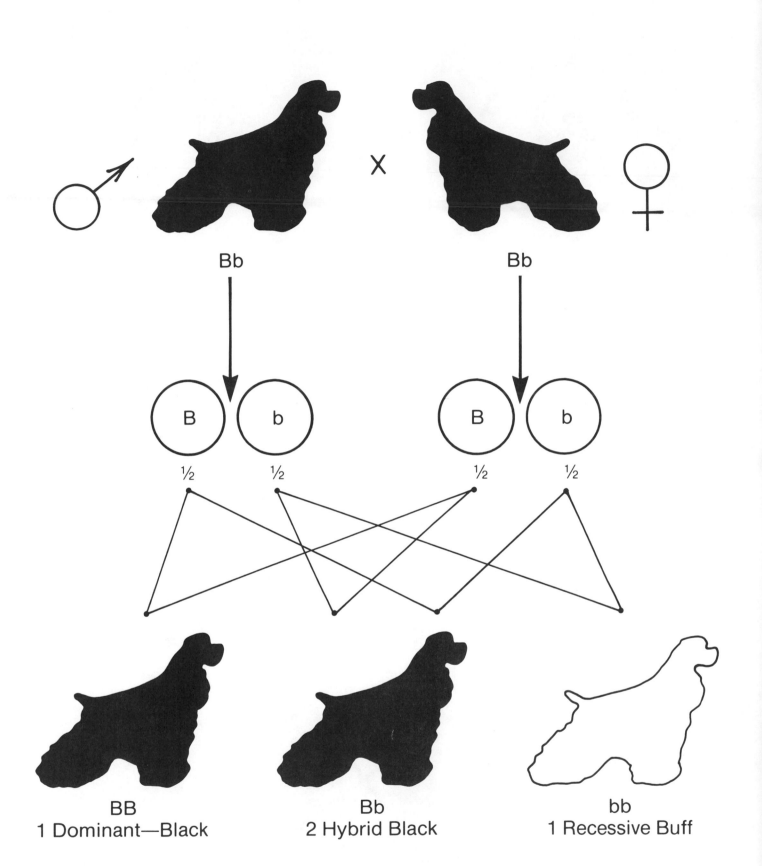

Bb   X   Bb

B   b   B   b

½   ½   ½   ½

BB
1 Dominant—Black

Bb
2 Hybrid Black

bb
1 Recessive Buff

Figure 3.

24

for coat color. Tall and short are alleles for height, etc.

If the two alleles in an individual are for the same expression of the trait (two black, two tall), the individual is said to be pure or homozygous for that trait. The term dominant is also often used. If the alleles for a pair are for different expressions of the same trait (one black, and one buff, one tall and one short), the individual is hybrid or heterozygous for the trait.

Thus two hybrid specimens that are black coated will produce, when mated together, some offspring that are buff in color, even though neither sire or dam shows this characteristic. The ability of the hybrid sire and dam to produce buffs is masked by the effects of the dominant black color, but is not affected in any other way by it. The two allelic genes are separated during mitosis (cell division and reduction which results in the formation of two new nuclei, each having the same number of chromosomes as the parent nucleus) by chance, two genes for the production of buff coat color recombine in one out of four offspring in the next generation. Then, the buff color appears in its full expression. Mendel called this result segregation, and he summarized the principle as "the law of segregation."

Let's move from the inheritance of a single trait to the inheritance of two traits simultaneously.

Let us breed a homozygous (pure) black dog that is tall (also homozygous) to a short buff specimen that is also homozygous for its traits. Naturally enough, we get tall black offspring, since those traits are dominant. The offspring are exactly like the black parent.

When you then take these hybrid offspring which are hybrid tall/hybrid black and mate them with other like specimens, the resultant types are quite interesting. There will be four different types produced. There will be a tall black type and a tall buff one. These types are new combinations of the two traits.

Continuing in this vein, and for all other traits as well, the distribution ratio turns out to be 9:3:3:1. This means that for every nine tall black dogs in a hybrid x hybrid mating, there will be three tall dogs with buff coats, three small dogs with black coats, and one short buff specimen.

A quick glance at the above will show twelve tall dogs to four short ones and twelve blacks to four buffs. Both demonstrate the 3:1 ratio already established for the inheritance of a single trait in which segregation occurs.

Mendel and later researchers also uncovered the fact that, for example, tallness is independent of coat color. This is called the law of independent assortment and is supported by the facts revealed by numerous experiments. Figure 3 shows how the principles of probability apply. Note that the probability of two or more related events is calculated by multiplying the individual probabilities. Thus if the probability of one event occurring is ¼ and the probability of a simultaneous event is also ¼ then the probability of the two occurring together is ¼ x ¼ or 1/16; that is, one in every sixteen.

As we have seen, some genes are dominant and will be seen in the offspring. Others are recessive and will not be outwardly apparent, yet can be passed on to the offspring to combine with a similar recessive gene of the other parent and thus be seen. Or they may be passed on to the offspring, not be outwardly apparent, but be passed on again to become apparent in a later generation. This is typical of the black/tan pattern in Cocker Spaniels.

The key to the differences between the various species lies in the total number of chromosomes peculiar to a species, and to the total number of and types of genes within the chromosomes. Scientists seem to agree that the number of chromosomes in the cells of each species is constant. In man the cells contain forty-six chromosomes, in the fruit fly, only eight, and in the dog, seventy-eight. Remember, these are total numbers, for each chromosome is part of a pair. Therefore, a dog has thirty-nine chromosome pairs. Within the chromosomes of the higher organisms are hundreds of thousands of genes (for higher organisms the exact number has not been determined), and each gene can be different.

The primitive or rudimentary germ cells multiply just as do cells of its substance to the nucleus of each of the two cells thus formed. Each spermatozoon and ovum has the total number of chromosomes peculiar to its species. If the primitive germ cell "produced by the union of a germ cell from either parent is to possess the number of chromosomes normal to a cell characteristic of its class," a reduction of the number in the primitive germ cell must be effected. To take care of this, Nature provides a special reducing process (a process which occurs only with cells that are to be used in reproduction) which is apparently solely for the purpose of taking from each of the parent cells one-half of its chromosomes. Many of the truly perplexing occurrences in breeding can be attributed to this special process of reduction. To make our points clear, it will be necessary to go further into this particular reducing process.

Propelled by the whipping motion of its tail, the spermatozoon, when deposited by the male organ, reaches the ovum of the female. Of the many spermatozoa which attach themselves to the exterior of the ovum, only one enters. When the spermatozoon enters the ovum, the chromosomes "coalesce" (go together so as to form one body) and the embryo comes into being. From this time on, the embryo grows and develops.

The combined chromosomes are the vehicles carrying all that is transmitted from parents to offspring. The lack of similarity in the offspring of two parents can be understood only when one realizes how the element of chance determines the possible combinations of chromosomes in the ovum.

The Airedale Terrier.

Form Follows Function

If you have ever designed anything with functional parts, you will know that structural design implies more than bare bones of anatomy. You know that a good design takes into account all factors that will help the structure serve its purpose. Similarly, the structural design of a dog must provide for all the needs of its owner.

In keeping with the principles of good architectural design, organic structure must take into account the specific properties that the animal uses in his work. These materials must be able to withstand the stresses implicit in the design. Therefore, no breeder of a dog designed to herd flocks would think of placing a thin unprotected skin where a tough layer of subcutaneous muscle and bristly coat should go. Here again, the inter-relationship of structure and function is obvious – the two go together. One of the most important things in designing and working with any breed is always to keep in mind the inseparability of structure and function. That is, the form of the animal must be designed for the function for which it had been originally bred. For example, the Cocker Spaniel has some major structural problems that must be addressed if it is to perform as its originators desired. Cocker breeders had changed their Standard to provide for a dog that is two inches shorter from withers to tail than from floor to withers. This creates a pretty, stacked dog but a badly engineered mover. Unless the shoulders are rotated far forward, the dog cannot get out of the way of its correctly engineered rear. This causes the dog to step either inside or outside of his front legs thus causing him to sidewind down the ring.

Mother nature, seeing breeders tamper with the natural design of things, has pitched in to help solve the problem. She has allowed them to breed a dog that could move correctly with the Standard's measurements. She has done this by rotating the pelvis and croup, thus throwing the angle of the rear quarters further back and allowing for more time for the rear leg swing so the front has time to get out of the way.

What are the consequences of this engineering change? First, logically enough, with the changed angle of the croup, we now have a terrier tail. How some purists howl about this, not appreciating that they caused the problem by making a Standard change that was improper for correct movement to result. The second consequence, again with the croup angle change, is that we don't have as many moving dogs who display a sloping topline. Now a level topline is what goes with the croup change.

In many instances, the function for which dogs were originally bred is not the function for which they are utilized today. Most dogs are kept in a house or apartment as the family pet and seldom have the opportunity to perform their specific skills. Many of the dogs are placed in groups today where they are not required to perform any specific function.

ORGANIC ENGINEERING

You can get a better understanding of the functional aspects of a breed of dog if you think of them in terms of engineering. Consider, for example, the role of the early breeders in England. They had two kinds of jobs. First, they tried to design a useful product, a dog who could go after upland birds, stay close to the hunter, have a good nose, be steady and have the ability to work in the field all day long. Don't forget, originally they had to help put food on the table. Only later were they hunted for sport. Then these early breeders had to find a way to manufacture these products. In bringing a new product into being, an engineer first lays out a method of operation. He might even design and build a new tool just for making this one product. With the breeder, he might bring in another breed and cross it and re-cross it and introduce others until he got the correct mixture. The breeder might have to go through dozens of developmental stages before turning out a satisfactory replica of the designed product.

But no matter how many steps you must take, a good product engineer (breeder) never departs from the intent of the basic design. He recognizes that the design has a special purpose which his efforts must serve. The English farmer who had to protect his livestock and fowl against the incursion of foxes who holed up in dens in rocky lairs, invented a sturdy little dog to take care of that problem. This dog had to get along with the pack hounds who were used to run the fox to ground. Added to the design was the necessity of having a skull and rib cage that were flat enough to allow him to squeeze into any crevice the fox could. And finally, he had to have punishing jaws to dispatch the fox and haul him out. This little dog was called the Lakeland Terrier. He is about the same size as the Cocker but certainly built for an expressly different function.

But whether we are talking about a dog breeder or an engineer, they both design their products or devise techniques to make use of certain basic designs. For example, an engineer must use only those geometrical figures that would yield desired structural strength. He must also use shapes that conserve on materials and yet provide for the greatest efficiency. Furthermore, he must also concern himself with simplicity of design. Therefore, whenever possible he must construct simple machines (levers, pulleys, and inclined planes) as such, rather than intricate combinations of these machines.

A dog or any living organism is its own engineer. Throughout its life, it constantly refers to a basic design and manufactures the product it needs. In so doing, it makes use of the same mechanical principles that underlie the operation of man-made devices. Consider, for example, the transmission of force. When an animal moves its moveable parts, it transmits force in much the same way that machines do. In so doing, the animal uses its built-in simple machines. You can see this quite clearly in locomotive structures and that is why judging the gait of a dog in terms of its ability to perform its function is so very important in the overall approach to judging dogs.

MOVEMENT

For many years, physiologists and even the vast majority of dog people believed that animals running at higher speeds would exact a higher *cost* in terms of energy burned – it didn't turn out that way! Recent studies have shown that animals use up energy at a uniform, predictable rate as the speed of movement increases.

As if that shattering piece of information wasn't enough – they found out that for any given animal, the amount of energy expended in getting from point A to point B was the same regardless of how fast the trip was taken. A cheetah running 100 yards at a top speed of 60 miles per hour, uses the same amount of energy as it would walking the same distance. The running is more exhausting because the calories are used up more quickly.

Size, however, does make a difference. Small dogs require much more energy per unit of weight to run at top speed than a Great Dane would. Small dogs appear to have higher *idling* speeds. The cost of maintaining muscular tension and of stretching and shortening the muscles is higher in small animals.

These same series of studies suggest that as much as 77 percent of the energy used in walking comes, not from the operation of the muscles themselves, but from a continual interplay between gravity and kinetic energy. From an engineering standpoint it seems that the body tends to rotate about a center of mass, somewhat like an egg rolling end-on-end or the swing of an inverted pendulum. The 30 percent of effort supplied by the muscles is imported through the limbs to the ground to keep the animal's center of mass moving forward.

At faster speeds, four-footed animals appear to be capable of calling into use a work-saving scheme that relies upon the elastic storage of energy in muscles and tendons. Some are better at it than others. Some are capable of storing more energy per stride than others.

During running or trotting the built-in springs for propulsion are the muscles and tendons of the limbs. When the animal has the need to move faster, he has the ability to use an even bigger spring. As the dog shifts from the fast trot to a gallop, he tends to use his body as a large spring to store more energy. He does not change the frequency of his strides, rather he increases the length of them.

SIMPLE BIO-MACHINES

Let us consider how the dog compares with man-made machines. The dog can be compared to combinations of simple machines and other mechanical systems found in any factory. A few familiar examples will quickly clarify this analogy. The dog's legs, for example, could be diagrammed as levers. The appendages of all animals, in fact, serve as levers. If laid out side by side, they present a rather special array of *machines*. As we have certainly seen, dogs from the Chihuahua to the Great Dane present a wide variety of angles and levers.

You would expect this because dog owners have widely different ways of life. Modifications in such bio-levers reflect the animal's way of life, so you would expect the Saluki's leg to be the kind of lever that gives the advantage of speed and distance; by the same token, you would expect the design of the front legs of the Dachshund, a burrowing animal, to provide for the multiplication of force, rather than the advantage of distance or speed.

Another simple machine that is easy to detect in nature is the pulley. You will find the living counterpart of the pulley wherever you find a muscle tendon joint apparatus. Whenever a tendon moves over a joint, it behaves like a pulley. Such mechanisms enable the dog to change the direction of force. A notable example of an application of the pulley principle is the action of the tendons and muscles in the dog's neck. When the handler "strings the dog up" on a tight lead, the ability of the dog to use that pulley correctly is gone. What you have looks like a spastic alligator moving.

Inclined planes are prevalent in all living things, but their presence is not always obvious. They frequently appear as wedges, which are made up of two inclined planes arranged back-to-back. The incisors of the dog, for example, are wedges. The cutting action of these teeth is an application of the wedge principle in nature. Another illustration is when a Standard calls for a sloping topline in movement. The sloping plane from withers to tail is designed to harness the thrust or drive from the rear quarters and move the dog along a straight line with power.

HYDRAULICS AND LIFE

Any person who has tried to dam up a creek or in some way tried to manage moving water has had experience with hydraulics. It involves the application of energy to practical uses. Frequently, therefore, hydraulics deals with the transfer of mechanical energy of moving fluids to the powering of machinery. It also deals with the use of pressure created by fluids (hydraulic pressure). All this finds an application in

The Gordon Setter.

biology, wherein fluid is of paramount importance. Applications of hydraulic pressure are evident in dogs. Certainly the pumping action of the heart as being responsible for the movement of blood through the circulatory system is an appropriate example.

A Standard asking for a deep chest and the front wide enough for adequate heart and lung space is telling us we need room for a pump big enough to keep the dog going under pressure all day long. This pump exerts pressure, directly or indirectly, on all body fluids. When the heart is in need of repair or is worn out, the blood pressure of the animal varies abnormally. When this happens, the animal finds it hard to maintain a proper fluid balance of its tissues and organs. The final result is interference with the movement of the materials of life.

Death can occur if the equipment designed to maintain hydraulic pressure fails in its function. As you may recall from your school studies of anatomy, it takes more than the pumping of the heart to maintain normal fluid pressure in an animal. The condition of the arteries and the veins is equally important. If these circulatory structures do not have the proper strength or elasticity, this condition could cause abnormal variation in the hydraulic pressure of the body. The arteries and veins are fluid conduits. Therefore, they must have a structural design that will enable them to withstand and adjust to sudden changes in hydraulic pressure.

As you may recall how effectively the design met the need, the walls of the arteries are designed to have heavier muscular construction than the veins because the blood being pumped under great pressure from the heart goes out through the arteries and returns under less pressure through the veins. Thus, the arteries can withstand greater pressure than the veins can tolerate. The arteries tend to be more elastic than the veins so they can react more quickly to changes in pressure and so regulate the movement of fluid to compensate for the change in the situation.

ORGANIC ARCHITECTURE

The shape of a building usually reflects its function. The design of its various parts (roof, doors, ventilators) also relates to special functions and so it is with the shape of the dog. In a large dog, the design often calls for a shape that will provide the necessary strength, compactness and capability to perform certain functions. For example, dogs such as the Rottweiler were used to haul heavy loads. They were designed with a shoulder construction and balanced size that would enable them to perform this function. On the other hand, a long and slender shape characterizes the coursing type of dog (Afghan, Greyhound, Russian Wolfhound and Saluki). This shape facilitates the faster movement of energy from place to place. The Beagle, on the other hand, is designed with a balanced shape to be neither a hauler or speed demon, but to go at a moderate pace for a sustained period of time.

STRUCTURE, SHAPE and SYMMETRY

As we have noted, overall body shape has a definite relationship to a dog's way of life. It relates, for example, to the use of energy. It also has to do with the animal's ability to relate to its environment and to perform the function for which it was originally bred. As you continue to study dogs, you will see more and more how the shape of things facilitates function. Take the opportunity to see how the smooth functioning of an animal or of its parts, relates to its survival.

As you look at your dog in the yard at home, in the show ring or out in the field working birds, look for the features of its design that might account for its survival and popularity. Look for the relationship of structural design to vital function. Ask yourself: "How is the shape of this animal related to the environment in which it has to live?" In searching for answers, go beyond the obvious facts and look for subtle relationships. Look for special problems. For example, in reading many of the breed magazines today, we find breeders bewailing the promiscuous breedings and the terrible things that have happened to their breed. They often point out their breed is no longer able to perform its primary function because of straight shoulders, over-angulated rears or too much coat. Their claim is the breed is no longer functional. FORM NO LONGER FOLLOWS FUNCTION! ... What are the breeders of today going to do about it?

Nature vs. Nurture

Natural Selection

We have learned over time that the Darwin/Wallace theory of evolution had come about by a process of natural selection. Natural selection is the process that results in the survival of those organisms best suited for their environment. Perhaps, even more important, those least suited are less likely to survive. Those best adapted would also leave more offspring than those less suited. These offspring, in turn, tend to be well adapted.

That's all well and good in the wild, but what about in a controlled environment such as ours where humans decide which traits will be bred for and preserved. Let's look at three of Darwin's line-of-reasoning steps to understand better our perspective.

• All organisms of the same species (breed) differ slightly from each other (and that makes dog shows and breeding programs).

• Thus, it is likely that some traits are more favorable for survival than others. These favorable traits allow certain individuals to live longer. In the process, they will leave more offspring than those without these traits. (In our man-controlled situation, those traits are selected by us through proving favorable traits in the show ring.)

• The favorable traits are passed on to the offspring. This increases the frequency of those traits in the population. After many generations, most of the members of this population have the selected trait. (An example might be the white blaze and collar of a certain bloodline in Springers that dominates the breed.)

Darwin hypothesized that because of competition those with unfavorable traits will have fewer offspring. Hence, he postulated, in time, unfavorable traits may even disappear. In our case, judges, by selecting the best show characteristics and breeders breeding for type, temperament and soundness, create an artificial environment but give nature a helping and accelerated hand.

Now that you're thoroughly comfortable with Darwinism, let me rock your boat a bit.

In 1984, a radical new theory of evolution called molecular drive was introduced. Although it probably won't replace Darwin's theory of natural selection, the molecular drive theory reported by Gabriel A. Dover, a biologist at the University of Cambridge, England, provides new insights into how random genetic mutations can modify the shape of an animal and possibly make it better able to survive. His theory of molecular drive assumes that changes in animal populations happen first, without regard to environmental changes.

Stephen Jay Gould, a Harvard University biologist, called the theory "radical" and "probably correct."

Dover points out that many genes come in multiple copies, and these multiple copies can interact with each other. If one (gene in the family) mutates (a change in the hereditary materials that may result in a change in the phenotype of the offspring), it can transfer that mutation to all copies.

There are at least three ways the mutations can occur: transposition, in which genes jump around on the chromosomes; unequal exchange, in which pieces of genes move; and, gene conversion.

In gene conversion, one member of a family mutates (for example, of 100 genes one mutates). The remaining 99 copies of the chromosomes are unchanged.

But because similar genes can interact with each other, a property only recently discovered, the mutant gene can convert all the others into the same mutation.

As more and more genes are converted, the body of the animal begins to change. (See the example of the giraffe that is explained later in this chapter under *The Role of the Environment.*)

As more and more copies of the mutation spread among the family of genes on the chromosomes, the change is further exploited.

The mutation happens first and spreads in the animal population and, Dover says, "the animal must shift his habitat to exploit the change." The change came first and the change in behavior second. That's the opposite of how Darwin explained it.

Darwin didn't know about genes, but he did know that there was substantial diversity in nature, and that changes could arise in an animal. It later was shown that genetic mutations caused these changes.

Darwin concluded that natural selection acted on these newly risen characteristics that helped the animal survive. Darwin theorized that there were small, gradual changes in related animals until they no longer resembled each other and evolved into a new species.

Dover's ideas about molecular drive theorize that there are

Setter Puppies

The Maltese.

rapid changes in the animal's genes – faster than known mutation rates. Dover is not abandoning natural selection, but believes that natural selection operates on the characteristics created by molecular drive.

We need to be aware that the molecular drive theory is just one of dozens of new findings complicating the traditional view of evolution. Many experts have felt that the classic theory didn't fit the new data coming out of the different fields.

For example, the belief that evolution proceeded gradually had already been challenged by Niles Eldredge from the American Museum of Natural History and Harvard's Gould because the fossil records seemed to show that there were bursts of rapid change.

It now appears that mass extinctions made a significant contribution to the development of new species, as occurred 65 million years ago when the dinosaurs apparently were wiped out by a major cataclysmic event, the exact nature of which is still being debated.

After that catastrophe, the smaller animals that survived, including small mouse-like mammals, proliferated and evolved into many new species.

Eldredge points out that "we are not looking for a simple theory." Rather, he expects that several related explanations will replace the simple models that dominated evolutionary thought since the 1930s.

The Role of the Environment

The environment plays a crucial role in natural selection. Darwin hypothesized that the environment acts as a selector on existing varieties. For example, the snow hare did not develop a white coat in response to the coming of winter; nor did it develop one because of the need to be camouflaged. Instead, winter changes in coat color enabled some hares to blend with the backgrounds. Those without such variations were more likely to be caught by predators. Thus, organisms may change or evolve in response to their environments. Changes in the environment may create a need for change. However, it is not sufficient to provide a desired change. A genetic potential must exist. It is the genetic potential of a population that produces variety. The environment can then select from that variety.

Let us use the giraffe as an example. We will begin with the short-necked ancestors. Among these, some might have had longer necks than others. This is an example of population variability. (In Golden Retrievers, for example, there are definitely three types: the tall, rather light-boned type, the big, heavy-coated bear type and a third, which is a compromise between the others.) Competition from other animals forced these giraffes to seek food from higher up in tree branches. (James Michener, in his book *Alaska*, points out a similar adaptation in the extra-long legs of the moose.) Those with longer necks would be favored in such an environment. In turn, they would survive longer, thus producing more off-spring than those with shorter necks. Offspring tend to be like their parents. Hence, they would also have somewhat longer necks than average. Over many generations, there would be a constant selective pressure by the environment. This would result in the longer necks of the giraffes that we know today.

Artificial Selection

The principles of natural selection had been in use long before Darwin's time. Early humans had no doubt used them to tame or domesticate certain animals. Using the principles of natural selection to domesticate wild organisms has been called "artificial selection." Organisms that had useful traits were selected by our ancestors, i.e., dogs that hunted and help put food on the table and dogs that herded or guarded flocks were thus favored. Continued selection eventually produced a wide range of useful plants and animals.

This improvement of species, of course, is dictated by human needs and desires, and thus artificial.

We know that the many varieties of dogs are all products of artificial selection. Once domesticated, variations in the species allowed selection for hunting, racing, herding, and many other uses.

The fact that artificial selection works, indicates that there is genetic variation in populations. This exists for almost every characteristic of the organism. The amount of variation in natural populations is much greater than that predicted by Darwin's ideas on survival.

Role of Sexual Reproduction

New mutations may occur in each generation. These are not the only sources of diversity. Because of sexual reproduction, chromosomes are constantly being shuffled into new combinations. Such mixing results in new genotype and phenotypes (the visible properties of an organism that are produced by the interaction of the genotype and the environment). These then can be acted upon by the environment.

As we have learned earlier, reproduction involves the union of male and female cells. Each reproductive cell contains one set of chromosomes. As these cells unite, the chromosomes are mixed. This recombination of genetic traits may produce new phenotypes. Such random assortment also results in new combinations of chromosomes in the reproductive cells. Recombination and random assortment account for a mixing of alleles (the two alternative forms of a gene for a mendelian trait) in a population. They do not, in themselves, cause evolution. The mixing results in new combinations of alleles. These alleles then can be exposed to selection at each new generation.

The nature vs. nurture argument has caused much debate regarding both humans and dogs for generations past. Dr. Ian Dunbar, a noted animal behaviorist and geneticist, writing in the October 1990 American Kennel Club *Gazette* points out: "We must accept both genetic and environmental effects as critically important in development, and it would be silly to consider one without the other. Rather than working against each other, let's accept the importance of both theoretical perspectives."

Dr. Dunbar is adamant that selective breeding could have a considerably greater beneficial effect if breeding stock were selected more carefully. The most common mistake is to select by phenotype instead of by genotype. Most people select prospective breeding stock by looking at show dogs, which by definition, obviously look good since they represent the best of the crop. To evaluate comprehensively a genotype and discover the genetic flaws in the line, it is important to view as many of a dog's relatives as possible, paying particular attention to the pet quality relatives. A preponderance of phenotypical problems in pet quality relatives is a good reason to suspect the genotype of all animals in the line.

Improved selection could go a long way towards the prevention of most physiological and physical defects.

Applying Genetics to Breeding Better Dogs

It has been said that the Standards of many breeds are recessive Standards. More simply stated, this means that everything that is *good* is recessive and everything that is *bad* is dominant. Of course, this is not entirely true even though it may seem to be so at times. But what about some of the bodily characteristics—knowledge of which could solve some breeder's particular problems.

In setting out to accomplish our aim of breeding the perfect dog, it is helpful to understand why each specimen differs somewhat from every other specimen.

Fortunately, more and more breeders are becoming increasingly aware of the necessity of acquiring knowledge of the basic laws of genetics.

One need not be surprised, then, after considering the immense number of possible chromosome combinations, in seldom finding two identical animals. Further, it can also be understood how it is possible for a high-class specimen to be produced by supposedly indifferent parents as a result of the combination of the best of material of each parent and the elimination of all that tends to bring about or produce inferiority.

On the other hand, it can be understood how the exact reverse might also be true. Renowned parents might produce mediocre offspring, the reason attributed to such an occurrence being a retention of chromatin productive of undesirable characteristics, and the elimination of chromatin productive of desirable characteristics. (*Chromatin* is the substance within the nucleus of the cell from which the chromosomes develop.)

In the more or less mysterious work of heredity, there is and must ever be a large element of chance. Chance determines what portions of the hereditary material will go to each offspring. One is not justified in assuming, however, that each chromosome is entirely different from all the others in the same or in another parent. The chances are they are largely similar. The difficulty arises in that they may be arranged in such a great number of combinations or sets and the arrangement of these combinations is beyond all human control.

If it is impossible to bring any influence to bear upon the manner of separating the portion of hereditary material which is to make up the new animal, then how is it possible to be assured of good results? By using for breeding stock only animals that give us good reason to believe that any selection from their supply of hereditary substances will contain a minimum of possibilities for undesirable characteristics. To reduce the element of chance in breeding, the breeder must limit his breeding by selection—by selecting and mating only individuals containing chromatin or hereditary material which holds the greatest possibilities for desirable characteristics and the least possibilities for undesirable characteristics. When these individuals are coupled (no matter what hereditary bodies are eliminated or combined by Dame Nature), the result is still for good and the chance of unwelcome qualities appearing is in the minority.

Practical geneticists have spent most of their time working on problems relating to agriculture and the improvement of valuable livestock. This is understandable, for the health and wealth of a nation are directly dependent upon the health and wealth of its agriculture. Therefore, relatively little work has been done in such fields as dog breeding. Great credit should be given to pioneers in this field, those scientists whose interest in dogs led to countless hours of study and the patient recording of their observations, experiences, and results in dog breeding, which work was largely and often entirely personally financed. The publication of the findings and theories of these scientists has added, bit by bit, to our current knowledge of canine genetics and has laid the foundation for many future investigations.

We have come to learn that the skeletal structure of a dog is determined by the interaction of a large number of genes while the color of a dog's coat may be determined by a single pair. It is no surprise that more is known about color inheritance than structural inheritance. Though the color of a dog's coat may be determined by a single gene or by a pair of genes, the skeletal structure of a dog is determined by the interaction of a large number of genes. It should not be difficult to understand why something as highly complex as the structure of a dog's head or body is not controlled by the actions of a single hereditary factor or pair of factors.

Let us take movement, for example. Needless to say, there is no one gene labeled "gait" which has the ability to determine whether an individual puppy will move properly or improperly. Rather, there are *countless* genes, working in harmony or against each other, which determine these facts.

What factors enable an individual dog to move in a way which has been designated as correct for its particular breed? Every breed has a characteristic gait, which is determined by its structure; not the structure of the legs, or the feet, or the hips, or the shoulders, but the structure of all of the parts of the dog. Thus the Chow moves with short steps and stilted action, the Pekingese and Bulldog "roll" along, and the German Shepherd covers ground rapidly with far-reaching steps and a "smooth" action.

These differences in gait are the result of differences in structure—the manner in which all the body parts are assembled in an individual.

There may be numerous structural faults which are responsible for a type of gait which is incorrect for the Bassett Hound. The hindquarters may lack the strength of bone and muscle to propel the rest of the dog forward properly, or they may be improperly placed or lack the proper angulation of hock and stifle to allow freedom of reach and a flexible stride. There are many other faults which could be responsible for an unnatural or incorrect gait.

As an example, faults of angulation may affect either the hindquarters or the forequarters, but they are most likely to affect both. If the hindquarters are affected, they lack the power to drive the body forward in a far-reaching, rhythmic stride. If the fault lies in the shoulders or front legs, the ability to take long steps with the front legs is impeded, and no matter how well-built the hindquarters may be, the animal will move in a way which suggests the front end is trying desperately to keep up with the hindquarters. To compensate for the lack of evenly distributed power and coordination, the animal may develop various habits which allow him to get to where he wants to go but which result in an awkward, choppy, or unbalanced way of moving.

Assuming the faults under discussion lie in the hindquarters, the question is, "How is angulation of hock and stifle inherited?" Again, the fact must be pointed out that whether a stifle is straight or well-turned, whether a back is long or short, or whether a foreface is deeply chiseled or built up with bone and muscle is *not* determined by the action of a single gene or pair of genes, or even, in all probability, by hereditary factors alone. When we seek to determine the manner in which any part of an animal's skeletal structure is inherited, we are not dealing with single-factor inheritance, but with *multiple-factor inheritance*.

Any attempt to explain multiple-factor inheritance fully would prove of little interest to readers who have had no training in advanced genetics. However, the following facts may serve to give a better understanding of this complex subject:

1. What we see and describe as a single character (a leg, foot, tail, etc.) is often affected and influenced in its development by *a large number of different and unrelated genes* which are capable of independent assortment (recombining with other genes in various ways at the time of reproduction).

2. It is extremely difficult to sort out the various genes which influence a particular character and to determine the specific effect each has on that character. In other words, just how important is the part each gene plays in the development of that particular character?

3. Since it is difficult to sort out these genes and identify them in relation to their importance in the development of a particular character, it is difficult to determine their manner of inheritance. Some genes have a direct, complete influence on the development of a character (*dominant genes*). Others have only a partial effect, being neutralized to some extent by the action of the opposing member of the pair of which it is one (*incompletely dominant genes*). Some genes are completely masked and have no effect unless such genes comprise both members of a given pair (*recessive genes*). In the study of any given character, only careful records obtained on a large scale will throw light on the differences between these types of hereditary action and influence.

4. The combination of multiple gene effects with environmental influences is the rule rather than the exception in such characters as body length, height, weight, head and muzzle development, tooth characteristics, foot size and shape, muscle and bone development, and such recognized "faults" as loose shoulders, flat ribs, cowhocks, weak pasterns, and splay feet. As an example, it has been found that body size depends upon some genes that affect all the tissues and upon others that influence only certain regions, such as the legs, neck, head, or tail. Then in addition, diet, exercise, and other environmental influences determine to some extent the degree to which these genes are able to stimulate and produce growth of the different tissues, organs, and body parts.

There are some one hundred and thirty breeds that are eligible for registration by The American Kennel Club. None of these breeds is "purebred" in the true genetic sense of the word; that is, all of them are subject to variations of form and type which may account for considerable differences in appearance between specimens of the same breed. Unlike certain strains of laboratory mice, which have been standardized by inbreeding and selection, and which are like peas in a pod, no breed of dog exists which reproduces its own kind without variations or differences which may be either slight or considerable in degree.

It is probable that the major differences which exist between breeds are due to independent genes which may be found in one breed and not in another. Therefore, the manner in which the multiple hereditary factors responsible for the construction of a Greyhound's body are inherited, may differ from the manner in which the countless genes which build a Keeshond's body are inherited. If breeders really want to know more about the manner in which such complex parts as the body, legs, head, and other structural parts are inherited, the following will be necessary:

1. Observations of a larger number of animals, resulting in careful and accurate records of the differences in structure which exist *within the breed*.

2. Accurately recorded breeding tests between animals of contrasting structural types, and recorded observations

The Siberian Husky.

of their resulting offspring. This may well require the crossing of breeds at one or more genetic research laboratories. In this way, extreme types can be compared and the inheritance of marked differences in structure can be studied.

3. The making available of these records to scientists who are qualified to analyze them. Obviously, the task of breeding and raising a large enough number of animals representing different breeds, the recording of observations of their structural types and the types of their offspring, is beyond the finances and ability of any one person or any one institution. However, such data could be collected by breeders at no additional expense and with a small amount of additional work. Each breeder's records could be sent to a central location at a scientific laboratory for tabulation and analysis and any resulting conclusions could, in turn, be made available to breeders.

What kind of questions pertaining to inheritance in dogs can geneticists answer right now? Information pertaining to a great variety of subjects is available, such as the color differences found in the coat, eyes, and skin of most breeds of dogs; differences in the length, quantity, texture, and distribution of hair; various reproductive problems such as fertility, fecundity, the production of stillborn or non-viable young, and such conditions as monorchidism and cryptorchidism; various abnormalities and malformations resulting from arrested development, such as harelip, cleft palate, cleft abdomen, etc.; such diseases as hemophilia and night blindness; differences in ear, eye, nose, jaw, foot, and tail characteristics; differences in size or length of leg, and other leg bone characteristics; differences in head size and shape; and numerous physiological and psychological differences resulting in characteristic patterns of behavior.

The Scottish Terrier.

It has already been pointed out that many of the characteristics in the above list are influenced by multiple genes and/or that they are affected in varying degrees by environmental factors. Therefore, the available information pertaining to most of these subjects is incomplete, though in some breeds and for some characteristics it is surprisingly extensive.

As was discussed in an earlier chapter, it is sometimes necessary to "take" one fault in a breed in order to "eliminate" another—a sort of "swapping" arrangement. The fault we have to "take" may be one that is easy to eliminate later on or it may not be anything very serious in the breed, even though it may "show" in an otherwise excellent specimen.

INBREEDING

Many breeders have skirted around the edges of inbreeding but have shied away from carrying it to its full fruition. As a means of finding which animals have the best genes, inbreeding seems to deserve more use than it has yet received. Not only does it uncover recessives more surely than any other method, but also it increases the relationship between the inbred animal and its parents and other relatives so that the animal's pedigree and the merits of the family to which it belongs become more dependable as indicators of its own genes than can be the case with animals which are not inbred.

Considerable inbreeding is necessary if family selection is to be very effective. As we have learned, the gene is the unit of inheritance, but the animal is the smallest unit which can be chosen or rejected for breeding purposes. To breed exclusively from one or two of the best specimens available would tend to fix their qualities, both good and bad. In fact, that is the essence of what happens under extreme inbreeding. Moreover, the breeder will make at least a few mistakes in estimating which animals have the very best inheritance. Hence, in a practical program, the breeder will hesitate to use even a very good stud too extensively.

The breeder also is far from having final authority to decide how many offspring each of his bitches will produce. Some of his basic stock may die or prove to be sterile or will be prevented by a wide variety of factors from having as many get as the breeder wants. Bitches from which he wants a top stud dog may persist in producing only females for several litters. Consequently, some specimens from which he really did not want so many offspring leave more to make up for the offspring he does not get from the dog he prefers.

The ideal plan for the most rapid improvement of the breed may differ from the plan of the individual breeder chiefly in that he dare not risk quite so much inbreeding deterioration. If the object were to improve the breed with little regard for immediate show prospects, then it would be a different story. Let's go into this in greater detail.

As we know, inbreeding refers to the mating of two closely related individuals. Most breeders practice inbreeding to a limited extent even though they may term it close line breeding. Actually, the breeding of half brother x half sister as well as niece x uncle or nephew x aunt is a limited form of inbreeding. For purposes of this discussion, however, inbreeding will refer to the mating of full brother x full sister, father x daughter, and son x mother. Most breeders probably consider these three categories as representative of true inbreeding.

It is not the purpose of this chapter to advocate or condemn the practice of inbreeding, but, rather, to ascertain what it cannot accomplish. It will also be the objective to present known facts and dispel some common fallacies.

It certainly would be interesting to know exactly what percentage of inbreeding does take place in various breeds and what results are obtained. Speaking in generalities, it would probably be safe to say that only one to two percent of all champions finishing within the past ten years were the products of inbreeding (brother x sister, father x daughter, son x mother) and perhaps that is being generous. On this basis, one would reasonably conclude that the practice of inbreeding on these terms is relatively rare.

In the breeding of domestic animals such as cattle, chickens, etc., as well as in plant breeding, inbreeding is regarded as a most valuable tool to fix a desired type and purify a strain. Scientific experiments have proven this to be a fact. This raises the question as to why inbreeding has not gained more widespread acceptance among dog breeders. By combining inbreeding with the selection of those individuals most nearly ideal in appearance and temperament, the desired stability of the stock is quickly obtained.

Breeding the offspring of the father x daughter or son x mother mating back to a parent is called "backcrossing." To illustrate this, suppose an outstanding male specimen is produced and the breeder's thought is to obtain more of the same type: the male is bred back to his dam, and the breeder retains the best bitch pups in the resulting litter. By breeding these bitch pups back to the excellent male (backcrossing), there is a good chance that some of the pups produced as a result of this backcross will resemble the outstanding sire greatly. In backcrossing to a superior breeding male, one may find some inbreeding degeneration in the offspring, but this is improbable according to Dr. Ojvind Winge in his book *Inheritance in Dogs*.

The mating of brothers x sisters is far more likely to produce inbreeding degeneration. This is because a brother x sister mating is the most intense form of inbreeding. Studies show that those breeders who have attempted to cross full brothers and sisters, for the purpose of fixing good characteristics in their stock, give very contradictory reports of their results. One will often find that the mating of brother x sister results in somewhat decreased vitality and robustness in the offspring.

It may happen that abnormal or stillborn individuals are segregated out in the litter if special weakening genes are carried in the stock. On the other hand, it is just as certain that one can be fortunate enough to avoid inbreeding degeneration. *Everything depends upon the hereditary nature of the animals concerned.* Inbreeding degeneration is of such a peculiar nature that it may be totally abolished by a single crossing with unrelated or distantly related animals. However, if it had made its appearance, the breeder should know it was present in the hereditary make-up of his stock.

Most of the studies on inbreeding are in agreement with one another. The decline in vigor, including the extinction of certain lines, follows largely the regrouping and fixing (making alike) of recessive genes which are, on the whole, injurious to the breed. However, along with the fixing of such recessives, there is also a fixing of gene pairs which are beneficial and desirable. It is a matter of chance as to what combination gene pairs a family finally comes to possess, except that selection is always at work weeding out combinations that are not well adapted to the conditions of life. There is a common belief that inbreeding causes the production of monstrosities and defectives. Seemingly reliable evidence indicates that inbreeding itself has no specific connection with the production of monstrosities. Inbreeding seems merely to have brought to light genetic traits in the original stock.

Among the most interesting and extensive investigations on inbreeding in animals is a series of experiments on guinea pigs begun in 1906 by the U.S. Department of Agriculture. Thirty-five healthy and vigorous females were selected from general breeding stock and mated with the same number of similarly selected males. The matings were numbered separately and the offspring of each mating were kept separate and mated exclusively brother x sister. Only the best two of each generation were selected to carry on the succeeding generations.

Two striking results followed this close inbreeding. First, each family became more like itself. While this was going on, there was a gradual elimination of sub-branches. Second, there was a decline in vigor during the first nine years, covering about twelve generations. This decline applied to weight, fertility, and vitality of the young.

During the second nine years of inbreeding, there was no further decline in vigor of the inbred animals as a group. This stability was taken to mean that after twelve generations, the families had become essentially pure-bred—that is, no longer different with respect to many genes. New mutations were not frequent enough to have effect. No evidence was found of inheritance of general vigor as a unit. The vigor of a family in one respect was

largely independent of its vigor in other respects. As a result of the inbreeding, members of each family came to be extremely alike with respect to such characteristics as hair color, eye color, and bodily conformation.

The theoretical rate at which continued brother x sister matings increase their alikeness has been calculated by a number of investigators. The most reliable calculations at hand indicate the reduction in the proportion of unlike gene pairs closely approximates 19.1 percent per generation after the first generation, in which the reduction is 25 percent. This rate is so rapid that after ten generations of brother x sister matings, starting with specimens that are 50 percent alike, about 94 percent of all gene pairs are alike. Therefore, such inbreeding produces its greatest effect during the earlier generations and relatively little effect if continued beyond ten to twelve generations.

What does all this mean in relation to breeding good dogs? From the foregoing data several conclusions are obvious. Inbreeding coupled with selection can be utilized to "fix" traits in breeding stock at a rapid rate. These traits may be good or they may be undesirable, depending entirely upon the individuals' hereditary nature. Inbreeding creates nothing *new*—it merely intensifies what is already present. If the hereditary nature of an individual contains undesirable traits, these will naturally be manifested when the recessive genes become regrouped and fixed. This applies to the desirable traits as well.

As previously described, the term *genotype* refers to the complete genetic make-up of an individual, in contrast to the apparent, or visible, type of the individual, which is called *phenotype*. In selecting puppies to retain for breeding stock, breeders must rely on phenotype because they have no way of knowing an unproven individual's genotype. Inbreeding can reduce genotype and phenotype to one common denominator.

Suppose that an outstanding specimen appears which is the product of inbreeding. What would this mean in terms of breeding? It would mean that this specimen has a greater chance of passing on his visible traits rather than possible hidden traits. Prepotent dogs and bitches are usually those that are pure for many of their outstanding characteristics. Since such a limited amount of inbreeding has been carried on in most breeds, prepotent specimens have become pure for certain traits more or less by chance, for they have appeared in all breeds as products of outcrossing as well as by line breeding.

Since line breeding, and especially close line breeding, is a limited form of inbreeding, the same good and bad points apply to line breeding but in a much more modified degree. The practice of inbreeding appears to be extremely limited in dogs, so one must assume that breeders are willing to trade slower progress for a lower element of risk with respect to degeneration.

The Telltale Gene

The day may not be far off when veterinarians perform genetic tests much as they do x-rays. In humans, genetic tests that could be exquisitely more revealing than a cholesterol count or blood pressure reading are now making their way from research laboratories into medical practice. Genetic testing is already a common part of obstetrical care and standard procedure for newborns. Would-be sperm donators face similar scrutiny.

And now the dog world is doing it. Every dog has genetic problems. Now, solutions may be in sight, and these solutions may be in a drop or two of blood.

Three leading organizations for dogs, The American Kennel Club, Morris Animal Foundation and the Orthopedic Foundation for Animals, have launched a study to seek the causes/cures for inherited diseases in dogs. It is being conducted by human geneticists at the University of Michigan and veterinary specialists at Michigan State University.

Some inherited disorders are minor, like eye color or coat patterns not recognized by the rules of that breed. Some, such as "water puppies" in bulldogs or skull deformities in small terrier breeds, kill puppies before or shortly after birth.

Others, like hip dysplasia, cataract, Progressive Retinal Atrophy or copper toxicosis are time bombs, crippling or fatal disorders ticking away in dogs that appear perfectly normal. Symptoms don't appear until later in life, often after a dog has been bred and passed the disorder on to another generation.

Dogs, like humans, have about 100,000 genes, any one of which can mutate or change. Fortunately, only a few mutations are harmful.

Until a few years ago, the only way to find out if a dog carried problem genes, especially recessive traits where carriers show no symptoms, was through test matings. A test dog was bred to a known affected dog. If any puppies had the disorder, the test dog was confirmed as a carrier.

New molecular genetics techniques let scientists examine genes directly under high-powered microscopes.

They don't have to find the exact gene that causes the problem. A new technique called molecular genetic linkage allows them to find "marker" genes. These marker genes are near the disease gene of interest, and are inherited along with the disease gene on the same chromosome.

With the ability to examine genes and their location on chromosomes, scientists learned that there is a great deal of similarity between species. Disease genes and markers linked in humans often are the same as those in rats, whales, monkeys and other species. Comparing disease markers in other species to similar diseases in dogs is a shortcut which may help identify disease genes more quickly.

By taking a blood sample and comparing it to the disease (markers) already discovered, scientists and later-practicing veterinarians (and if the dog's parentage is known) will be able to identify all dogs with the gene whether it is recessive or dominant, and whether the dogs are carriers or are affected.

One of the major breakthroughs of this kind of study will allow superior animals, which may be carriers, to continue to be used in breeding programs when caution is used. With a trained veterinarian's guidance, the new test will allow breeders to avoid breeding another carrier dog, or to select non-affected or non-carrier offspring for future breeding. On an unscientific note, it may also end witch hunts in a breed where many popular studs stand accused.

The potential impact of genetic testing is tremendous. In only a few generations, a breed can be rid of harmful genetic traits - an option not open to human geneticists, who seldom have as much success convincing their clients to select mates based on genetic compatibility.

The advance of genetic testing will pose unique challenges to breeders of purebred dogs. In many ways, genetic information is unlike any other medical data. It may forecast illness years in advance of symptoms. And because many genetic tests are still imperfect predictors, the risk of a future health problem may have to be expressed only as an increased probability, not a certainty, adding to the difficulty of making decisions. The incomplete dominance and degree of penetrance of cataract in American Cocker Spaniels comes to mind.

Once the experimentation is over, the genetic testing and counseling services will need to shift eventually from university settings to primary care veterinarians. Unfortunately, genetics has historically had a low priority in medical and veterinary school training. This indicates the need for a large scale training program for in-practice vets and added study in colleges of veterinary medicine.

George Brewer, M.D., one of the principal investigators at the University of Michigan, indicated that genetic diseases are difficult to control because so many of the carriers are "hidden."

Dominant genes are like bicycle tires. If one is "flat," or defective, it is easy to see, so dogs with dominant genetic problems are not bred. Continuing the analogy, recessive genes may be likened to automobile headlights. The driver sees light whether one or two headlights are burning. The problem is visible only if two lights burn out – or if the animal receives two defective genes. Carriers – those with one headlight burned out – can't be distinguished from normal dogs.

A third type of genetic problem is even more difficult to detect. In polygenic diseases, such as hip dysplasia, the problem is caused by a defect in more than one gene.

Genetic counseling in humans produces little change in the gene pool, Dr. Brewer said. People still have children in most cases, even if they know they carry genetic defects. Dog breeders, on the other hand, can make a substantial change in the gene pool of their breed by refusing to breed dogs with defects.

In developing probes or "markers" for disease genes, the teams of researchers are concerned about the diversity of dog breeds. They hope that the same probes will work in Great Danes and Chihuahuas. To date, those that have been developed seem to be successful in a variety of dog breeds.

Dr. Brewer envisions a canine resource library in Michigan that can be used by canine veterinary investigative teams working on specific diseases and by dog organizations which wish to work to eradicate major genetic problems.

The science behind the newest genetic tests dates back less than 20 years to the beginning of genetic engineering. Armed with the ability to cut, splice, and transplant genetic material, scientists set to work deciphering the estimated 100,000 genes tucked into the nucleus of virtually every human (and dog) cell. Collectively, genes comprise the complete set of chemical instructions for making a human being or a dog (or any other creature for that matter). Each gene codes for the production of a single polypeptide (a protein compound); untold thousands of proteins give the body function and form.

Even a tiny genetic error can derail protein production, resulting in disease or deformity. In humans, more than 4,000 inherited disorders are due to single-gene defects. (Many more are thought to be influenced by multiple genes or by a combination of genes and environment.) I have long held this theory regarding cataract in the American Cocker Spaniel.

Locating a specific disease-associated gene on one of the 78 chromosomes gives researchers the basis for a diagnostic test. With gene in hand, it may be possible in later studies to identify the protein for which it codes, a giant step toward understanding the disease and developing treatment for it.

The Best to the Best

The preceding chapters dealt with building a foundation of knowledge. How best to apply this knowledge in a practical way is the real test of the breeder. Interestingly, very few scientific reports are available that go into detail about developing strains of dogs which have been established deliberately under research conditions. There are three such reports which will be described.

The author is indebted to the J. B. Lippincott Company (publishers) and Marcia Burns and Margaret N. Fraser (authors) for permission to quote from their 1966 book, *Genetics of the Dog*, which reported on these studies.

The projects resembled each other in many ways. In all, the breed concerned was a Working breed and success at work was the essential criterion by which the dogs were judged. In the case of Dr. Kelley's Boveagh strain of Border Collies in Australia (1949), one type of work only was required of the dogs—namely, shepherding. In the second example, the Fortunate Fields German Shepherd Dogs, each dog was tested for suitability in a number of vocations and trained for that work for which it showed most aptitude. Authors Humphrey and Warner (1934), although primarily concerned with the breeding of outstanding Working Dogs, gave considerable attention to the relationship between conformation, show points, and working ability. They detail their conclusions as to the inheritance of particular attributes. In this chapter we will focus on their breeding system.

The third and much more recent attempt to establish, by scientific methods, an outstanding strain of Working Dogs is that of Guide Dogs for the Blind, Inc., at San Rafael, California. In this work by Clarence Pfaffenberger (1963), a Cocker Spaniel breeder and exhibitor of some note, full advantage was taken both of previous knowledge—particularly that derived from similar work of Fortunate Fields—and of the then-current researches of the Roscoe P. Jackson Memorial Laboratory. (The author also has made extensive use of the work of the Jackson Laboratory done in the 1940s.) The cooperation which developed between practical dog breeders and trainers and leading scientists led to very rapid advances, such that the percentage of dogs successfully completing their training as guide dogs rose from 9% in 1946 to 90% in 1958. As compared with Fortunate Fields, the selection process was simplified by ignoring show points and most structural features, and depending almost entirely on the results of behavior tests applied to young puppies. Attention was paid, however, to selection for optimal size for the job, and to selection of dogs without hip abnormalities. Analysis of the first year's records revealed a strong correlation between high scores in "fetch and eye tests" and subsequent success in guide dog work. Scores in these tests then were used to guide selection of breeding stock, and pedigree analysis subsequently showed that the majority of high-scoring animals were descended from certain bloodlines. Among German Shepherd Dogs, a certain sire was found to be prepotent, and a policy of line breeding to this dog was followed. It has been found that the highest percentage of this bloodline (up to 48%) gives the highest percentage of good test scores, and many 100% litters (every puppy successfully trained as a guide dog) have now been bred. No "bad" effects of inbreeding have occurred so far. The accumulated data led to the conclusion that the qualities which enabled a puppy to score high in the tests—particularly the fetch test—are inherited as quantitative characters.

It is a very significant fact that the geneticists concerned with these three strains did not start with any exact knowledge of the mode of inheritance of particular characteristics in their dogs. In some instances, after many years' work, the authors express the opinion that certain characteristics are probably inherited in a simple Mendelian manner, either as dominant or as recessive factors, but even in these few instances they do not claim that the mode of inheritance has been proved with certainty. In the meantime, before even that knowledge of Mendelian factors became available to them, the main object of their work had been achieved, for they had, in fact, succeeded in developing superior strains of dogs. They have done this far more rapidly and with a far greater degree of success than is usually attained even by the above-average dog breeder; indeed, very few breeders have ever equaled their achievements. (Of course, it must be kept in mind that most dog breeders do not have the resources, both money and staff, to accomplish what has been noted above.) However, the average dog breeder can, to a great extent, by emulating the techniques used, elevate his breeding stock to a much higher state of perfection.

What each of these reports shows is careful recording, objective analysis and assessment of the characteristics of each dog, and rigid selection of breeding animals on the basis of performance, pedigree, and, where possible, some kind of progeny test; then line breeding to animals proven as outstanding producers. These have been the bases of success in all of these projects. There is nothing in these methods which is obscure or beyond the reach of any intelligent dog breeder.

(In previous chapters we commented on the use of observation, measurement, and analysis. In fact, using these same techniques, we bred twenty-four champions from twenty-three litters and had stud dogs which sired over sixty champions.)

Genetical theory influenced the investigators mainly in two matters: the emphasis on progeny testing as a method of distinguishing genotype from phenotype, and the calculations of inbreeding coefficients.

Calculation of inbreeding coefficients is based on the assumption that each animal receives one-half of its inheritance (genotype) from each parent. While this is not strictly correct, it, in general, holds true. Obviously, every gene a dog gets from its grandparents must come through its parents, so that at the time of fertilization the whole of its inheritance is derived from its parents, although not necessarily quite equally from each. The purpose of an inbreeding coefficient is to give a measure of the increase in homozygosity—i.e., the increased opportunity for the similar genes to reach the progeny through both parents. Think of it as a number of dice in a dice box, with the possible numbers on each dice ranging from one to six. Each cast of the dice will give a certain proportion of each number according to random probability theory. By reducing the proportion of low numbers in the box and increasing the higher numbers, each throw naturally enough will produce only a greater number of high numbers. That is what we seek in breeding—to increase the odds of getting the genes that we want (higher numbers) and of producing an animal that is homozygous for the traits we want.

Kelley found that certain matings, which would have resulted in pups with an inbreeding coefficient of more than 25%, were infertile or produced weak pups, although animals with a coefficient of about 20% were highly satisfactory. He therefore concluded that 20% inbreeding was the maximum which could be used safely in this *particular strain,* and by calculating inbreeding coefficients in advance, he was able to avoid matings which would be dangerously close. No exact safety limit was established in the Fortunate Fields dogs, but inbreeding coefficients were used for guidance in a similar way. In both strains, a number of separate line bred families were developed and then matings were made between these inbred families. In the Boveagh dogs, the families were all closely related and descended from the same foundation animals, with a slight infusion of unrelated bloodlines introduced from time to time to prevent too-close inbreeding. This is called "controlled heterosis." The Fortunate Fields strain began with a large number of foundation animals which were little related to each other, so that there was less danger of excessive inbreeding since the families within the strain were not so closely related as in the Boveagh dogs. In later generations, however, it probably would be necessary to introduce a small amount of outside blood. In the major strain of German Shepherds at San Rafael, three lines have been established. These three lines can be interbred if necessary, although only one is very strongly inbred (48%).

Kelley, in describing the development of the Boveagh strain, does not give any analysis of the qualities required in his dogs, other than success at everyday shepherding work and at sheepdog trials. The only other quality mentioned is short coat, which is desired because it is considered more suitable than the rough coat for Australian conditions. The foundation animals were selected because of their temperaments and high working ability, and if any outcross was found to introduce any fault of temperament, that dog and its descendants were immediately discarded from the strain. (How many of us do that, especially in a prized breeding in a small kennel?) All pups were allowed to see and to work sheep when about ten weeks old, before they knew their names or had been controlled in any way, and pups for retention were selected at that time, on the basis of the extent to which their instinctive behavior was similar to that which is held ideal for adults. This probably is the most important factor in selection. Attention also was paid to any special signs of intelligence, such as unusual ability to escape the kennel enclosure.

Humphrey and Warner, on the other hand, give very great detail concerning the qualities required, and developed a scoring system by which the assessment of each dog was expressed. In all, thirty-two traits were listed for each dog, of which the great majority were concerned with structural characteristics or other physical attributes such as color. However, the single trait of temperament was given such a high proportion of the total score that no animal failing in this respect would be passed as a breeding animal. (As a breeder, I once made the mistake of being captivated by a young male dog. He had all of the physical attributes required by the breed Standard. His color was perfect. After an intense retraining period, he did show and complete his championship. He quickly sired five champions in his first three litters. However, they had both temperament and physical problems. The stud dog was promptly retired and all persons owning his get were notified. All of these problems could have been avoided if, following proper breeding discipline, the dog had been discarded.) The only qualities penalized under temperament by Humphrey and Warner were shyness and distrust. Other psychological traits such as intelligence, willingness, and aggression were not weighted in the total score, but were scored separately, since it was not considered desirable that dogs having low scores in these traits should be eliminated, for breeding animals were selected and paired with each other entirely on the basis of calculations (the formula for which is given in their book) derived from the detailed records and scoring system. The main pressure of selection was against bad temperament (shyness) and was successful in that there was a rapid drop in the proportion of shy dogs produced in the strain after the first generation. Traits which followed an upward trend (improvement) included intelligence, ability to smell, willingness to work, energy, and aggressiveness, while fighting instinct was reduced by selection against it. In the foundation animals there was a negative correlation between show points and good temperament, but this was reversed in the third generation when a positive correlation appeared. A higher proportion of successful workers was produced in later generations.

It is apparent from the above that breed changes can take place. Some breeds look the same today as they did when the original Standards were written. Others today look entirely different from the original forebears. Selective breeding has successfully changed the type in the direction desired by breeders, giving shorter backs and deeper muzzles, and well-up-on-leg specimens.

Again in Humphrey and Warner's work, several interesting statistical correlations are revealed by analysis of the accumulated data. Chest development (depth and forechest) was correlated with good health, and so was flank development. Distrust was correlated between light eyes and high intelligence, despite selection in favor of dark eyes. Nevertheless, there is no evidence that light eyes are necessarily correlated with intelligence in other strains or breeds, and the authors concluded that no reliable association between structural and functional traits existed.

Examination of the pedigrees of the top producers and show winners invariably reveals the fact that successful dogs have always been produced by line breeding to famous animals.

It should be noted, however, that in some cases a famous stud dog was so widely used in his day that in subsequent generations it becomes difficult to find an individual that does not trace back to him—and this is true of the average and poor members of the breed as well as winners. In such a case the dog hardly can be said to have founded the winning bloodlines, though he may, like Obo in Cocker Spaniels (with a boost from Red Brucie), practically have founded the breed.

Prepotency, although usually a characteristic of

The Pointer.

The Bulldog.

somewhat inbred strains, does not occur equally in all members of a strain or family. Some individuals have a strong tendency to reproduce their general type or to produce outstanding offspring when bred to many different mates. Dogs and bitches with this tendency are extremely valuable to their breed.

The prepotency of a breeding animal may be attributed to several causes. The animal may carry dominant genes for a few conspicuous characteristics, such as black color, long coat, and sloping top line. There may be a general resemblance of the offspring to one parent in some physiological trait, such as the disease resistance of the Bull Terrier, and this is generally associated with a resemblance in type. Prepotency in so-called quantitative characters is generally the result of inbreeding, or, in

breed crosses, of one breed having been established longer than the other. Environmental conditions during development may favor the exhibition in the offspring of qualities characteristic of one parent rather than those of the other parent.

As all breeders can appreciate, the prime concern is with the adult dog or bitch. The appearance or performance of the puppy is of little significance except as an indication of what the puppy will be like at maturity. The appearance and performance of the adult animal are, however, the outcome of many influences.

We've learned how easily a promising puppy can be ruined by bad rearing, and even more evident is the influence of training on the performance of Working Dogs.

If at any time it was possible to assess the merits of every living individual in a breed, giving a numerical score to each dog according to its quality, results would range from bad to excellent, and if the scores were plotted on a graph, the result would be a bell-shaped curve approximating a normal curve of distribution. The diagram below illustrates such a curve. The quality of any specimen produced by a breeder could be plotted similarly, and the aim should be to produce a line which has a merit-curve skewed to the right of the distribution curve of the breed as a whole. However, if success in the show ring is the aim, the curve for comparison is not the breed as a whole but the narrower, more select group of other show specimens. This is the level of quality one must equal or exceed.

If the quality of two specimens to be bred together places them both near one extreme of the curve—whether both are exceptionally good or exceptionally bad—their progeny will tend to be nearer to the average of the breed than the parents are, although the range of the litter will be toward the parents' end of the curve. If one parent is

Example of a normal Curve.

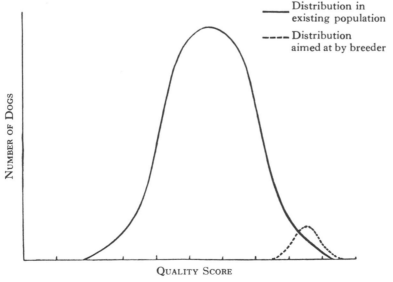

———— Distribution in existing population

- - - - Distribution aimed at by breeder

Number of Dogs

Quality Score

Figure 4.

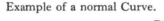

46

exceptionally good and the other bad, the tendency is for the range of quality of the litter to be similar to that of the breed or line as a whole. A very mediocre bitch thus tends to produce some puppies better than herself even if her mate is equally mediocre. And if she is mated to a champion stud dog, not all of the credit for the improved quality of the litter as compared to their dam should be given to the dog. Similarly, when two champions are mated together, they cannot be expected to produce a litter in which all of the puppies are as good as the parents, although the range of the litter should be at the top end of the quality curve, and the best pup as good as, or better than, the parents.

There is always danger in talking in terms of tendencies and averages—danger that these will be taken as rigid and absolute. Part of the "art" of breeding lies in the selection of mates which will "nick" with each other and produce offspring which revert little or not at all toward the average of the breed. Once the tendency toward the "drag of the race" is recognized, the breeder judges his success by the range of merit in his puppies rather than the production of a few brilliant individuals among a lot of duds. The importance of the *worst* puppy of each generation then becomes apparent: if the worst puppies produced in the fourth generation of your line are just as bad and just as numerous as the worst in your first generation, you have made no real progress, even though you may have bred a champion.

In conclusion, a concrete breeding plan can now be synthesized from the work of Kelley, of Humphrey and Warner, and of Pfaffenberger:

(1) Decide on a few traits which are regarded as essential and on any faults considered intolerable. Whatever the breed, disease resistance, fertility, and the absence of genetic faults must be included as essentials, and certain character failings, such as viciousness, extreme nervousness, and hysterical or epileptic tendencies must be condemned.

(2) Develop a scoring system in which selected virtues and faults are scored in accordance with (a) their importance to your purpose or breeding aim, (b) their rarity or wide occurrence in the breed as a whole. Virtues which are well established in the breed and present in every individual need not be scored. As certain traits, rare at first, become established in your line, their scoring may be reduced in order that greater weight and attention may be given to some other trait. Or the scoring system may remain the same, with attention in matings being concentrated on scores for individual traits which require improvement.

(3) Line breed consistently to the best individual produced until a better one is produced. Then line breed to that individual. The virtues of an outstanding dog or bitch can be conserved only by inbreeding to it while it is

still living, but close inbreeding should be resorted to only when an animal of exceptional qualities and no outstanding faults is available. If inbreeding results in unsatisfactory litters, this does not condemn the favored animal but merely indicates that less close matings should be made. Wide outcrosses should not be resorted to after establishment of a line, but some outside bloodline may be introduced, for example by the use of an animal sired by a dog of the line from an unrelated bitch. In the foundation animals, relationship need not be close. In fact, wide outcrosses will give more variation and therefore greater possibility for selection of desirable combination of traits. Every animal to be used in the breeding program must pass rigorous assessments for individual excellence as well as average excellence of its relatives, including its progeny when known.

In following a line breeding program, it becomes desirable to find a way of expressing the closeness of inbreeding and the amount of influence which any animal in the pedigree may be expected to have on the offspring of a particular mating.

A common method used is to credit the sire and dam with 50%, each grandparent with 25%, each great-grandparent with 12.5%, each great-great-grandparent with 6.25%, etc. Thus, if the same dog sires both the sire and the dam of a litter, that dog contributes 50%, or as much as if it had itself sired the pups.

In addition to the percentage contributed, however, it is important to know how many times the same individual appears in a pedigree, and especially whether heredity derived from him (or her) can reach the offspring through both parents. If any individual appears in the pedigree of both the sire and the dam of a litter, inherited factors derived from that individual may reach some of the offspring through both parents (this truly is inbreeding), but this is the less likely to happen the further back the common ancestor is in the pedigree. If a certain individual occurs many times in the pedigree of one parent but not at all in the pedigree of the other, then the litter is not inbred, even though the percentage of inheritance of that individual may be high, and his influence therefore greater than that of any other individual in the pedigree. The percentage of inheritance cannot, however, exceed 50% without inbreeding.

The term "line breeding" is usually understood to mean building a pedigree in which one individual occurs repeatedly, but it is possible to line breed to several individuals at once. It is not possible to line breed without inbreeding to some extent, but it is possible to inbreed without line breeding in this sense of the term—for example, by mating brother to sister in every generation. Some breeders, however, would call the latter line breeding, on the grounds that the animals mated belong to the same bloodlines.

The Keeshond.

Test Tube Puppies . . .
A New Day Dawning

When a normally quiet microbiologist in Illinois heard that the Supreme Court had ruled in his favor (June 1980) on a court test regarding new forms of life created in the laboratory, it was a landmark in jurisprudence and in science.

Dr. Ananda Mohan Chakrabarty of the University of Illinois celebrated a significant step in the new science of genetic engineering. His radical invention—a microorganism that consumes oil spills—does not, however, include gene-splicing—the manipulation of DNA (deoxyribonucleic acids) the genetic substance that determines hereditary traits. He stated, "I simply shuffled genes, changing bacteria that had already existed. It's like teaching your pet cat new tricks."

Skeptics still question recombinant DNA research, on scientific grounds as well as irrational ones. (Columnist George Will calls gene-splicing "A form of impudence against the cosmos.") Chakrabarty feels "that maybe someday genetic technology may be used to create a super-race, but government can't regulate that any more than it can crime."

Nationally syndicated columnist Nickie McWhirter, who writes for the Knight-Ridder newspapers, takes a more mischievous approach. She states, "I see no evidence that nature gives a fig leaf about genetic mutation or that she has any particular plan for it either. Let the kids alter this gene and that one. Do it through natural irradiation—Ms. Nature is the champion synthesizer and the most capricious creator. Her discards and experimental life forms fill our Natural History Museums."

What is the genetic code of DNA that we read so much about?

A genetic code is a simple four-character code that spells the recipe for all life on earth.

The code appears along two, long twisted chains of DNA (Deoxyribonucleic Acid). They contain the four base codes: A, E, T and G.

Many scientists believed that the chromosomes held a chemical code for life and heredity, but some thought life was too complicated to be coded by lifeless chemicals.

Eventually, most scientists agreed that a mere 20 amino acids built the proteins that make up life. Proteins are the things cells are made of and what makes them run. They are the enzymes that take things apart (digest a dinner) and the enzymes that put things together (build a muscle). Twenty amino acids may not seem like enough to do all that, but all the English books and magazines and newspapers in the world are in a code of only 26 letters.

The natural question was: "What kind of genetic code could spell out the recipe for life?" Scientists, such as George Gamon, Nobel prize-winning physicist, applied the skills of cryptography to help break the code. Gamon asked himself how many four-character bases it would take to code the 20 amino acids. Four would make only four amino acids. A pair such as AG or TC would make up only 16 codes (4 X 4). But triplets (ATC) would make 64 different codes (4 X 4 X 4), plenty to make the 20 amino acids. It was a good guess. In 1961, eight years after Watson and Crick discovered the double helix structure of DNA, scientists learned how the bases coded for life.

The four bases appear in sets of three. For instance, TCG codes from the amino acid Tryptophan are found in milk and were formerly sold in health food stores as a sleeping aide. Some amino acids can be made by up to six different codes. None of the 64 possible triplet codes is wasted.

The four bases are connected in a long chain that runs along the three feet of DNA in each cell. Thousands of bases make up a single gene in a chromosome. At the end of each gene is a stop code so the cell knows where one gene ends and the next one begins.

Somehow the triplets code for protein that makes a dog or a pumpkin. Proteins aren't made directly from the long chain of bases in a gene. Rather, the gene is the master plan, like an architect's original blueprint and copies are given to the carpenters and plumbers to work from. The codes are cheap and plentiful, a little is lost if one is damaged. In the cell, the copies are called messengers RNA and are taken to the construction site by the wagon load. The RNA works like a child stringing a necklace, attaching little amino acids one after the other in a long chain until the protein is formed.

What does all this genetic tinkering mean to us in the dog game? What is possible? What might happen? Can we use genetic engineering to clone (the replication of identical specimens by artificial means) a dog?

It seems to me that we are long past the time of merely scoffing at such ideas. Cloning of a mammal may lie in our immediate future and chances are good that it could be a dog.

Work along these lines starting with animal cells really began in 1962 when Dr. John B. Gurdon of Oxford University extracted nuclei from cells found in the tissue-lining of the intestines of a frog. He transplanted these nuclei into frog eggs from which the nuclei had been removed. A number of these eggs developed into normal, perfectly healthy adult frogs, which proved that cells in the intestine contain all the genetic information required for normal development. This method of transplanting nuclei into frog eggs has formed the basis of a whole range of important experiments designed to investigate the control mechanisms which are exerted on genes. This research has produced some bizarre and rather disturbing results, but it also is providing scientists with essential information on what actually goes wrong in a cell when it becomes cancerous, or produces birth defects and metabolic disorders of a genetic nature. Understanding the control process might be the first step towards putting it right when it goes wrong.

Gurdon, in his original experiments, was actually able to stimulate a frog egg to produce a tadpole without any fertilization into an egg from which the nucleus had been removed. Supposing the transplanted nuclei all come from the cells of one particular frog, all the eggs will develop into tadpoles containing exactly the same genetic information as the one original frog, and these tadpoles will grow into absolutely identical frogs. Such "genetically identical individuals" are described as members of a "clone." In fact, this is exactly what Dr. Gurdon did, and by doing so he brought us one step nearer to turning the fiction of Aldous Huxley's "Brave New World" into reality.

Before attempting to understand cloning or mononuclear reproduction, we need to review once more the process of reproduction. In ordinary canine reproduction there is an ovum or egg from the female and a sperm cell from the male, each with a nucleus containing thirty-nine pairs of chromosomes, the filaments on which the genes, hundreds of thousands of them, are strung like beads. The two nuclei merge, and we have a fertilized egg cell with double the chromosomes we started with. The chromosomes duplicate themselves, duplicating each of their genes, and the cell divides, one set of identical chromosomes going into each resulting cell. This duplication and division which occurs again and again is called *mitosis*.

In sixty-three days we have the billions of cells of the complete organism. They've evolved to perform different functions—to become bone or skin or blood or hair, to respond to light or heat or tension, and so on—but each of those cells, each of the billions of cells that constitute the dog, contains in its nucleus exact duplicates of an original set of seventy-eight chromosomes, half from the dam, half from the sire; a mix that is absolutely unique—the blueprint, as it were, of an absolutely unique individual.

In mononuclear reproduction, the nucleus of an egg is destroyed, leaving the body of the cell unharmed. This is done by radiation and takes microsurgery of the highest order. Into the enucleated egg is put the nucleus of a body

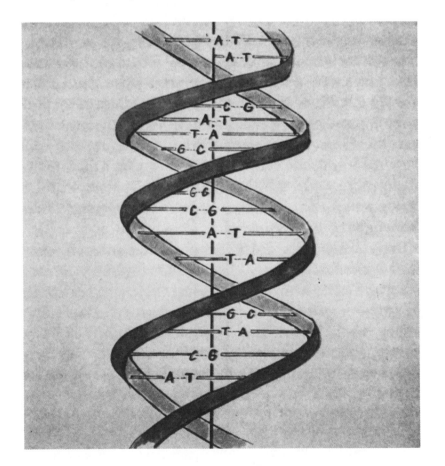

Figure 5.

50

The Doberman Pinscher.

The Pug.

cell of the organism to be reproduced (not a sex cell). We now have exactly what we had at this point in natural reproduction: An egg cell with seventy-eight chromosomes in its nucleus; a fertilized egg cell which, in a nutrient solution, proceeds to duplicate and divide. When it reaches the second division of cell stage—it can be implanted in the uterus of its "mother;" who isn't its mother at all, biologically speaking. She supplied an egg cell, and now she's supplying a proper environment for the embryo's growth, but she's given it nothing of her own genetic endowment. The puppies, when born, have neither father nor mother, only a donor—the giver of the nucleus—of whom it's an exact genetic duplicate. Its chromosomes and genes are identical to the donor's. Instead of a new and unique individual, we have an existing one repeated.

One scientist has already produced seven cloned female mice through this method. However, males cannot be cloned this way, stated Dr. Clement Markert of Yale University, a pioneer in this field. Nevertheless, cloning of mammals "should be possible very soon."

Indeed, in late 1975 at the Department of Zoology in Oxford University, Dr. Derek Bromhall fertilized an egg cell of a rabbit with the nucleus of an ordinary non-reproductive cell, not sperm. He had succeeded in doing the same thing with a rabbit egg that Dr. Gurdon had done thirteen years earlier with a frog egg. Fertilizing a rabbit egg cell this way is much more difficult than doing the same thing with a frog egg. For one thing, a frog egg is about one thousand times larger than a rabbit egg and this makes the micro-injection of a transplant nucleus a difficult and delicate procedure. Also, a frog egg naturally develops outside the body, whereas a rabbit's egg needs special treatment if it is going to survive outside the rabbit's womb.

Dr. Bromhall's experiments showed that it was possible for the sperm substitute *not to fuse with the egg nucleus but to totally replace it and the egg develops according to the genetic information contained in the sperm substitute nucleus.* It is not difficult to imagine how this technique could be used to produce rabbit clones. So far, no attempt has been made to grow these fertilized rabbit egg cells into animals, so we don't know what these creatures would look like if they were encouraged to develop, but it is highly probable that they would grow up looking like ordinary rabbits. In fact, they would be a set of absolutely identical, ordinary rabbits.

The imagination can conjure all sorts of frightening prospects, but it is always important to remember that genetic engineering has a positive side to it. The experiments with animal clones may also have a positive contribution to make. Dr. Bromhall's work is likely to find application in cancer research, where it is essential to discover the role of the nucleus when a cell becomes malignant. If the nucleus of a cancer cell were used to fertilize an egg cell, then valuable information could be obtained on the relative importance of the nucleus and the surrounding cytoplasm in determining the cancerous nature of the cell.

Now, with the recent Supreme Court decision, will the scientific community turn its attention toward human engineering? The only barriers at the moment are the values of the scientific community, which are focused on the ethical question of human reproduction. The artificial reproduction of a dog is merely a step along the way.

Horticulturists have used cloning for years as a way to short-cut generations of crossbreeding and perpetuate desirable specimens. Anyone who has taken a cutting from a plant and repotted it to grow a new plant has cloned. But horticulturists have gone one step further and grown batches of identical plants from minute tissue cultures.

All this raises the spectre of cloning top winning show dogs in the near future. Should this be biologically possible, it raises innumerable questions for the kennel clubs of the world and the registration of purebred dogs.

It is not a large step in the imagination to think of the possibilities for using cloning in dogs to preserve "desirable" specimens, chosen perhaps by the various breed clubs. This technique could be used to select especially high quality dogs and then produce dozens, or hundreds, of members of the clone.

Assuming that a decision *could* be made concerning the desirability of perpetuating certain outstanding specimens in each breed, what might the impact be? If what we think about genetics and evolution is correct, nature seems totally unconcerned with any individual. The important unit seems to be the species. As a result of sexual reproduction, species seem to obtain the selective advantage of genetic variability.

Robert Schimke, a Stanford biologist, pointed out, as did many scientists, that by constantly recombining genes through natural reproduction, species evolve and adapt to their changing environment over hundreds of thousands of years.

If you stop the recombination from occurring by assuming that each member of a species will be the same, you stop evolution. "In time that undoubtedly means extinction because the environment is going to change. With a pool of nearly infinite combinations of genes, immense variability and potential are available." Without genetic variability a species becomes completely adapted to one set of environmental variables. It is apparent then, "If you continue to clone individuals without recombination, that's sheer evolutionary disaster."

Dr. Roger Pedersen of the University of California Medical Center has been quoted as saying, "It is precisely genetic diversity which has given sexual beings success, biologically."

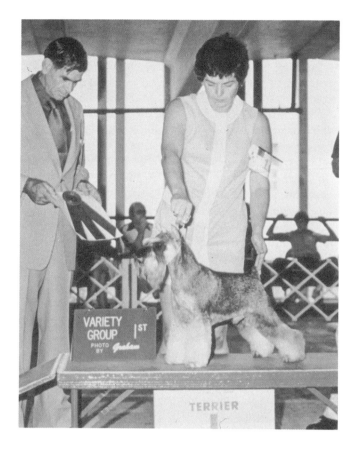

The Miniature Schnauzer.

The Borzoi.

"Any attempt to select for certain characteristics is done at the expense of other characteristics. One of the first things to go is fertility, lifespan, general health and viability," he says.

Pedersen pointed out some of the current difficulties with cloning a mammal, let alone a human being.

"I am certain no one has cloned a human being such as suggested in a novel published in 1978," says Pedersen. "The basis for my certainty is what I know are the difficulties of dealing with mammalian embryos.

"Frogs compared to mammals boast large eggs, with small nuclei and embryos that develop in spring water without requiring implantation into a foster mother, all of which makes them easier to clone than mammals."

But even the frog experiments, he goes on, have not been complete successes. "Every experiment where they transferred an adult nucleus ended in death during the tadpole stage, and they have done thousands."

It follows, then, that a dog embryo formed by borrowing a nucleus from an adult specimen would live only three or four weeks after conception if it followed the pattern of the frog.

These frog clones which have lived to adulthood have been formed by borrowing the nucleus not from adult frogs, but from other embryos and tadpoles.

This would seem to mean that even if the method worked in dogs, by the time the individual is old enough so that its quality as a show dog was known, it would be too late to clone it.

"You could fantasize about technical improvements, but the main problem is this biological problem," Pedersen says. "Nuclei do mature during embryonic and fetal development and they're no longer the same as they were in the egg. By the time you could recognize a desirable feature you might want to clone, it's too late. That is the lesson from the frog."

However, some of the technical difficulties are already making way when it comes to mice. As an example, Dr. Peter Hoppe, a researcher at the Jackson Laboratory in Bar Harbor, Maine, who, like Dr. Markert of Yale, is working toward cloning mammals, announced he could probably successfully clone mice within a month (July 1978). He would not, he said, because he didn't care for the public attention, and, perhaps, outrage he would bring upon himself.

However, in 1981, Hoppe and Dr. Karl Illmensee, at the University of Geneva, Switzerland, actually did clone a mouse. The procedure was described in the journal, *Cell*, Jan./Feb. 1981.

Hoppe's cloning was a two-generation process. He formed a batch of genetically identical mice by removing mouse eggs and sucking out the genetic contribution of one parent by microsurgery. They are not clones, since the genetic contribution left is one that has already recombined—it is a new combination of the genes inherited from its mother or father mouse.

But if he repeated the operation, mating the mice and removing the male contribution, he would have produced mice who were identical twins to their mother.

Other researchers are working on different approaches which may bring them to the same point, the ability to clone a mammal.

Dr. Allan Campbell, Professor of Biology at Stanford University, feels that among the possibilities of failure which would have to be considered, is whether genetic tampering could lead to abnormalities in the fetus.

"If there were a way to reproduce beef stock the way you reproduce a prime pear tree, I don't think this would raise any apprehension," Campbell said.

If scientists did reach this point, would it mean that breeders (and their veterinarians) would be able to select the specimens to be cloned from a catalog and then stamp them out *ad infinitum?* Could it mean that as an individual breeder I would have to be willing to let my breed club or maybe even a nation's kennel club decide which specimens were a desirable source of nuclei? Certainly it is obvious that we are acquiring the technical skills for genetic engineering before we have formulated the policies for its use.

I firmly believe that The American Kennel Club, as the guiding force in American dogdom, should take the lead in concert with other international bodies to appoint a distinguished panel of laymen and scientists from among the dog fancy to develop guidelines regarding further experimentation, registration, and acceptable breeding practices. Unless we give serious thought to this problem *now*, the scientific community will not have the necessary input that is required to make considered judgments. Cloning mammals to produce herds of better beef cattle may be all right, but I have grave reservations about cloning purebred dogs as an accepted reproduction process.

I would suggest that the guidelines themselves be a compromise between undue restrictions on research and the obligations to protect the integrity of registration of purebred dogs in each country. Most likely they could carry no legal force and offer no sanctions other than, perhaps, restrictions on admission to registration in cooperating countries. No restriction of academic or scientific freedom need be implied beyond what any individual or group accepts when its deeds potentially affect others.

This appointed body should look upon itself as advisory only. It should make immediate contact with the scientific community through the respective National Institutes of Health and offer its considered recommendations and advice. It is urgent that communications be established between the governing bodies of the various national kennel clubs and their scientific communities in the very near future.

Reproduction Techniques of the Future Here Today

Much has been made of the announcement by AKC in April of 1981 that artificial insemination in dogs was now economically and scientifically feasible and that a viable means was at hand to promote the distribution of male dog's sperm. Under certain approved and controlled circumstances, get resulting from such artificial insemination could be registered with AKC. Such a major breakthrough is to be heartily applauded.

For many, many years, research into preserving a stud dog's spermatozoa had produced less than favorable results. Much of this research had been supported by AKC itself. Dog sperm does not take kindly to lengthy storage. Artificial insemination with dogs is much more successful—namely, pregnancies happen with greater certitude—if fresh semen is used. If chilled and then warmed up again, the spermatozoa are still satisfactory, but less so. If chilled for longer periods, there is a further loss; no greater number of malformations are created, but something vital is lost with the passage of time in a frozen state. Bull semen is different and lasts extremely well in these circumstances.

The practical application of artificial insemination in horses, cattle, sheep, and pigs was developed in Russia during the first decades of the twentieth century. Semen was collected from the male by a variety of means and preserved for several days outside the body. More rapid progress became possible in 1950 when it was shown that bull semen could be deep frozen at -79 degrees centigrade with solid carbon dioxide and later thawed without serious effect on fertility, provided that a certain amount of glycerol was added before freezing. Later, the use of liquid nitrogen made it possible to store semen at about -196 degrees centigrade. Calves have been produced from semen that has been frozen for more than ten years, and it seems possible to increase the period of storage indefinitely.

While the current state of the art of preserving dog semen is nowhere near that advanced, we know from our experiences with the bull what may be possible. The same problems that faced the preservation of dog semen were faced in the deep freezing of boar semen, but these difficulties appear to have been overcome.

The advantages of using frozen semen in dogs was lucidly stated by Dr. Stephen W. J. Seager and C. C. Platz, Jr., in their June 1981 article in the *American Kennel Gazette*, titled "1,143 Puppies." They point out that:

1. Frozen semen will eliminate the costly, dangerous, and time-consuming effort involved in shipping dogs by road or air, which not only exposes them to the hazards of disease, infections, and injuries, but may also result in death during shipment. It is becoming more difficult to ship dogs by air, since a number of airlines will not transport dogs weighing over eighty pounds, nor during certain holiday periods or under certain weather conditions. Also, extremes in temperature must be considered.

2. Frozen semen will save breeders money since it can be kept in the frozen state relatively inexpensively for many years.

3. Frozen semen will relieve the responsibility of having someone else's in-heat bitch on the premises, with all of the hazards that poses.

4. Frozen semen will be of benefit to the stud dog owner who wants to breed but does not have the experience, or the time, and does not want the responsibility of someone else's dog.

5. Frozen semen will help prevent the spread of venereal disease, which sometimes results from natural breeding. Also, with an increase in canine brucella and other infectious diseases, breeders may be forced to use artificial insemination with fresh or frozen semen.

6. Frozen semen will allow genetically superior dogs to reproduce even if they suffer physical handicaps as a result of injury or disease that may not allow natural mating. Thus, a stud's genes can be passed on to future generations or can be used widely, permitting many more bitches to be bred with his frozen semen than could be possible by natural means. When superior males are identified as having the ability to pass on good genes, such studs could be used widely to improve their respective breeds.

7. Frozen semen banks will allow breeders from distant places to breed to a particular male. They may be unwilling or unable to afford to ship their female, or the breed may be too large to ship by air, and the distance too great to transport the bitch by automobile.

8. Shipping frozen semen will greatly reduce the number of health certificates needed for shipping females.

9. Frozen semen will allow a stud dog owner to have his dog used for breeding even when it is not convenient to have him used normally, such as during a busy period of the year (show circuits), vacation time, etc. Breeding a bitch can upset a male to the point where he will not show well. To solve this problem, semen can be collected for freezing during a period when he is not actively campaigning. This factor is most important in that semen can be collected from the dog when it is most convenient for the owner.

10. Frozen semen will allow champion or field trial dogs to have semen stored at an earlier date at more convenient times. Some champions and many field trial dogs do not obtain titles until six or seven years of age. To wait until that time to collect and freeze his semen can result in the dog's not being able to produce satisfactory ejaculates for freezing. By this age, the majority of dogs have passed their natural breeding prime and have

relatively few years of breeding life remaining. It must be emphasized that in order to acquire optimum sperm quantity and quality, semen should be collected from the stud while he is in his reproductive prime. Freezing semen from potential champions at an earlier, more nearly prime age will allow the semen to be utilized at a much later date if the sire turns out to be as good as expected. It should be pointed out that, so far, none of the dogs used in testing in the first through fifth generations of frozen semen litters have experienced any congenital or acquired defects that could be attributed to the semen-freezing process.

11. Frozen semen offers the possibility of breeding outstanding sires which have long since been dead. National breed clubs could recognize and nominate outstanding sires whose semen could be available to club members.

12. Another important factor is progeny testing, which is widely utilized in commercial animal breeding for testing superior sires. This has never been widely used in dogs, primarily because not enough progeny could be produced for statistical testing within the natural breeding life of the stud.

13. Frozen semen facilitates and enhances line breeding and inbreeding that would not have been possible without frozen semen. Such breeding, coupled with sound genetic advice, application, and vital principles, will assure improvement of breeds.

14. Frozen semen would allow researchers to store potential animal models. This is especially important in large colonies of dogs used in genetic research where identical models are to be available for study in order that a possible cure can be discovered for diseases that afflict both dog and man.

American dogs have made their presence known throughout the world. Breeders in such far away countries as Australia, Sweden, New Zealand, etc., have made remarkable strides in successfully introducing the breeds to their countries. There is, however, a major problem in importing high-quality breeding stock. Stringent quarantine rules make it extremely difficult and financially prohibitive to import quality stock. Now, at long last, there may be a solution to this problem. Artificial insemination has been approved by the AKC under certain controlled conditions for use in this country. However, shipping semen over long distances has proven to be a formidable task.

In October and November of 1986, Howard H. Furumoto, D.V.M., Ph.D., writing in *Ilio*, Hawaii's dog magazine, cast a new light on the problem:

Recent research on canine semen preservation and storage offers Hawaiian dog breeders a promising future *[as well as foreign countries and continents that maintain strict quarantine regulations such as the state of Hawaii requires]*. The technology and expertise are available today to overcome the hitherto insurmountable barriers of time, logistics, and statutory requirements when considering the importation of new bloodlines.

To properly understand and appreciate the significance of these advancements, a short review of the evolution of the two methods of semen preservation are in order.

When approval was granted by the American Kennel Club to legitimize registration of litters conceived by stored semen and artificial insemination, the way was opened for Hawaii's breeders *[and breeders of other countries]* to take advantage of the golden opportunity presented by the new technology. Here, at last, was an AKC-accredited program which provided the means to circumvent the quarantine requirements and to eliminate the expense, inconvenience, and stress of shipping animals to and from destination points. An added attraction for many breeders was the preservation of valuable bloodlines for posterity by the establishment of frozen semen banks.

The original work on frozen semen was done by Dr. Stephen Seager and co-workers at the University of Oregon under the auspices of the American Kennel Club. The widespread interest he created led to *[a collaboration with the University of Hawaii]*. The objective was to determine whether or not we could duplicate the results obtained by Dr. Seager and his co-workers with the additional variables of air-shipping frozen semen and bitches in estrus cycle. Much to our disappointment the four bitches shipped to Hawaii and inseminated with frozen semen shipped from Oregon failed to become impregnated. Subsequently, other investigators have reported similar negative results.

Because of the unreliable results obtained from the insemination of stored semen, canine theriogenologists began searching for more productive methodologies. Two such programs came to my attention. *[One effort was led by]* Dr. Frances Smith who had obtained her Ph.D. from the University of Minnesota. Her dissertation was based on the successful development of a semen extender which prolongs the viability of spermatazoa for up to seven days after collection without freezing.

Dr. Smith is widely recognized by dog breeders throughout the continental United States for her work with top line-breeding stock of various breeds. In her experience she has been just as successful in obtaining pregnancies with the use of the newly formulated extended semen as with natural breeding.

The second source of information *[led me to]* Mr. George Govette of the Cryogenics Laboratories in

Chester Spring, Pennsylvania. Mr. Govette has earned the reputation of being the foremost frozen semen specialist in the country, having successfully registered 44 litters out of the approximately 50 now recognized by the AKC by this method. In addition, he has reported successful frozen semen usage in Japan.

Gleaning germane information from both sources, Dr. Furumoto wrote a second article in which he briefly described the methods employed in semen collection, extension, preservation, storage, and preparation for artificial insemination.

He then projected the long-term benefits and potential hazards of these new technologies as they relate to breed improvement.

Semen Collection

Semen is collected for a number of overlapping reasons – for qualitative and quantitative evaluation, for immediate insemination when natural breeding fails or cannot be used due to physical and psychological inhibitions, for extending the volume of semen, for semen preservation and storage and for legal reasons (quarantine restrictions).

To collect semen, it is generally helpful to excite the dog with the scent of a bitch in estrus. Ejaculation is usually performed by digital manipulation and the semen is collected in a graduated sterile collecting tube fitted to a funnel-shaped latex sleeve which is held around the penis.

Three distinct fractions are observed from the ejaculate. The scant first fraction is clear and is secreted by the glands of the urethral mucosa; the opaque second fraction is secreted by the testicles and contains spermatozoa; the third and most voluminous fraction is clear and is secreted by the prostate glands.

Qualitative and quantitative evaluations are made after the semen is collected. The volume and turbidity of the semen are noted. Microscopically, the sperm concentration, motility, ratio of live to dead sperm cells and the shape and size are evaluated. Fresh undiluted semen is used for immediate artificial insemination.

Semen Extenders and Semen Preservation

After semen evaluation, semen of good to excellent quality is selected for preservation by one of two basic methods: chilling or chilling and freezing. In both methods, a vehicle – or media for dilution and maintenance called "semen extenders" – is used.

A great deal of research has been done to determine which media serves as the best semen extender. Various combinations of sterilized skim milk, homogenized milk, egg yolk, glucose, sodium citrate, sodium bicarbonate, potassium chloride and other substances have been used. The tremendous success in conception rate obtained by Dr. Frances Smith is the direct result of her newly developed and tested semen extender.

Fresh, undiluted semen maintains its viability for 24 to 48 hours. Beyond this period, the viability of the semen may be prolonged for approximately 4 more days by suspending it in special media known as semen extenders and chilling. The viability of spermatozoa may be continued over an indefinite period of years by freezing the semen after it is suspended in a suitable vehicle (semen extender). By a gradual chilling process spermatozoa are conditioned for freezing at -70° C. The extended semen suspension is then shaped into pellets by placing single drops into super-cooled styrofoam wells. Enough frozen pellets are placed in each vial to yield about 50 million spermatozoa. Each vial is properly identified and stored at -70° C in a liquid nitrogen tank.

An alternative method of preservation is to pipette the extended semen into straws, one end of which is presealed. When the straw is filled, the top end is sealed and the semen is conditioned for freezing as with the pelletized semen, frozen, and stored.

Preparation for Insemination

The reverse of cooling and freezing is carried out to prepare frozen semen for artificial insemination. A suitable number of pellets or straws are selected to yield 100 to 300 million spermatozoa and gradually thawed to ambient temperature. At this point, an evaluation of the thawed semen quality is made. If viability and motility are satisfactory the semen is introduced in the anterior vagina or cervix of the bitch. At least two inseminations usually 24 to 48 hours apart is recommended.

Long-Term Benefits of Extended and Frozen Semen

In the context of [foreign countries with] quarantine restrictions, the greatest advantage to be derived from the use of extended and frozen semen is the by-passing of the trans-oceanic shipment of stud dogs and their confinement in [government] quarantine facilities for a specified period of time (10 days beyond the last insemination date). Extended or frozen semen [on the other hand] may be shipped in special compact containers over long distances.

Another attraction of extended and frozen semen is the flexibility and convenience of synchronizing semen shipment with the optimal breeding period in the estrus cycle of a prospective bitch. This advantage is particularly applicable when long distance shipment of stud dogs and bitches is involved in conventional breeding programs.

Venereal diseases, particularly canine brucellosis and transmissible venereal tumor may be circumvented, simply by the process of screening out potential carriers in the collection process.

By far the most significant benefit to accrue from extended and frozen semen is the concentration of proven or select gene pools for the improvement of the breed to more rapidly attain that elusive goal known as the ideal breed standard. By extending and freezing semen many more bitches can be inseminated with "matching" semen which would complement the desirable qualities of the sire and dam.

Disadvantages of Extended and Frozen Semen

In addition to the purely technical difficulties of implementing an artificial insemination program which *[uses]* extended and frozen semen, the success rate among breeders *[so far]* has been very limited.

The greatest concern regarding frozen and extended semen is the potential for intensifying or replicating undesirable genetic traits. Just as much as the potential for breed improvement over a shorter period exists, there is also the danger of perpetuating undesirable heritable traits, i.e., juvenile cataracts, subvalvular aortic stenosis, hip dysplasia, etc. within an abbreviated time frame. Therefore, a great deal of selectivity and objectivity must be exercised in the utilization of preserved semen. Any abnormal offspring must be dealt with objectively and decisively and either euthanized or neutered so that the genetic defect will not become established within a given line or breed.

Another area of concern is the requirement for meticulous attention to details of proper identification and documentation. One only needs to refer to the AKC regulations on "Registration of Litters Produced Through Artificial Insemination Using Frozen Semen" to appreciate the complexity of the stringent regulations.

Conclusion

Notwithstanding the objectionable features of semen preservation and storage, the technical and scientific feasibility of their application to canine reproduction have been amply demonstrated. The acceptance of the program depends – to a large extent – on the interest and support of dog breeders and the professional and technical competence of veterinarians to deliver the "goods" when the chips are down. Ultimately, the success of the program depends on the development of special interest and expertise in the handling of extended and frozen semen form collection to insemination.

Success breeds success. Nowhere is this truism more important than in the pioneering *[use of these techniques]*.

ARTIFICIAL INSEMINATION USING FRESH SEMEN

The American Kennel Club will consider an application to register a litter resulting from artificial insemination provided both the sire and dam are present during the extraction and insemination.

The certifications on the form below must be completed and submitted with a litter registration form. If the dam was leased at the time of mating, the lessee must file a "Report of Lease of Bitch for the Purpose of Whelping a Litter" card with AKC.

For information regarding the registration of litters whelped as a result of artificial insemination using Frozen Semen, contact: **The American Kennel Club, Attn: Dept. B, 5580 Centerview Drive, Raleigh NC 27606**

CERTIFICATION OF BREEDING BY ARTIFICIAL INSEMINATION USING FRESH SEMEN

Required with each application to register a litter whelped as a result of an artificial mating.

1) TO BE COMPLETED BY OWNER, CO-OWNER OR LESSEE OF DAM:

I certify that I am the owner ( ) co-owner ( ) or lessee ( ) of the female _____
(Breed)

_____; and that on _____
(Registered Name/Number of Bitch)   *(Date)*

I artificially inseminated (or authorized _____ to artificially inseminate) said bitch
(Name of Authorized Person)

to _____; that I did ( ) did not ( ) witness the artificial
(Registered Name/Number of Sire)
breeding, and that no other male serviced my bitch prior or subsequent to this artificial breeding during the bitch's season.

Signature _____

Printed Name _____

Address _____
          (Number and Street)

_____
(City)   *(State)*   *(Zip Code)*

2) TO BE COMPLETED BY OWNER OR CO-OWNER OF SIRE:

I certify that I am the owner ( ) co-owner ( ) of the male _____
(Breed)

_____; and that on _____
(Registered Name/Number of Sire)   *(Date)*

I extracted semen (or authorized _____ to extract semen) from my
(Name of Authorized Person)
dog for the purpose of inseminating the bitch named above; and that I did ( ) did not ( ) witness the artificial breeding.

Signature _____

Printed Name _____

Address _____
          (Number and Street)

_____
(City)   *(State)*   *(Zip Code)*

3) TO BE COMPLETED BY PERSON AUTHORIZED TO EXTRACT SEMEN:

I certify that on _____ I extracted semen from the above identified male for the purpose of
(Date)
inseminating the above-identified female. The named bitch was present during the collection process.

Signature _____

Printed Name _____

Address _____
          (Number and Street)

_____
(City)   *(State)*   *(Zip Code)*

4) TO BE COMPLETED BY PERSON AUTHORIZED TO INSEMINATE:

I certify that on _____ I inseminated the above identified female with semen collected from the
(Date)
above identified male. The named male was present during the insemination process.
This artificial breeding was effected at the following location: _____

_____

Signature _____

Printed Name _____

Address _____
          (Number and Street)

_____
(City)   *(State)*   *(Zip Code)*

R 94-4 (2/91)

ARTIFICIAL INSEMINATION USING FRESH EXTENDED SEMEN

The American Kennel Club will consider an application to register a litter resulting from artificial insemination of the bitch using fresh extended semen provided the semen is extracted and extended by a licensed veterinarian; the insemination of the bitch is performed by a licensed veterinarian and the litter is eligible for registration in all other respects. The semen must be extracted from males within the USA and shipped to points within the USA only.

The certifications on the form below must be completed and submitted with a litter registration application form and a litter registration fee. If the dam was leased at the time of mating, the lessee must file a "Report of Lease of Bitch for the Purpose of Whelping a Litter" card with AKC.

CERTIFICATION OF BREEDING BY ARTIFICIAL INSEMINATION USING FRESH EXTENDED SEMEN

1) TO BE COMPLETED BY OWNER, CO-OWNER OR LESSEE OF DAM:

I certify that I am the owner (   ) co-owner (   ) or lessee (   ) of the female _____
_____ (Breed)

_____ ; and that on _____
(Registered Name/Number of Bitch)   (Date)

I authorized_____ to artificially inseminate said bitch with semen
(Name of Licensed Veterinarian)

extracted from_____ ; that I did (   ) did not (   ) witness the artificial
(Registered Name/Number of Sire)

breeding, and that no other male serviced my bitch prior or subsequent to this artificial breeding during the bitch's season.

Signature_____

Printed Name _____

Address _____
(Number and Street)

_____
(City)   (State)   (Zip Code)

2) TO BE COMPLETED BY OWNER OR CO-OWNER OF SIRE:

I certify that I am the owner (   ) co-owner (   ) of the male_____
(Breed)

_____and that on _____
(Registered Name/Number of Sire)   (Date)

I authorized_____ to extract semen from my dog for the purpose of
(Name of Licensed Veterinarian)

inseminating the bitch named above; and that I did (   ) did not (   ) witness the artificial breeding.

Signature_____

Printed Name _____

Address _____
(Number and Street)

_____
(City)   (State)   (Zip Code)

3) TO BE COMPLETED BY LICENSED VETERINARIAN AUTHORIZED TO EXTRACT AND EXTEND SEMEN

I certify that on _____ I extracted semen from the above identified male which semen was
(Date)

extended and shipped to _____.
(Name of Person or Veterinarian to whom shipped)

Signature_____

Printed Name _____

Address _____
(Number and Street)

_____
(City)   (State)   (Zip Code)

4) TO BE COMPLETED BY LICENCED VETERINARIAN AUTHORIZED TO INSEMINATE:

I certify that on_____ I received the semen collected from the above identified male and
(Date)

inseminated the above identified female with that semen. This artificial breeding was effected at the following location: _____
_____

Signature_____

Printed Name _____

License No. _____

Address _____
(Number and Street)

_____
(City)   (State)   (Zip Code)

R 207-1 (2/91)

REGULATIONS APPLYING TO THE REGISTRATION OF LITTERS PRODUCED THROUGH ARTIFICIAL INSEMINATION USING FROZEN SEMEN.

These Regulations shall supplement the "Regulations for Record Keeping and Identification of Dogs."

Each person* engaged in the collection, freezing, storage, shipping and insemination of frozen semen shall follow such practices and maintain such records as will preclude any possibility of error in identification of any individual dog or doubt as to the parentage of any dog or litter.

RECORDS:

To provide a source of reference for the registration of litters of pure-bred dogs produced by artificial insemination, using frozen semen, applications for which have been made, or may later be made, to the American Kennel Club, and to assure the accuracy of such applications, certain minimum records must be kept.

All required records shall be made immediately, when dog has been delivered for the purpose of semen collection, at time of shipment of frozen semen, and insemination of same; shall be kept on forms devoted to that exclusive purpose; and shall be consecutive, accurate and up-to-date. Such records shall be maintained for a period of no less than five years from the point in time when the last of the frozen semen from a given donor-dog is used.

NOTE: At this time there are no provisions for registering litters that result from imported frozen canine semen.

RECORDS TO BE KEPT BY COLLECTOR:

A. Dog Identification:

Breed
AKC registered name and number of donor-dog
Sex, color, markings of donor-dog (include tattoo, if any)
Color photographs of donor-dog (full front and full side views)
Date of birth
AKC registered name and number of sire and dam
Name and address of owner of donor-dog
(AKC suggests that collector also keep a health
work-up of donor-dog as part of donor-dog's
identification)

B. Collection of Semen:

Date on which donor-dog was received
Owner's authorization of semen collection
Date semen collected, frozen and stored
Number of breeding units stored
Form of semen storage (Pellets, Ampules, Vials, Straws, etc.)
Container in which each breeding unit is stored shall be
indelibly imprinted to show: Breed, AKC registration
number of donor-dog; Date semen collected

C. Disposition of Semen:

Identification of shipped semen
Number of breeding units shipped
Name and address of person to whom semen shipped
Authorization of semen owner for shipment
Date(s) semen shipped

D. Collector shall also maintain records of all transfers of ownership of stored semen. (See Section VI below re: Transfer of ownership of semen.)

II RECORDS TO BE KEPT BY OWNERS OF DONOR-DOGS:

In addition to the records required to be kept by owners and breeders, as provided in AKC pamphlet "Regulations for Record Keeping and Identification of Dogs," owners of dogs from which semen has been collected, frozen and stored, shall include the following:

AKC registered name and number of donor-dog
Date dog shipped to collector
Name and address of collector
Number of breeding units collected, frozen and in storage
Location of semen storage
Transfer of ownership of semen (see Section VI below)

III RECORDS TO BE KEPT BY OWNERS OF SEMEN OF DONOR-DOGS WHEN BREEDING HAS BEEN ARRANGED:

Identification of semen (Breed, AKC registered name and number of donor-dog, date semen collected)
Number of breeding units authorized for shipment and insemination
Date of shipment
To whom semen shipped
AKC registered name and number of bitch to be inseminated
Name and address of owner of bitch

IV RECORDS TO BE KEPT BY BREEDERS:

In addition to the records required to be kept by owners and breeders, as provided in AKC's pamphlet "Regulations for Record Keeping and Identification of Dogs," owners (or lessees) of bitches inseminated shall include the following:

Name and address of veterinarian who handled insemination
AKC registered name and number of bitch inseminated
Date(s) of insemination
Identification of semen (Breed, AKC registered name and number of donor-dog, date semen collected)

V NOTIFICATION TO AKC BY COLLECTOR:

A. Collector:

The AKC shall be immediately notified by collector of collection and freezing of canine semem. Such notification shall identify donor-dog by its breed; AKC registered name and number; the number of breeding units collected; date stored; address of storage facility; name and address of owner of donor-dog.

B. Collector/Semen Bank:

The AKC shall be immediately notified by the collector/semen bank whenever semen is shipped for intended use. Such notification shall include the identity of the donor-dog by its breed; registered name and number; the number of breeding units shipped; the identification of such breeding units; the name and address of the person to whom the units were shipped, and the date of shipment.

VI TRANSFER OF OWNERSHIP OF SEMEN:

Records required to be kept by owners of dogs from which semen has been collected and stored, and records required to be kept by collector (if semen is held in storage) must also note transfers of ownership of semen. Such records to include:

Authorization of transfer
Number of breeding units transferred
Date of transfer
Name and address of new owner

The AKC shall be immediately notified of such transfer of ownership of frozen semen.

VII LOCATION OF STORED SEMEN:

In the event semen is stored at a facility other than the facility at which it was collected, frozen and initially stored — or — in the event all or part of the collected frozen semen is transferred to a new owner (see Sections II and VI above), the owner or new owner shall immediately notify AKC. Such notification shall include:

Identification of semen (Breed, AKC registered name and number of donor-dog, date semen collected)
Number of breeding units relocated
Date transferred to new storage facility
Name and address of storage facility

VIII CERTIFICATION:

The AKC shall require such certifications from the semen owner, owner (or lessee) of bitch, and veterinarian who inseminated bitch as shall be necessary to support an application for registration of a litter of dogs produced by the use of frozen semen.

IX INSPECTION:

The rules provide that the AKC or its duly authorized representatives shall have the right to inspect the records required to be kept and the practices required to be followed by these regulations and to examine any dog registered or to be registered with the AKC.

X PENALTIES:

The rules provide that the AKC may refuse to register any dog or litter or to record the transfer of any dog, for the sole reason that the application is not supported by the records required by these regulations.

The rules also provide that the Board of Directors of the AKC may suspend from all privileges of the AKC any person who fails to observe the above regulations.

---

* Chapter 3A Section 1 of Rules Applying to Registration and Dog Show defines "Person" as "...any individual, partnership, firm, corporation, association or organization of any kind."

R-198-2 (11-85)

61

Collection/Storage Facilities — Frozen Canine Semen

Listed below and on the reverse are the names of the collection/storage facilities whose record–keeping practices have been examined and found to be in compliance with AKC's regulations applying to the registration of litters produced artificially using frozen canine semen. **Note well, however, that the AKC neither licenses, sponsors, nor endorses these facilities.** This list was revised July 22, 1991.

ARIZONA

Int'l Canine Semen Bank – AZ
2611 W. Northern Ave.
Phoenix, AZ 85051
(602) 995-0460

CALIFORNIA

Canine Cryobank
340 State Place
Escondido, CA 92029
(619) 739-1091

International Canine Genetics
3854 Santa Rosa Ave.
Santa Rosa, CA 95407
(707) 573-1893

International Canine Genetics
Dr. Charles Cantrell
10661 Ellis Ave., Ste. F
Fountain Valley, CA 92708
(714) 963-5504

International Canine Genetics
Dr. Janice Kane
807 B Davis St.
Vacaville, CA 95687

Spermco, Inc.
490 W. Durham Perry Rd.
Tracy, CA 95376
(209) 835-3259

GEORGIA

University of Georgia
College of Veterinary Medicine
Athens, GA 30602
(404) 542-9368 or 542-3221

ILLINOIS

Herd's Merchant Semen
7N330 Dunham Rd.
Elgin, IL 60120
(312) 741-1444

ILLINOIS (continued)

Int'l Canine Semen Bank – IL
Rte. 78 N.
Virginia, IL 62691
(217) 452-3006 or 323-2978

Seager Canine Semen Bank, Inc.
329 Sioux
Park Forest, IL 60466
(312) 748-0954

Triple S Cryo Genetics
University of Illinois Trail
Box 217
Philo, IL 61864
(217) 684-2900 or 253-3202

IOWA

Iowa State University*
Dept. of Veterinary Clinical Sciences
Theriogenology Section
Ames, IA 50010
(515) 294-1500

KENTUCKY

Premier Veterinary Services
Box 607
Shelbyville, KY 40065
(502) 633-2000

MASSACHUSETTS

Mill Valley Veterinary Clinic*
224 Mill Valley Road
Belchertown, MA 01007
(413) 323-9201

Westford–Ho Cryoservices
Elizabeth F. Trainor, DVM
Lovett Rd.
Oxford, MA 01540
(508) 987-2110

An asterisk (*) denotes a newly added facility

MINNESOTA

Crossroads Animal Hospital, Ltd.
Frances O. Smith, DVM PhD
14321 Nicollet Ct.
Burnsville, MN 55337
(612) 435-2655

OHIO

Int'l Canine Semen Bank – OH
34910 Center Ridge Rd.
N. Ridgeville, OH 44039
(216) 327-8282

OREGON

International Canine Semen Bank
Northwest Center
PO Box 651
Sandy, OR 97055
(503) 663-7031 or 633-1257

PENNSYLVANIA

Cryo–Genetics Laboratories
Ludwig's Corner, Rte. 100
Box 256–A
Chester Springs, PA 19425
(215) 458-5888

International Canine Genetics
271 Great Valley Parkway
Malvern, PA 19355
(215) 640-1244
1-800-248-8099

SOUTH CAROLINA

Cryo Tech International, Inc.
Rte. 1, Box 386
Abbeville, SC 29620
(803) 446-8787

TENNESSEE

Collierville Canine Genetics*
(formerly Spring Creek Ranch)
POB 633
Collierville, TN 38027
(901) 853-0550

University of Tennessee
College of Veterinary Medicine
POB 1071
Knoxville, TN 37901
(617) 546-9240

TEXAS

Int'l Canine Semen Bank – TX
1236 Brittmoore
Houston, TX 77043
(713) 468-8253

United Breeders Service
PO Box 211
Lubbock, TX 79408
(806) 745-3419

VIRGINIA

Roanoke A. I. Laboratories, Inc.
8533 Martin Creek Rd.
Roanoke, VA 24018
(703) 774-0676

WASHINGTON

Preservation, Inc.
17706 49th Pl. SE
Snohomish, WA 98290
(206) 568-8894

WISCONSIN

International Canine Genetics, Inc.
Dr. David Schabdach
c/o Dr. Ed Graham
1026 280th St.
Glenwood City, WI 54013
1-800-248-8099

International Canine Genetics, Inc.
Dr. Robert M. Brown
Jackson Area Pet Hospital
3370 Jackson Dr.
Jackson, WI 53037
(414) 677-3112

An asterisk (*) denotes a newly added facility

The ASCOB Cocker Spaniel.

New Life Forms

According to the article, "Gene Splicers to Try New Animals," by Charles Petit (*The San Francisco Chronicle*, 5/26/87) the unnatural world of gene juggling is finally about to trample, flutter and hoof it from laboratory to barnyard:

"We're trying to make cows do things Mother Nature never even thought of," said Thomas Richardson, professor of food science at the University of California at Davis.

It may be quite a while before some company patents six-legged sheep and corners the market on leg of lamb, but some strange animals are on the way as scientists learn to mix and match genes from totally unrelated species or insert genes invented from scratch.

Basic research in farmyard gene splicing got a hefty boost last month from a Commerce Department ruling. It extends to horses and cows and man-made animal variations the sort of patent protection already given genetically engineered crops and microbes.

Patents may be given to farm animals that carry genes not normally found in the species and put there artificially without cross breeding. Patent Office officials say they have 15 such applications in hand already, but they will not give details.

The benefits of genetically altered animals are obvious: Increased productivity through gene splicing could greatly lower prices. It may ease hunger worldwide by giving farmers in Third World nations hardy, productive crops and livestock that do not need expensive fertilizers or feeds.

Potential Dangers

However, some experts warn that uncontrolled use of genetic engineering on farm animals may be hazardous for both farms and the natural world.

Plunging prices could send farm economics into a tailspin. If rich farmers and corporations use patents to monopolize efficient agriculture, they could put the final nail in the coffin of the American small family farm. In addition, novel living things intended for the farm could conceivably disrupt or even destroy populations of some wild animals.

"We don't know what the effects will be," said Robert Colwell, an ecologist and professor of zoology at the University of California at Berkeley. "Almost every new gene will probably pose no danger at all, but is almost good enough?"

Richardson, who brainstorms with graduate students among racks of flasks and beakers and DNA sequencing equipment, has been around a long time and knows milk. But his UC Davis students know genetic engineering. "Jeez, I gotta ask them sometimes how some of the science works," said the middle-aged professor. "I just set the agenda."

Graduate student Sang Oh is altering the DNA code on a cow gene so that enzymes can more easily digest milk particles. Why? Faster, better cheese.

Once made, the new version is to be cloned, isolated and put back in cow embryos. If it all works, the embryos will be implanted in adult cows, develop into calves, and grow to become dairy cows programmed to make milk primed for the cheese maker. Their offspring will inherit the same abilities.

Another student is laying plans for cows whose milk does not contain lactose, a substance that millions of non-milk drinkers cannot tolerate. Yet another Richardson student is designing a gene that should put more iron-rich protein lactoferrin in milk right out of the cow, making it more nutritious and more resistant to spoiling.

The 'Super Mouse'

The first and most famous example of a dramatically altered higher animal was a *super mouse* that grew to twice normal size three years ago when embryologist Ralph Brinster of the University of Pennsylvania and biochemist Richard Palmiter at the University of Washington put rat growth hormones in mouse embryos.

Since then, genes for rat and cow and human growth hormones have been put in rabbits, pigs, sheep and even fish. A rat growth hormone gene will not make a cow ratlike, but if it churns out enough hormone, it may make a cow that produces more milk, or a steer that makes steaks quicker.

Results so far are less than perfect. More than 50 pigs in pens outside the USDA office in Beltsville, MD are suffering arthritis and the bone deformities of a condition called acromegaly. The pigs, despite their defects, are "a little more efficient in their use of feed, they are leaner than normal, but they don't grow any faster," said Harold Hawkes, the USDA scientist who grew them with genes provided by Palmiter.

Technically, the pigs are patentable, but *they're not real useful.*

"They actually produce too much of the hormone. It's turned on all the time," Hawkes said.

At a time when research is mushrooming – at UC Davis alone, 40 people in half a dozen labs are working on creating genetically healthier livestock – critics contend that no one is watching over the process.

There is no clear overall government watchdog to regulate new higher forms of life.

"I sure wouldn't want to be the one to sort out that bag of worms around patents and regulation," Hawkes said.

Even last month's patent ruling is unclear at the practical level.

If, for instance, a genetically altered Guernsey cow that produces low-fat milk is patented, what happens if one such cow is crossed with a Brahman bull? Does the patent follow the gene wherever it goes, covering any crossbred offspring that also carry the novel trait?

New Territory

Will farm beasts be put through regular gene checks to make sure that farmers pay all due royalties and license fees? Can current technology find all artificially introduced genes in an adult animal? "We just don't know, this is all new territory," said Kate Murashige, a biochemist and patent attorney in Palo Alto.

The Washington-based Foundation on Economic Trends, headed by Jeremy Rifkin, has joined forces with 11 animal welfare organizations – including the American Humane Society – to protest the patent ruling. Rifkin called it "morally repugnant" to allow corporations to monopolize the genetic code of all life.

"The most amazing thing to me is the hubris involved in patenting an animal so you can say this is my animal, when all you have done is add one gene among the billions of genes produced by millions of years of evolution and thousands of years of breeding by farmers," Colwell said.

One of the most startling sights at Davis is in a pen in a barn at the edge of campus. Is it a sheep? Is it a goat? It is both. In fact, it is literally a smorgasbord. Its head – the animal is a she but whether nanny or ewe is uncertain – has the markings of a goat. It's flank is a patchwork of wool and matted goat hair.

Biologist Gary Anderson created the chimera – from the mythical Greek creature made partly of goat, lion, serpent and other assorted parts – by joining two microscopic goat and sheep embryos before the cells began differentiating into types of tissue such as nerve, skin, muscle and bone. He put the combo in a sheep's womb.

The sheep cells and goat cells divided and grew into different tissues, sometimes making islands of pure goat or pure sheep in the creature, sometimes mixing more or less evenly. "Somehow, they knew not to make extra legs, or leave out the heart," marveled Anderson.

The animal, of no particular good in the barnyard, shows that the immune systems of different species do not reject each other if they grow together from the embryo stage.

The new extension of the patenting law was prompted at the University of Washington by a bid to patent oysters that do not reproduce but are commercially attractive because they are edible year around. Unlike normal oysters, they do not lose their flavor during breeding season.

Ironically, the oyster patent was turned down because the mollusks do not have new genes, just extra copies. Nonetheless, the Seattle team is going ahead with modifications of the oysters and plans to test them in Pacific waters in Oregon and Northern California.

Kenneth Chew, director of aquaculture at the University of Washington, said he does not see any way to prevent introduction of genetically altered species of fish into the world's oceans.

"We obviously don't want to compromise the natural stocks," he said, "but I think with careful planning, just like in land farming, we can develop a better product. The world has to be fed. Just as long as people sit down and talk about it rationally, there is a place for all this."

Another article, "Calves Genetically Engineered," written by Keith Schneider and appearing in *The New York Times* (no date on newspaper article) explores this issue further:

A team of scientists has produced the nation's first genetically engineered calves, a milestone in using advanced genetic technology to alter food-producing animals.

Four calves born in the last 15 months on a farm near Marquez, Texas, 120 miles north of Houston, have genes from other species, including one from humans.

Researchers expect the genes, inserted into fertilized eggs removed from the womb, to speed growth and make cattle leaner. The four calves are a first step in understanding how direct genetic manipulation of the chromosomes of cattle will affect meat and milk.

In producing the genetically engineered calves, which look no different from ordinary calves, scientists in the United States now have completed their goal of inserting foreign genes into the chromosomes of every important food animal.

The breakthrough holds the promise not only of eliminating many steps in the long and costly process of cattle breeding, but also of directly producing superior livestock with traits that until now have existed only in theory.

But federal regulators said they had several concerns about how the genetic transformations might affect the quality of meat and milk. These issues are being reviewed by the Department of Agriculture.

Animal welfare groups and some family farm groups have been worried as well about the new technology's potential to harm animals, the environment and smaller producers who could be forced out of business.

The procedure has been done in pigs, sheep, goats and chickens. But scientists say the genetically engineered calves represent a significant step in using the technology because cattle are much more complicated to work with and far more important to the nation's farm economy.

Farm specialists say the technology holds vast promise for altering production practices and changing the structure of the $35 billion beef industry and the $20 billion dairy industry in the United States.

For instance, cattle companies could offer McDonald's beef animals specially designed to produce more meat for hamburgers. Kraft may have the opportunity to operate dairies with its own trademark breed of cows that produce milk specifically intended for producing cheese. And farmers could gain animals far more resistant to diseases and stress, making it possible to halt or sharply curtail the use of toxic drugs and dangerous antibodies.

"This technology has tremendous implications," said Caird E. Rexroad, a research physiologist at the Department of Agriculture's Beltsville Agricultural Research Station in Beltsville, MD., who produced genetically altered sheep.

"For the time being, most people are looking at improving efficiency; the amount of feed it takes to produce a pound of meat. In the future, we're looking at manipulating growth and other characteristics," Rexroad said.

But Michael W. Fox, a veterinarian who is vice president of the Humane Society of the United States, had another point of view.

"We have 2 billion cattle, 1.6 billion sheep and goats and 800 million pigs in the world today," he said. "That population needs to be drastically reduced because of adverse environmental impacts. This focusing on enhanced productivity might look good to investors, but is the last thing the world needs."

The genetically engineered calves were developed by a group of Texas researchers let by Bert O'Malley, a cell biologist from the Baylor College of Medicine in Houston; Robert Hammer, a research physiologist at the Howard Hughes Memorial Institute in Dallas, and Ken Bondioli, a senior scientist at Granada BioSciences, Inc., an affiliate of Granada Corp., a cattle breeding and food company in Houston.

Darold F. McCalla, president of Granada BioSciences, which financed the research, said his company had not been eager to disclose the breakthrough until now because not enough animals had been produced. He said Granada also was concerned about the reaction of animal welfare groups and others who oppose biotechnology development.

Two other research groups have said they produced genetically engineered calves before the American group.

One group led by Robert Church, a medical biochemist, at the University of Calgary in Alberta, said it developed a calf in June 1986 that had a human gene that produced the protein interferon as a way to improve disease resistance.

The Canadian group has reported three generations of gene-altered animals, 23 males and females in all, Church said in an interview from his office in Calgary.

An East German group from the Academy of Agricultural Sciences in Dummerstorf reported the birth of a genetically engineered calf January 19, 1988.

The Toy Poodle.

The Standard Poodle.

The Stud Dog

The dog you select to stand at stud should have certain things going for him. First, he should be masculine in appearance and, at least your appraisal, to conform closely to the breed Standard. A major mistake made by breeders is to keep a dog that is overdone in some features in the hope he can overcome a bitch with deficiencies in these areas. It doesn't work that way. Breeding an oversize dog to a small bitch in the hopes of getting average-sized puppies is a futile effort. The hallmark of a good breeder, one who understands basic genetics, is breeding to dogs who conform to the Standard. Extremes should be avoided like the plague. They only add complications to a breeding program down the road.

Second, it is extremely important that the stud dog come from an unbroken line of producers on both his sire's and dam's sides. Unbroken means that at least his sire, grandfather and great grandfather have produced 10 or more champions each. If his sire is still young, he may not have hit that mark, but from reading the magazines and seeing his offspring an intelligent breeder can tell if he is going to make it. This unbroken line helps to ensure that he is likely to be homozygous (containing either but not both members of a pair of alleles) for his good traits. An unbroken producing bitch line is frosting on the cake. It's usually more difficult to find because bitches have fewer offspring. So, when a dog is found that has unbroken producing lines for three generations on his sire's and dam's sides, there is an excellent chance of having a prepotent stud.

The third consideration is appearance. Let's face it, if the male is not constructed right or if his color is not quite right, he is not going to be a great show dog. While the dog doesn't have to be a great show winner to attract the bitches, it helps. Believe me, it helps. There are outstanding examples of non-titled dogs being excellent studs. However, they are few and far between.

There is more to breeding than just dropping a bitch in season into the stud dog's pen and hoping for the best.

First off, let's talk about a subject that never seems to be addressed in the literature about stud dogs, the psyche of the dog. Young stud dogs need to be brought along slowly. If he is a show dog to begin with, he is most likely outgoing and the "gung ho" type. If he is not, please do not think about using him at stud. Behavior traits such as shyness and lack of aggressiveness are transmitted to the next generation just as beautiful necks or slipped stifles are.

Early on he should be taught to get along with other male dogs. Do not put him in with an older male too early. If you do there is a good likelihood that he will be intimidated and it may harm his prospects of being a good stud. Good stud dogs have to be aggressive in the breeding box. Dogs who have been intimidated early seldom shape up. However, running, playing and even puppy fighting with litter mates or slightly older puppies doesn't seem to have a detrimental effect.

The young male, until he is old enough to stand up for himself, should be quartered first with puppies his own age and then introduced to older bitches as kennel mates. It's not a good idea to keep him in a pen by himself. Socialization is extremely important. Time for play as a puppy and a companion to keep him from boredom helps his growth and development.

His quarters and food should present no special problems. Serious breeders all feed their dogs a nourishing and balanced diet. Study after study in colleges of veterinary medicine and by nutritionists at major dog food companies, have shown that the major brands of dry dog food come as close to meeting the total needs of the dog as any elaborately concocted breeder's formula. Each of you has probably learned to add three drops of this and two teaspoons of that, but honestly, a good dry food does the trick. Many breeders spice up the basic diet with their own version of goodies, including table scraps, to break up the monotony or to stimulate a finicky eater. However, for the most part, this is more cosmetic than nutritional. If it makes you feel better, feed him those extra goodies. Do not get him fat and out of condition. That could do terrible things to his libido.

A very important aspect of being the owner of a stud dog is to make sure he can produce puppies. Therefore, at around 11 to 12 months of age it's a good idea to trundle him off to the vet's for a check on his sperm count. This will tell you if he is producing enough viable sperm cells to make sure he can fertilize eggs in the ovum of a bitch. Sometimes it is found that while a stud produces spermatozoa, they are not active. The chances of this dog being able to fertilize an egg is markedly reduced. While this problem is usually found in older dogs, it happens often enough in young animals to be of concern. Thus, the sperm count exam is important, and should be done yearly.

Since we are dealing with the breeding of a warm-blooded mammal, there is a need to be concerned with his general health. Sexual contact with a variety of bitches exposes the dog to a wide variety of minor infections and some major ones. Some, if not promptly identified and treated, can lead to sterility – and there goes the farm. Other non-sexual infections and illnesses, such as urinary infections, stones, etc., can also reduce a dog's ability to sire puppies. Since it is not desirable for any of these things to happen, stud -dog owners need to watch their young Romeos like hawks.

It's a good idea to have your vet check all incoming bitches. While checking them for obvious signs of infection, especially brucellosis, he can also run a smear to see when they are ready to breed. The dog should also be checked frequently to see if there is any type of discharge from his penis. A dog at regular stud should not have a discharge. Usually he will lick himself frequently to keep the area clean. After breeding, it is also a good idea to rinse off the area with a clean saline solution. Your vet may also advise flushing out the penile area after breeding, using a special solution.

The testicles and penis are the male organs of reproduction. Testicles are housed in a sac called the scrotum. The AKC will not allow dogs who are cryptorchid's (neither testicle descended) nor monorchids (a dog that has only one testicle descended) to be shown.

The male's testicles are outside the body because the internal heat of the body could curtail the production of sperm. There is a special muscle that keeps them close to the body for warmth in cold weather and relaxes and lets them down to get air cooled in hot weather.

In the male fetus, the gonads, or sex organs, develop in the abdominal cavity migrating during gestation toward their eventual position. Shortly before birth they hover over an opening in the muscular structure of the pubic area through which they will descend to reach the scrotal sac. This external position is vital to the fertility of the animal, for production of live sperm can only proceed at a temperature several degrees cooler than normal body temperature. The glandular tissue of the testes are nourished and supported by arteries, veins, nerves, connective tissue and ductwork, collectively known as the spermatic cord. The scrotum acts as a thermostat.

As noted above, there are many involuntary muscle fibers that are stimulated to contract with the environmental temperature, pulling the testes closer to the body for warmth. Contraction also occurs as a result of any stimulus that might be interpreted by the dog as a threat of physical harm - sight of a strange dog, being picked up, etc. This contraction does not force the testicles back up into the abdominal cavity of the adult dog because the inguinal rings have tightened and will not allow them to be drawn back up. The tightening of the rings usually occurs at about 10 months of age.

There are a number of reasons why a dog may be a monorchid or cryptorchid. For example, the size of the opening through the muscles may be too small to allow for easy passage of the testes, or, the spermatic cord may not be long enough for the testes to remain in the scrotum most of the time, and as the proportions of the inguinal ring and testes change in the growing puppy, the time comes when the testes may be trapped above the ring as they grow at different rates. Also, there exists a fibrous muscular band which attaches both to the testes and scrotal wall, gradually shortening and actually guiding the testes in their descent. Possibly this structure could be at fault.

The important thing about all of this is to help the prospective stud-dog owner learn about the anatomy of the reproduction organs of the dog. From the foregoing is it any wonder that many puppies are described as being down one day and up the next?

Next time you place that favorite male puppy up on the grooming table be wary when probing for all of his standard equipment. The scrotal muscles may contract and the still generous inguinal rings may allow the disappearance of the parts sought.

Great luck, a youngster has been found that has IT, and you decide to let the world share in the good fortune of owning him. It's a good idea to get him started on the right foot with a cooperative, experienced bitch, one of your own preferably. By introducing the young and inexperienced stud to a *woman of the world*, his first experience will result in an easy and successful breeding. Like all males, his ego will soar as a result. This is important. He needs to have the feeling of accomplishment and success. A feisty, difficult bitch the first time around could very well frustrate the youngster and as a result he may not be too enthusiastic about future breedings. Remember, you want a confident and aggressive stud dog in the breeding box. There will be difficult bitches to come so it's best to bring him along slow and easy until he will be a match for those fearsome females.

When the bitch is ready to breed (as your stud gains experience he will not pay too much attention to her until she is really ready) both animals should be allowed to exercise and relieve themselves just before being brought together. Its also a good idea not to feed them before mating. Bring the bitch in first. The place should be quiet and away from noise and other dogs. Spend a few minutes petting her and telling her how wonderful she is. Then bring the dog in on a lead. Do not allow him to come lunging in and make a frustrated leap at her. This can cause her to panic and bite him out of fear.

After a few minutes of pirouetting around together, she throwing her vulva in his face and he, with his ears curled on top of his head, trying to lick fore and aft, take off the lead. Allow them to court for a few minutes. She should tell you she is ready by being coquettish and continually backing up into the dog.

Now comes the important time for the future success of the young stud. The dog needs to learn the owner is there to help and should not back away from breeding the bitch just because someone is holding her.

Having planned ahead, there will be a large non-skid rug on the floor. Place the bitch on the rug, add a little Vaseline around the vulva and face her rump toward the dog. Pat her on the fanny to encourage the dog to come ahead. Generally speaking, he will. As a rule he will lick her again around the vulva. Some dogs are truly considerate lovers, they will go around to the front and gently lick at the bitches eyes and ears. These are true gentlemen. However, this will get him nowhere, so again encourage him to come around to where the action is. If he is unsure of himself, lift the bitch's rear and dangle it in front of the dog's nose.

Encouraged and emboldened, the male will mount the bitch from the rear and begin to probe slowly for the opening to the vulva. Once he discovers it, he will begin to move more rapidly. This is a critical time. Some young dogs are so far off the target they never get near the right opening. It's time to gently reposition the bitch so he can have a better angle. This may occur any number of times. He may get frustrated and back off. Don't get excited, this is normal in a young dog. He may even get so excited and confused that he swings around and tries to breed her from the front. This approach never ends successfully.

Get him back on track. Show him the business end again and encourage him to proceed. By now you have noticed a red, bone like protuberance sticking out from the penis sheath. This, of course, if the penis itself. When, as a dog continues to probe and finds the opening, he will begin to move frenetically. As he moves in this fashion, a section just behind the pointed penis bone begins to swell. It is capable of great enlargement. This enlargement of the bulbous takes place due to its filling with blood, and it becomes some three times larger than the rest of the penis. In this way the dog, once having penetrated, is tied to the bitch; it is entirely due to the male, the bitch having no part in the initial tying.

When a tie has occurred, the semen is pumped in spurts into the vagina. The bitch then helps to keep the penis enlarged as she begins to have a series of peristaltic waves which cause a slight tightening and relaxing of the vagina. Some males will stay tied for up to one hour and others for as little as five minutes. A five-minute successful tie is just as satisfactory as a longer one because the semen has moved up through the uterus and fallopian tubes to the ovarian capsules by the end of five minutes.

Once the dog and bitch are successfully tied, the male characteristically tries to lift his rear leg over the bitch and keep the tie in a back-to-back position. Some dogs merely slide off the back of a bitch and maintain a tie facing in the same direction. One thing you can count on, they will not stay in one position for any length of time. If someone were to chart the moves of a dog and a bitch during a 30-minute tie, it would look like break dancing at its best. Because of this, it's a good idea to have two people involved at this point. One at the bitch's head and one at the male's.

Every now and then a fractious bitch will be sent for breeding. She can be frightened about being shipped or just plain spooked by a variety of things. Certainly one doesn't want the dog to be bitten by a frightened bitch nor to have one's fingers lacerated. The easiest solution to this problem is to tie her jaws loosely with wide gauze. This muzzle should tie behind her ears to make sure it doesn't slide off. Pet her, reassure her, but hold her firmly during the breeding so she doesn't lunge at the dog.

After the tie has been broken, there sometimes will be a rush of fluid from the bitch. Don't worry about it, the sperm is well on its way up the fallopian tubes. Place the bitch gently in a quiet pen, apart from other dogs, and give her fresh water and an opportunity to relieve herself. The dog should be petted and told how well he has done. This is also a good time to flush out his sheath, and if your vet has recommended any medication, apply it now. Then, he too should be put in a separate, quiet pen with fresh water. It is not a good idea to put him back with a group of male dogs. The opportunity for a serious fight is greatest at this time. The other dogs smell him and get quite upset that it wasn't their turn.

How often can the dog be used at stud? If the dog is in good condition he should be able to be used every day for a week. Some serious breeders who, when faced with many bitches to be bred to a popular stud, have used the dog in the morning and the evening for at least three days. If a dog is used regularly he can be used from day to day for a long time. However, if a dog is seldom used, he should not be expected to be able to service day after day for any great length of time.

Nature is most generous with sperm. In one good mating a dog may discharge millions, and by and large, a copious amount of sperm is produced in dogs who are used regularly. Dr. Leon Whitney in his book, *This is the Cocker Spaniel*, describes a stud left with a bitch who copulated five times with her, and remained tied at least 18 minutes each time.

All this Olympian activity may be possible for a short time, but for good health and good management, three times a week in normal use seems about right. Most breeders would give their eye teeth for such a popular stud. An individual bitch should be serviced twice – once every other day – for the best chance of conception.

For some breeders to breed to a stud of their choice is often difficult, especially in countries that have quarantine restrictions. In the United States, the basic cost of shipping, the possibility of the dog being booked, the chance of making connections with a popular stud who is out on a circuit being campaigned, etc., all these problems can produce a great deal of frustration. The use of frozen sperm opens up many new possibilities. Owners of popular stud dogs should definitely look into it. At the time of this writing, there are 29 AKC-sanctioned collection stations. There should be many more in the near future.

Collecting sperm from dogs is not like collecting from cattle. One collection from the latter produces enough to inseminate more than 100 cows. The largest amount collected at one time over the many years of research in dogs was 22 vials. Usually two to three vials are used to breed a bitch on two to three occasions while she is in season.

The estimated time to store enough semen to inseminate 30

bitches differs by age, health, and sperm quantity and quality. Estimate approximately a month for a young dog, approximately three months for a dog of eight or nine years of age or older. Collection is still time consuming.

It doesn't take one long to recognize that, in the early stages, those males of outstanding quality will make up the main reservoir of the sperm bank. It is suggested by the collection centers that collection be done at a young age - three to five years.

Limitations in quality and quantity due to old age lengthen the period necessary to store enough sperm for even a few bitches. In addition, the daily routine of a dog's life may limit freezability: The settling down in a new environment, changes in diet/water, minor health problems, etc. It is also not uncommon to get poor freeze results from a stud dog that has not been used for a month or longer. For the dog, once he settles down, the process of collection is a pleasant experience.

The following information on artificial insemination written by Diann Sullivan is reprinted by permission of *The Labrador Quarterly* (Hoflin Publishing Ltd., 4401 Zephyr St., Wheat Ridge, CO 80033-3299):

Artificial insemination [AI] has been recognized as possible in dogs for some two hundred years. Semen is collected from the male and introduced into the reproductive tract of the female. When done properly, it is as successful as natural mating. It will not spoil a dog or bitch for future natural breedings and in fact, may desensitize a bitch to accept penetration.

The main reason for AI failure is that it is used all too often as a last resort after trying and failing at natural breedings, when it is too late in a bitch's cycle for her to conceive. The use of artificial insemination as a back-up to a natural mating where a tie was not produced helps assure that as complete a mating occurred as was possible. Bitches who have had a vaginal prolapse and may have scar tissue present after the protruding vaginal wall has been clipped and healed, may reject intercourse due to pain. It is also very useful when the stud dog manager finds he has a spoiled bitch in or one who has had little association with other dogs. Using an AI when natural mating is somehow impossible will provide a satisfactory service versus frustration on everyone's part.

The equipment needed includes one pair of sterile gloves (available through a pharmacy or your doctor), one inseminating rod (through dairy stores or International Canine Genetics), one 12 cc or 20 cc syringe (from stores, pharmacies), one artificial vagina and collection tube (ICG) or the sterile container that housed the syringe, a small piece of rubber tubing to attach the rod to the syringe and a non-spermicidal jelly (K-Y). To sterilize equipment after use, wash thoroughly in warm water and a drop or two of mild liquid dish soap. Rinse well with distilled water and dry completely with a hair dryer to avoid residual minerals that act as a spermicide.

On a safe surface within reach, lay out the package of sterile gloves, not touching the left glove to contamination. Glove your right hand with the right glove. On the sterile paper that the gloves are wrapped in, dispense a little jelly. Attach the collection tube to the smallest end of the artificial vagina (AV). Be sure it is securely in place. Roll down two plus inches on the large end of the AV to make it somewhat shorter. Place the AV and attached tube next to your body. We have the stud dog waiting in a crate within reach until the bitch is securely muzzled and standing ready.

The stud dog handler sits comfortably on a stool facing the bitch's left side. I use my left hand to support her stifle and can hold her tail out of the way with the same hand. Using the right hand, the stud dog helper pats the top of the bitch and encourages the stud dog to "get her!" The thumb and forefinger of the right hand grasps the bottom of the vulva to open it for easy penetration of the dog's erect penis, as he is actively mounting. When he is fully penetrated, the right hand can then hold the bitch's hock to add to the support the left hand is giving to her left stifle.

The stud dog may dismount without a tie occurring. If he is fully erect and dripping seminal fluid, the pre-warmed AV is slipped over his penis and held in place with the left hand. The right thumb and forefinger grasp the penis above the bulbous enlargement and apply steady pressure as the penis is pulled down and back for duration of the collection. If a collection is preferred without allowing penetration, the dog is stimulated into erection as he is actively mounting the bitch. Grasping the penis back behind the developing bulbous will produce thrusting at which time the AV is slipped over the enlarging penis. If collection is being done without an AV, the penis is brought down and back and the syringe container tube is carefully held under and away from the tip of the penis. The pressure from the right hand around the bulbous will cause the ejaculation which is carefully caught in the casing. Watch the collection tube fill. When you see a significant third and clear portion on top of the settled, thickened sperm, withdraw the AV.

Put the stud dog away in a kennel or area with enough room for him to safely retract his penis and in a clean environment. The bitch handler should sit comfortably on his stool and left the bitch's rear up over his knee so her rear is tilted up significantly.

Attach the inseminating rod to the syringe securely. Cut the rods to make them easier to handle. Slip the smooth end of the rod into the collection tube and all the way to the bottom. VERY SLOWLY (so as not to rip off those little sperm tails), draw up the seminal fluid into the syringe. Draw up an extra few cc's of air.

Carefully place the syringe and rod back inside your shirt for warmth, and carefully glove the left hand and apply the pre-dispensed K-Y jelly to the left fingertips.

Palm up, carefully insert the left third (middle) finger in and up to where the cervix can be felt. Gently slip your third fingertip just through the cervix. Carefully glide the inseminating rod along the palm side of the third finger to where the smooth tip can be felt by the fingertip. SLOWLY, use the syringe to pass the seminal fluid into the bitch. If you notice leakage, gently pass the finger tip and rod tip in a little further and continue to inseminate. Leaving the third finger in place during insemination acts as the body of the penis to block fluid loss.

Remove your finger after two minutes and continue to massage the vulva every thirty seconds or so, maintaining the tilt of her rear end for at least ten minutes. The massage of the vulva causes her vaginal canal to contract and pull the fluid up.

Crate the bitch for at least one hour after the breeding.

If the dog's sperm count is good and the sperm has good motility, breed three to four days apart to allow for the complete rebuilding of the stud dog's sperm count.

We must each continue to learn new and improved techniques to facilitate healthy pregnancies and practice methods that improve conception rates. Utilizing simple artificial insemination as a back-up to unsuccessful natural matings or as a choice in difficult matings increases the number of successful litters. AI allows the stud dog manager a reliable choice to assist his mating strategy for each bitch. AI is extremely useful in achieving a breeding early in the estrus, near when she may be ovulating. Following with either a successful natural mating or another successful AI every three or four days throughout her standing heat, would help insure that active sperm is available to the ripening ovum.

It is wonderful to receive the phone calls reporting the arrival of a litter that would not exist without the use of artificial insemination. Its reliability is constantly reinforced, and plays a strong role in improving conception rates.

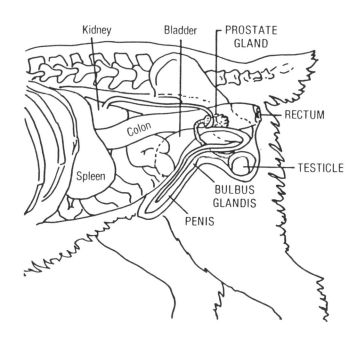

Figure 6.

The Whippet.

The Smooth Fox Terrier.

Prenatal Care and Whelping

Proper planning makes breeding a fascinating pastime. The mark to be aimed at in dog breeding is improvement—improvement in your own stock; improvement in the quality of the puppies you raise; and, finally, improvement in the breed itself. After you have decided to breed your bitch at her next season, start thinking ahead—your objective being to have the bitch in the very best possible physical condition before she is bred in order to maintain her health during the gestation period so that her offspring will greet the world in the pink of condition. Four to six weeks in advance is not too soon. Have her checked thoroughly by a competent veterinarian for general condition: coat, development, the presence of internal parasites, possible anemia, etc. Then if it is found, say, that she is anemic, measures should be taken at once to build her up so that she will be in prime condition to perpetuate her kind. Internal parasites should be evacuated to the best of your ability. In other words, everything within your power should be done to get the bitch in A-one condition for her new responsibilities.

It is best to check for internal parasites again just prior to breeding the bitch. But if you belong to the "never do today what you can put off until she is in whelp" school, remember that the deadline for worming is within the first three weeks after the bitch is bred. If you forgot it, then omit the worming and gather gray hairs worrying over those wormy puppies.

In the early stages of pregnancy—that is, the first three weeks—a bitch requires very little extra care. Her diet must be a well balanced one containing adequate quantities of protein, carbohydrates, fat, minerals, and vitamins. Meat, eggs, and milk contain the essential amino acids not necessarily found in prepared foods and vegetables, and should be the principle constituents of her diet. Cooked meat is preferable to raw, and vegetables should be fed either raw or only slightly cooked in order to preserve valuable vitamins. Beef, liver, horse meat, eggs, milk, and vegetables provide the necessary food substances and may be combined with various prepared cereals to round out a well balanced diet for your bitch. As soon as a bitch is bred, start her on a calcium preparation and vitamin D. Some breeders prefer a capsule—

dicalcium phosphate with iron and vitamin D—one per day for the first four weeks, then two per day for the remainder of the period. From these the bitch will get adequate amounts of calcium in an easily metabolized form, together with iron to combat any tendency toward anemia, and the essential vitamin D. In addition, continue any vitamin-mineral supplement you have been giving all along.

From the first to the third week, the bitch in whelp should be fed twice daily, using her usual quantity of food but in divided feedings. After the third week, the quantity should gradually be doubled. After the seventh week, the bitch should be fed three times daily without increasing the quantity—small feedings being the rule so as not to over-distend the stomach at any one feeding. In the last trimester, the bitch should not be given hard-to-digest foods. Above all, she should not be overloaded with food. Toward the end of the pregnancy, the diet should be slightly laxative in an attempt to help the bitch eliminate extra waste products from her system. A pinch of sodium bicarbonate should be added to the drinking water throughout the entire period but is most essential during the last week. This has a tendency to reduce the danger of acid milk, which causes the death of not a few puppies. Starting three days before she is due to whelp, it is well to give the bitch a teaspoonful of milk of magnesia each day to aid in the evacuation of waste from the intestinal tract.

During the first trimester, the bitch can exercise as usual. After the fifth week, it is well to restrict any violent exercise such as fast and continuous running. The bitch should be walked briskly twice daily on a lead. Do not permit her to romp with other dogs. In general, she should be treated with kindness and consideration.

There is no sure, early sign to ascertain whether or not your bitch is in whelp. The presence of foeti cannot be determined before four weeks, at which time they may be the size of hickory nuts. By laying the bitch on her side facing you, placing one hand underneath with the other on top of her abdomen, and then moving the fingers gently along the abdomen, you can often feel the swollen tubes on each side. The breasts begin to enlarge with milk content toward the end of the sixth week.

Beginning about one week before the bitch is due to whelp, clean her teeth daily, using a mixture of table salt and sodium bicarbonate. This tends to lessen the possibility of navel and other infections in the newborn puppies. Keep the bitch's skin as free as possible from any eczema, lice, fleas, or ticks, but do not use insecticides this late in her pregnancy.

As to the time of whelping, nature gives a few hints. Two to three days before the pups are coming, the shape of the bitch changes. Instead of resembling a sausage, her weight tends to shift lower down in the body and often her hip bones become quite prominent. Her nipples begin to swell and usually you can express milk from them.

It is customary to conclude that a bitch will commence whelping sixty-three days after she is bred. This is not a hard and fast rule. Some bitches whelp on the fifty-ninth day, some on the sixtieth day, etc. If the bitch has been bred twice, this complicates matters even more, for there is no way to determine whether one should count from the first or the second breeding. Therefore, it is well to be watchful from the fifty-ninth day of the first breeding onward.

Some common signs that whelping is about to commence are: refusal of food, shivering, panting, restlessness, digging, staring wide-eyed, and a slight, clear

The Dalmatian.

vaginal discharge. Any or all of these indications may be present. The most reliable indication that whelping time is near is the bitch's temperature. Normal temperature is 101.5 degrees. There is a definite lowering of the temperature when whelping is at hand. When the temperature falls below 99 degrees, it is almost certain that there is not much longer to wait. A bitch's temperature may even fall as low as 96 degrees at this point. During the final week it is not uncommon for the temperature to fall to 99 degrees at night only to go back up by morning. This can result in many sleepless nights. However, when the temperature goes below 99 degrees and keeps on dropping, it is safe to assume the bitch will commence to whelp.

About one week before the bitch is due, she should be bathed thoroughly, with special attention being paid to cleaning her breasts. If she has an extremely heavy coat, the hair around the breasts should be massaged with baby oil to loosen accumulated crusts and this should be followed by a good bath with mild soap—no disinfectants. The place of whelping should be quiet and out of the way, such as a utility room, unused room, or one in which there is little traffic. A suitable box should be provided and the bitch encouraged to sleep in it at least a week before the puppies are due so that she becomes accustomed to it. It should be of sufficient size to house dam and puppies, and preferably it should be raised slightly off the floor to avoid drafts and to facilitate cleaning the box. Other supplies which will be needed are: a good-sized stack of clean newspapers, clean but expendable towels, sterile scissors, cotton, tincture of merthiolate, baby oil, sterile thread, pencil, writing paper, scale (if possible), alcohol (for sterilizing and cleaning scissors), a fairly small cardboard box, easily obtainable at the supermarket (be sure it hasn't contained insecticides), hot water bottle or heating pad, and brandy and an eyedropper for stimulating the sluggish puppy. These supplies should be gathered and set out beforehand so they will be available immediately when needed. The whelping box should be lined with many thicknesses of newspaper so that the bitch can utilize her instinct to make a nest if she is so inclined. A container for the disposal of waste should also be available.

Some bitches approach whelping and handle the entire process with equanimity and dispatch. They know, by instinct, exactly what to do and proceed to do it with little or no assistance. Others do not. For this reason, a bitch should not be left unattended. If it will not be possible for someone to be with her, prior arrangements should be made with the veterinarian to assume the responsibility. Even if the owner plans to be in attendance, it is wise for him to notify his veterinarian so that the latter may be "on call" and easily located. Whelping usually takes place at night, although there are exceptions to this rule.

The onset of whelping should not signal the start of a

neighborhood party to view the event. The bitch should not be bothered with outsiders, and this rule should hold for at least two weeks after the puppies are whelped. Ideally, only one person should stay with the bitch, but it is sometimes easier for two people to work together, especially if the puppies come rapidly.

Assuming that the bitch's temperature has dropped and she is exhibiting several of the symptoms mentioned previously, the breaking of the water signals the onset of true labor. Sometimes this is very obvious and sometimes a sharp eye is needed to detect it. Suddenly, the bitch appears to be sitting in a puddle of water, or, sometimes, the bag of water extends from the vulva like a balloon. When the latter happens, do not interfere with it. Allow it to break of its own accord. The amount of fluid varies—it may be scanty or profuse. If the bitch is restless, digging up her papers and constantly moving around, the breaking of the water is not so obvious, and, therefore, a careful watch is necessary. There is usually a show of fluid before the arrival of each puppy. After the water has broken, the first puppy should arrive any time from a few minutes to half an hour later. If half an hour goes by and a puppy has not arrived, it is not necessarily cause for concern unless the bitch is "straining." Straining is an obvious muscular contraction, is fairly slow and steady, and is characterized by an arching of the back and raising of the tail—the bitch is obviously working to expel something. The bitch may strain once and then rest for a few minutes. The next time she might strain twice or three times in succession. Usually, by the time she strains five or six times in succession, the puppy is about to be whelped. The bitch may strain either lying down or in a squatting position and puppies are whelped in either position.

If a puppy is not whelped after twenty minutes of straining, something is usually wrong. It could mean that the puppy is being presented sideways and has turned, or is abnormally large, requiring assistance, etc. Call the veterinarian, bundle the bitch into the car (along with an assistant if possible, in case the puppy arrives along the way), and proceed to the veterinarian's office. Should this happen during the night, call the veterinarian (this is why he should be "on call") and he will come to your home or have you meet him at his office.

When the puppy arrives, the normal presentation is head first. The head of the newborn puppy is the largest portion of it, so that when the head arrives first, the remainder of the puppy slips out easily. A puppy sometimes arrives quickly and with force and is dumped unceremoniously on the floor of the whelping box. At other times, a bubble appears to emerge from the bitch, becoming larger each time she strains. The puppy will emerge entirely enclosed in the sac, and will seemingly dangle between the bitch's hind legs. Quickly grasp the end closest to the bitch and pull firmly but gently. This will also dislodge the afterbirth, or placenta, which is still within the bitch.

It is not uncommon for the new arrival to greet the world feet first. This is called a breech presentation. This can make things a little more difficult but usually can be handled fairly easily. When the head arrives last, it has a more difficult time passing through the opening. When the feet protrude and dangle from the vulva and the rest of the body does not immediately follow, grasp the hindquarters of the puppy with a clean towel and with gentle pressure slowly rotate the body and pull gently as the bitch strains. This can sometimes be aided by elevating the bitch's front legs slightly and massaging her abdomen (gently) from front to rear in the milking manner. If you are not able to dislodge the puppy and it keeps slipping back into the bitch, get her to the veterinarian.

Regardless of the manner in which the puppy arrives, it should emerge enclosed in a sac. Generally, the sac is intact, but sometimes it is broken in the process of whelping. Attached to the sac is the afterbirth, which is a blackish mass almost as large as the puppy. Sometimes the afterbirth is retained or becomes dislodged temporarily. It is vital to account for an afterbirth for each puppy that is whelped. If the afterbirth does not follow immediately after the whelping of the puppy, it might appear just before the whelping of the next puppy or the one after that. As each puppy is whelped, note on paper the time of arrival, the sex, and whether or not there was an afterbirth. This will avoid confusion should one or more of the afterbirths be delayed. Some bitches are eager to eat the afterbirth and others are not. There are two schools of thought about this: one says yes and the other says no. If the bitch does not eat the afterbirth, wrap it up in newspaper and dispose of it.

As soon as the puppy emerges completely, the sac (if intact) must be broken immediately. Some bitches assume this responsibility as a matter of course, while others will not. Some bitches are over-zealous and will bite the cord too close to the puppy's navel. For these reasons it is probably best for the attendant to assume matter-of-factly the responsibility for breaking the sac and cutting the cord (with sterile scissors). It is best to keep the puppy lower than the dam while cutting the cord, so as to prevent the contents within the cord from draining away. The new puppy should then be gently but firmly rubbed with a dry, clean towel so that it will give out a lusty yell. The end of the cord (which should be about an inch in length) can be touched with Merthiolate and tied off with a small piece of light-weight string (which has been immersed in a dish of alcohol). The ends of the string should be cut short so that the dam can't pull on them and damage the puppy's navel. The cord will dry and drop off in about two days. After the puppy has been rubbed somewhat dry, it should be given to the bitch to lick and admire.

Sometimes a puppy is whelped that appears lifeless, or nearly so. When this happens, stimulate it by vigorous but gentle rubbing or immerse it (except for the head, of course) in cold water and quite warm (not scalding) water and keep alternating until the shock stimulates the puppy to gasp and squeal. A drop or two of brandy or whiskey placed on the tongue will also help. If the puppy has swallowed some of the fluid from the sac, it will sound wheezy or bubble from the nose and/or mouth. This fluid from the sac must be expelled or it can result in an artificial pneumonia. Grasp the puppy firmly in both hands and swing it up, head first, over your head and then down between your knees. Repeated but gentle swinging will produce a centrifugal force which will help expel the fluid. An infant syringe can also be used to suck excess fluid from the nose and mouth.

When the bitch becomes restless and concerned with the next arrival, remove the puppy to the small cardboard box in which you have placed the hot water bottle or heating pad (covered with towels) but keep it within the bitch's sight. The bottom of the box should feel warm to the touch but not hot.

Often two puppies will arrive fairly close together and then there will be a longer wait for the next one to arrive, or they can be spaced fairly evenly—every twenty minutes or half an hour.

After all the puppies have been whelped, allow the bitch (force her if necessary) to go outside to relieve herself, but be sure to go with her and stay with her in the event that another puppy should be whelped unexpectedly while the bitch is out-of-doors. Some bitches welcome the opportunity to relieve themselves during the whelping as well. Following whelping, the bitch should have a clear, red discharge which will last about two weeks or so, diminishing gradually.

After all the puppies are whelped, if the discharge is blackish or greenish in color, something is wrong. The cause may be retained afterbirth or part of one, or a decomposing dead puppy. Even though everything appears normal after the bitch is through whelping, it is a wise procedure to take her to the veterinarian for a shot of pituitrin to expel anything that might have been retained. This eliminates the possibility of infection. At this time the veterinarian can also confirm that all the puppies have been whelped.

Sponge off the bitch's underside and clean her up after all the puppies have arrived. Clear away all the messy papers and put fresh, clean bedding in her box. Use something like toweling which will provide a rough enough surface to give the puppies needed traction to nurse. Keep the bedding clean at all times. If possible, weigh each puppy and note the weights on paper. It is a good idea to check weights daily to see that all the puppies are gaining. The first few days they should gain at least a half ounce per day. Daily weighing makes it easy to spot a puppy that isn't doing well.

After the entire litter has been whelped, offer the bitch a light meal, such as chicken soup or broth. The bitch should settle down, allow the puppies to nurse, and keep them clean, with their bodily processes functioning normally, by licking them.

Place each puppy on a breast and make sure they all know how to eat. With normal, robust puppies, this usually comes naturally when they are headed in the right direction toward the food supply. Others might have to be shown how by actually placing the nipple in their mouths (making sure the tongue is under the nipple) or by squeezing a few drops of milk onto their tongues. If the bitch will not settle down and you know for sure that all the puppies are whelped, consult the veterinarian, for the bitch may require a calcium shot to ward off a pre-eclampsia type condition. The veterinarian may prescribe a tranquilizer to calm the bitch down so she will allow the babies to eat. Healthy, contented puppies are quiet. When puppies cry or whine continually, something is wrong. If there is any concern, check with the veterinarian. Keep the puppies warm at all times and out of drafts.

All puppies are whelped with a wax-like plug in the rectum. This might be expelled immediately after whelping or when the dam begins to lick the puppy. It is necessary that this be expelled within a few days at the latest, and expelling the plug can be aided by gently massaging under the tail with a piece of cotton soaked in baby oil. Whether or not the plug has been expelled can sometimes be determined just by lifting the tail and looking. If a dot of brown is showing, the plug usually is still retained. These plugs can be several inches in length, so if a piece is expelled, it might not be the entire plug. This situation could cause constipation, which would account for a restless, unhappy puppy—in which case, consult your veterinarian.

In some breeds, the tails are docked early, depending on the puppies' size and condition and on the feelings of the veterinarian. So again, consult with him, and also, be sure he understands the right length for the breed.

After labor has begun, if there are indications of a long and drawn out whelping—that is, no puppy but *no* straining, or if two hours elapse between puppies but it appears there are more to be whelped, consult your veterinarian as to the advisability of administering a pituitrin shot. In appropriate circumstances this will speed up the labor process considerably. Sluggish labor is usually due to "uterine inertia" or lack of muscle tone encountered more often in older bitches and those not in the best of physical condition. Sometimes a short walk around the room or in the yard (on leash!) will stimulate labor. Allowing an earlier arrival to nurse (if the bitch is willing) sometimes stimulates labor, also.

Sometimes nothing seems to work. It is time to consult with your veterinarian. A cesarean-section operation may be necessary. The most common reason for a cesarean-section is uterine inertia. Dr. Samuel Beckman, in his article on cesarean-section in *Pet Focus* (Vol 2 No 2, 1990), describes this term as a uterus that does not contract at all or has weak contractions that do not force the fetus out of the uterus. Uterine inertia may prohibit labor from starting or it may develop after prolonged straining with or without the delivery of part of the litter.

If medical therapy (shots to encourage the uterus to work harder) is not successful, Dr. Beckman recommends that preparations should be made for a well-planned cesarean-section:

As with many surgical procedures, the success of a cesarean section depends to a large degree on attention to the details of patient care before and after surgery, not just during the surgical procedure.

A heated chamber with the capability to administer oxygen should be ready to receive the newborns. As much preparation as possible of the female should be done before anesthetic administration, but the temperament of the dam may affect how much can be done at that time. If possible this includes insertion of an intravenous (IV) catheter for fluids and emergency drug administration and clipping of the hair on the belly and around the vulva.

Many safe anesthetic drugs are available these days, and the selection in each patient depends on the patient and the experience of the veterinarian. Regardless of the drug chosen it is important that the dam have a tube placed in her trachea (windpipe) for the delivery of oxygen during the surgery and to help inflate her lungs when she is lying on her back with a large heavy uterus pressing on her diaphragm.

After the patient is anesthetized and placed on her back on the surgery table, a final antiseptic washing of her abdomen is done to kill any bacteria on the skin. An incision is made between the mammary glands from her umbilical scar (belly button) to the brim of her pelvis. When the incision has been extended into the abdomen cavity, the uterus is easily identified because it is so large. A single incision is made into the body of the uterus and each puppy or kitten is 'milked' out of the uterine incision. Sterile hemostatic clamps are clamped on the umbilical cord and the newborn is handed to an assistant. For each newborn delivered a separate placenta (afterbirth) must also be removed from the uterus. After the entire litter has been removed from the uterus, the uterine and abdominal incisions are sutured closed.

If the pet's owner has decided prior to surgery to have the surgeon perform an ovariohysterectomy (spay), then that may be done before closing the abdomen, if the patient is stable and would not be harmed by the increased surgery and anesthesia time. Rarely, the uterus may need to be removed because it was severely damaged during prolonged straining or because of severe infection or loss of blood circulation.

As each newborn is handed to the assistants, it is dried off with a sterile towel and rubbed briskly to stimulate it to breath. After a few minutes the hemostatic clamps are removed from the umbilical cord. If bleeding occurs a suture is tied around the cord to stop it. Iodine is applied to the end of the umbilical cord to prevent infection. The newborn is put into a chamber with a temperature of 90 degrees F after it is breathing normally. It is kept there until the dam has recovered from anesthesia enough to nurse the litter and keep them warm. With modern anesthetic techniques, this may be as soon as 20-30 minutes after the conclusion of surgery.

Now you need to get her and the puppies home. It's a good idea to have another small box with a hot water bottle in it when you go to the veterinarian so any puppies delivered there can be taken care of.

Mary Donnelly, writing in the March 1987 issue of *The Min Pin Monthly*, says to take a crate along to bring the bitch home if she has to have a cesarean:

If you feel the trip from the vet will take an hour or more, you may consider giving the puppies the opportunity to nurse before you leave the office. This will also help you see if you will have any problems introducing them to nursing. You can take a supply of formula with you in the event you have to feed or supplement them.

Once home, the dam should be your first concern. Position her on her side with her back flush against the side of the whelping box. Don't worry, she won't be going anywhere for several hours. With the pan of warm cleaning water, dip your disposable towel and clean any blood from her incision or vaginal area. Because she has had a C-section, she will bleed a bit more than she would from a normal birth. (In a normal birth the bitch will have a blackish discharge at first turning to bright red shortly thereafter). Those little pups won't take long learning to explore the dam so you must keep her clean until she can take over. If you will notice her tongue is probably hanging from the side of her mouth. Take a bowl of clean water and dip a cloth in, squeeze most of the excess water back into the bowl and just moisten her tongue and mouth. NEVER put water into her mouth at this point. She could choke because her natural reflexes are on vacation because of the anesthetic."

Don't leave the puppies alone for too long a

period. They will get cold and hungry. There are a number of things that need to be done promptly. Begin with the smallest ones. Use toenail clippers and take the tips off their nails to preclude their causing problems with the stitches. Eliminate as much discomfort for the dam as possible. Once this is done, introduce the puppy to his dam. Let it sniff and try on its own to fit a teat to nurse. If the pup needs help, gently open its mouth and squeeze a bit of milk on the pup's tongue. (Even without a C-section some pups have to be shown how to do it and others just dig right in.) If the puppy won't cooperate, go ahead and give it a bit of formula. Continue this process until all the puppies have had their toenails cut and have been fed.

It is important to remember that YOU must do everything for the puppies. The bitch may be out of it anywhere from 6 to 12 hours or more. This is normal. During the time she is helpless, someone must carefully watch her and care for the puppies at the same time. Let's hope you'll have help and shifts can be rotated. If not, roll up your sleeves.

As soon as the puppies are fed and the bitch has been cleaned up again, help the pups to eliminate their waste. Dip a cotton ball in warm water, squeeze out most of the excess and gently rub it on their bellies. This should produce urination. Do the same around the anal area for a bowel movement. (This doesn't always work for there is a "plug" in there that is a bit hard to initially dislodge.) If there is not initial success in getting a bowel movement, be patient and try tickling the anal area with a swab. If that doesn't work, don't be too alarmed for the dam will soon be awake and will take care of this.

Generally, most puppies are worn out by now and ready to curl up next to their dam and go to sleep...but you can count on one or two little brats to be obnoxious and climb on her or try to see what's on the other side of the box. Let them explore but try to convince them to stay in the heated area. The dam is not going to grab them and cuddle them, so you want to keep them warm. They expected life to be different and are finding out that their mother isn't doing her job. Go ahead and clean the bitch again while they explore and cast longing eyes at the bed nearby. NO!! you can't go to sleep yet.

Try and moisten the bitch's mouth again. While taking care of business be aware if the bitch feels cold to the touch. Once all the puppies have settled down for a nap, you can drape a light sheet over the dam and the puppies. (Do not attempt to do this with a dam who has not had a C-section.) Now it's possible to lay down. There is a specific way to lay down. (Why should this be easy?) Stretch out but be sure you are close enough to the box so a hand can rest against the bitch. It is not advisable to fall asleep but since you are exhausted, it will happen anyway. The bitch will undoubtedly wait until you have just fallen asleep to wake up. (Just like she had her emergency section at 3:00 a.m.) Hopefully, you will feel her stir and awaken.

Just because she starts to stir does not mean she is anywhere close to being left alone. Do NOT let her stand on her own right away. She is not in control. She may think she is but she could fall and injure herself and/or her puppies.

Usually the first time she stirs she will not need to relieve herself. She may or may not be interested in her litter. In most cases, she is going to be convinced to go back to sleep. Offer her a bit of water but not too much. Too much water at this time can cause nausea. Just about five good laps is all she needs. Be assured she needs cleaning again and the pups have been awakened and want to eat. So take care of this all over again.

Some dams will shake as they come awake. More often than not this is caused by the anesthetic. This shaking can be slight or strong. In the event she shakes to the extent it could cause injury to the puppies, calm her by petting and covering the puppies a bit away from her. If at any time the shaking is too much, or there is a concern for any reason, call the veterinarian.

When the bitch really becomes restless she won't be talked into going back to sleep. Try to judge by the control she exhibits as to how stable she is. Take her outside when she becomes too restless. On her first trip carry her. Place her in a safe area and be ready to assist her should she fall.

The rest of the recovery consists of your attention to the dam and the safety of her and her litter. If you are patient and see her through her time of need, she will eventually ease you right out of a job.

Now, whether the puppies have arrived normally or by C-section they are pursuing normal puppy behavior. Their primary concerns are keeping warm and being fed. A healthy dam will be able to take care of those needs. Be sure to keep a keen eye on both the dam and the puppies; watch for signs of distress. Crying, being unable to settle down, or looking bloated all portend trouble for the puppies. Call the vet. Watch the bitch to see if her discharge turns from a blackish color to bright red. See if she has milk and if the puppies can nurse from her. It is extremely important to stay vigilant for the next three weeks. It's a critical time.

As a breeder, it is helpful to understand how the size and sex of the litter is determined. One of the most informative and entertaining articles I have read on the subject was written by Patricia Gail Burnham, a Greyhound breeder from Sacramento, California. Her article, "Breeding, Litter Size and Gender" appeared in an issue of the *American Cocker Review*, and I will attempt to paraphrase the information so that it is most applicable.

The number of puppies in a litter at whelping time is determined by several different factors. In the order in which they occur:
1. The number of ova (gametes) produced by the dam.
2. The number of ova that are successfully fertilized and implanted in the uterus.
3. The prenatal mortality rate among the embryos while they are developing.

It is not possible to end up with more puppies than the number of ova that the bitch produces. As a bitch ages, the number of ova will often decrease. Bitches don't manufacture ova on demand the way a male dog can manufacture sperm. All the ova a bitch will ever have are stored in her ovaries.

In each season some of them will be shed (ovulated) into her uterus for a chance at fertilization. Elderly bitches quite commonly produce two- or three-puppy litters. Sometimes, just living hard can have the same effect on a bitch as old age.

If a bitch does produce a large number of ova, what happens next? The ova need to be fertilized. If they are not fertilized, or if they are fertilized and not implanted, they will perish. If a bitch ovulates over an extended period of time and she is bred late in her season, then the ova that were produced early may have died unfertilized before the sperm could reach them, and the result can be a smaller litter.

Sometimes there is a noticeable difference in birth weight. It is a good idea not to consider the small ones runts. They may have been conceived a few days later than their larger litter mates, and may grow up to be average-sized adults.

All the puppies in a litter are never conceived simultaneously, since all the ova are not released at once. Ovulation takes place over an extended period, so at birth some of the puppies may be 59 days old while others may be 64 days old. A few days difference in puppies of this age can create noticeable differences in size.

The mature size of a dog is determined by its heredity and its nutrition. Its size at birth is determined by the size of its dam, the number of puppies in the litter, and their individual dates of conception. The small puppies could just be more refined than the others and could always be smaller. Only time will tell.

The sire is always responsible for the sex of the offspring. The rule applies equally to people and dogs. While dams are often blamed for not producing males, they have nothing to do with the sex of their offspring. If the bitch determined the sex of the offspring, then all the puppies would be bitches, because the only chromosomes that a bitch can contribute to her offspring are those that she and every female has, homozygous (XX) sex chromosomes.

What's the difference between boys and girls? It's not sugar and spice and puppy-dog tails. It's the makeup of their sex chromosomes. All of the chromosome pairs are matched to each other with the exception of one pair. Dogs (and people) each have one pair of chromosomes that may or may not match. This is the chromosome pair that determines sex. Sex chromosomes may be either X chromosomes (which are named for their shape) or X chromosomes that are missing one leg, which makes them Y chromosomes (again name for their shape.)

All females have two homozygous X chromosomes. They are XX genetically. All males are heterozygous (unmatched). They have one X and one Y chromosome to be XY genetically.

In each breeding, all ova contain an X chromosome, which is all a female can donate, while the sperm can contain either an X or a Y chromosome. If the X carrying ovum is fertilized by an X carrying sperm, then the result is female (XX). If the X carrying ovum is fertilized by a Y carrying sperm, then the result is a male (XY).

What influences whether an X or a Y carrying sperm reaches the ovum to fertilize it? The Y chromosome is smaller and lighter weight than the X chromosome. This enables the Y chromosome-carrying (male) sperm to swim faster than the heavier X carrying (female) sperm. This gives the male an edge in the upstream sprint to reach the ovum that is waiting to be fertilized.

As a result, slightly more than 50 percent of the fertilized ova are male. More males are conceived than females. However, things even up, because males have a higher mortality rate than females, both in the womb and later.

What if ova are not ready and waiting when the sperm arrive? If sperm have to wait in the uterus or fallopian tubes for an ovum to arrive, then the odds change. Female sperm live longer than male ones. As the wait increases, the males die off and leave the female sperm waiting when the ovum arrives.

This is the reason that some breeders advise breeding as early as the bitch will stand to maximize the chance for female puppies. The idea is to breed, if she will allow it, before the bitch ovulates. This allows the male sperm time to die off and leaves the female sperm waiting when the ova arrive. Whether this is a basis in fact is not known.

What can influence the number of males and females in a litter other than the time of breeding? The age of the sire can influence the gender of the puppies. As a stud dog ages, all his sperm slow down. Instead of a sprint, the race to fertilize the ova becomes an endurance race in which the female sperm's greater life span and hardiness can offset the male sperm's early speed advantage. When they are both slowed down, then the male sperm's higher mortality rate gives the female sperm the advantage.

Technological breakthroughs continue to cascade upon us from the nation's laboratories since the advent of gene splicing. Now we find that emerging technology will allow sex selection of the fetus in humans. If it can be easily done for humans, it's a lead pipe cinch it can happen in dogs.

According to an article by Eve Glickman (*The Oregonian*, 6/18/91), a freelance writer from Philadelphia, it is now possible in the laboratory to separate the X and Y chromosomes in a man's sperm with 75 percent accuracy prior to conception. Since the male's X chromosome produces a girl and the Y a boy, artificial insemination can be used to improve mother nature's odds.

To date, the Ericsson technique named after its originator, physiologist Ronald Ericsson, has been used primarily by couples trying to eliminate sex-linked genetic diseases in their families. Others opting for the procedure have been those desperate for a son after having several daughters or vice versa. A moral medical dilemma is shaping up in the medical community.

In dogs it would be possible in a short time to not only choose for sex but for color, height, etc.

I can foresee the dramatic reduction in males produced by breeding kennels. After all, who needs excess males if we can get good bitches, and who says our top show bitches have to carry a litter if we can implant her eggs in the womb of a surrogate bitch. No more time out from the shows to whelp litters, blow coat and the like.

Are we overstepping the bounds of medicine? Are we going too far in tinkering with mother nature? Are we going to change the whole face of the breeder's art?

Breeders of today are faced with problems and wondrous solutions that were not known to breeders before the discovery of DNA and gene splicing. Like it or not, the age of medical "miracles" is upon us. As usual, technology has outrun man's ability to control it. To the best of my knowledge, there are no "appointed" organizations, committees or what have you, within dogdom, thinking through the implications of these discoveries. The AKC has none, nor does FCI (the international body of dog clubs), the US Department of Agriculture or the Federal Drug Administration. Events are outrunning our ability to control them.

The Japanese Chin.

Problems Associated with the Birth, Growth, and Development of Puppies

CAUSES OF DEATH IN NEWBORN PUPPIES

Whether or not a puppy develops along normal lines either before or after birth depends entirely on its environment and on the hereditary characteristics and tendencies which have been handed down by its parents. We all know that puppies which are fed inadequate, unbalanced diets not only fail to grow properly but also may develop nutritional diseases and structural distortions such as anemia, rickets, etc. The diet provided for the growing puppy constitutes part of its environment. If the diet is unsuitable, it may be said that the puppy's environment is unfavorable for proper development.

An unfavorable environment may seriously hinder normal development before birth as well as after birth. The prenatal environment provided for the growing embryo may be unsuitable because the mother has been improperly fed and cared for during pregnancy or because she is infested with worms. Even though Nature will rob the mother to feed the unformed young, the puppies may be so lacking in vitality as the result of malnutrition that they are either born dead or die shortly after birth. Newborn puppies which are suffering from malnutrition are not necessarily skinny puppies. They may be well formed and appear to be healthy, but like adult dogs which have waxed fat on an unbalanced diet and lack of exercise, they may be anemic and so weak that they are unable to cope with the difficulties encountered during birth and unable to adjust themselves successfully to the new environment. Puppies which are born with worms acquired from the bitch may not show signs of illness until they are three or four weeks of age, when they will sicken and die very quickly. Because information concerning the proper care of the bitch during pregnancy and prevention of worm infestations is readily available today, malnutrition and parasites should not be major causes of puppy losses.

Injuries received either before or after birth may result in the death of one or more puppies in a litter, in spite of the fact that every precaution may have been taken to prevent such injuries. Also, especially in the case of a large litter but even in a small or average size litter, the embryos may be crowded together too closely to allow for proper development, resulting in distortions or in the premature birth of small, weak puppies.

Carelessness on the part of a nervous or inexperienced bitch undoubtedly accounts for the loss of many puppies which are born alive and which appear to be strong and healthy at birth. Even the best of mothers may occasionally sit or lie on a puppy, crushing or smothering it. While some bitches will quickly retrieve a puppy which wanders away from the warmth of the nest, others will refuse to do so. The wanderer may very easily become chilled and so weakened that when, by chance, it finds its way back to the nest, it is unable to compete with the stronger members of the litter or to nurse properly. A whelping box which is so arranged that it enables the mother to settle herself comfortably and with safety to the puppies and which prevents wanderers from becoming lost, will help lower the mortality of newborn puppies. A prospective brood matron should be selected not only on the basis of her pedigree, conformation, and personality, but also on the basis of her ability to whelp and raise a litter of normal puppies successfully.

The bitch's endocrine system, which is responsible for the secretions of such important glands as the thyroid, pituitary, adrenal, and reproductive glands, may fail to work properly during pregnancy because of disease or hereditary factors, resulting in the arrested development or malformation of the embryos or in the premature birth of the litter. Abnormal functioning of the endocrine system may also cause various mating and whelping difficulties, such as dystocia (painful or delayed delivery), and lack of an adequate milk supply, which may account for puppy losses. If an inadequate amount of endocrine secretions (hormones) is produced within the unborn puppy itself, its development may be temporarily or permanently stopped at any stage. If development is arrested in the early stages, the partly formed embryo or embryos affected may be aborted or reabsorbed by the bitch, or they may lie dormant in a "petrified" state awaiting the termination of gestation. If development is arrested in later stages, the embryo may be born alive but malformed.

Many so-called "freaks" are the result of arrested development during the embryonic stage, resulting in such malformations as harelip, cleft palate, cleft abdomen, cleft skull, etc. All of these malformations are the result of the parts of the embryo failing to unite properly during development. If this failure is complete, any part of the embryo may be disunited by a deep cleft which may affect one side of the body more than the other, or may affect both sides equally. If the growth of the embryo is retarded in a very late stage of development, only a slight cleft or other malformation may mar its perfection.

An analysis of litter records done by the Roscoe B. Jackson Memorial Laboratory indicates a higher percentage of puppies are stillborn or die shortly after birth in the first litter than in the second, third, fourth, and fifth litters. In a study of 337 litters, the percentage of dead puppies in the first litter was 5.7 percent, while in the fourth litter the percentage was 2.0 percent and in the fifth litter 2.8 percent. Because the cause of death could not be determined accurately in most cases, it is assumed that inexperience on the part of the bitch in whelping and caring for her first litter is partly responsible for the higher death rate. After the fifth litter, however, the death rate increased considerably, the percentage of dead puppies in the sixth litter averaging 18.7 percent. The number of "seventh litter" records obtained was too small to have any great significance. However, the steady decrease in incidence of death until after the fourth or fifth litters indicates intrauterine conditions in older bitches are more likely to be unfavorable for the production of normal young.

Harelip occurs more frequently than any other one malformation with the exception of undershot jaws. Because harelip may not be recognized readily, all puppies which are born dead or die unaccountably before reaching weaning age should be examined carefully. Harelip may or may not be accompanied by cleft palate. The two sides of the face may be disunited by a deep cleft extending from the nostril to the back of the roof of the mouth. (Though both the upper and lower jaws may be affected, harelip usually affects only the upper jaw.) The cleft may be on the right or left side of the palate or there may be two clefts, one on each side. On the other hand, if the growth of the embryo is retarded at a later stage of its development, the defect may consist of merely a "split lip" condition. Regardless of whether the condition consists of a deep cleft or a slight one affecting the lip only, it is often accompanied by malocclusion (abnormal position) of the teeth, as well as by other deformities.

Almost all puppies affected with harelip are stillborn or die within a few weeks of birth. Harelipped puppies which are born alive may be normal in other respects, but because they are unable to nurse they soon die of starvation. In attempting to suck, air is drawn through the cleft in the lip or the roof of the mouth, and the puppy is unable to draw the milk properly and swallow it. In a very few cases, puppies born with harelip have been raised successfully on a bottle, and one has been reported which overcame its handicap and managed to nurse from its dam in spite of the fact that the roof of its mouth, as well as the upper lip, was cleft. In the latter case, a surgical operation was later performed which repaired the palate cleft, though the malposition of the teeth and the split lip could not be corrected.

Very little is known of the manner of inheritance of this deformity. That most cases of harelip are caused by the influence of hereditary factors there is little doubt, for the defect appears very definitely to occur in certain families and breeds and not in other families and breeds. In mice, harelip has been found to be caused by recessive genes. If harelip in dogs is caused by the influence of recessive genes, those genes must be carried by both sides of the family before the condition can be expressed in the offspring. Harelip may occur occasionally as the result of an environmental (prenatal) accident, but if it occurs fairly regularly within a particular family of dogs, the breeder must assume the cause to be hereditary and select against this lethal characteristic.

During the first few years that we were breeding dogs, we had no difficulties whatsoever with stillbirths and deaths of newborn puppies. Does this sound familiar? It should because we've heard it from others, over and over again. If one of our bitches whelped six puppies, that was it—we (and she, of course) raised six puppies. During this time, whenever we'd hear of another breeder who lost puppies shortly after whelping, we'd be convinced that the losses were due to carelessness in supervision and care on the part of the breeder. After all, we had no difficulties, so that had to be the reason. This, too, should sound familiar, for we have heard many other breeders echo this exact thought.

Suddenly, the shoe was on the other foot, and believe me, it didn't feel good. Our first losses occurred when one of our bitches whelped a litter of five. This particular bitch had previously whelped two litters of six each and had raised both litters with ease. We lost two puppies from this litter of five—a bitch and a male. I'm sure that upon reading this some of you will say, "What's so unusual or terrible about that?" Breeders who are able to have five or six or even more litters per year are able to compensate for a certain percentage of loss by reason of overall quantity produced. Those, like ourselves, who were limited to one or perhaps two litters per year can be left with a breeding program that is all but nil. In this particular breeding we had wanted a bitch pup very much, and the bitch we lost was the one and only female in the litter. All previously made plans had to be put aside and we were back where we had started from. There is always the nagging thought that those that do not survive might be the outstanding ones. Who knows? They may be—and for this reason alone, none of us can afford to lose puppies.

We felt badly about these first losses, and in our

particular case we knew they were not due to carelessness in supervision and care. I might add that we began to view our fellow breeders' losses with more compassion, as well. Our next litter saw two survivors out of five puppies whelped. Next we raised four out of six, which seemed to be an improvement. However, from then on the situation went from bad to worse. We raised one puppy out of a litter of five, we lost an entire litter of three, etc. Losing that litter of three affected us deeply in a rather personal way that is difficult to explain. We just wanted to stop breeding rather than continue to subject ourselves to this type of discouragement. There is nothing more discouraging than to plan a breeding with all one's hopes, theories, and ideas riding on it and then not even have the opportunity to see how it might have developed. This is to say nothing of what happens to one's breeding program or the finances that are involved.

Our particular losses were all due to the same cause—artificial pneumonia caused by fluid in the lungs. We are well aware that not all puppy losses are due to this particular cause. However, the more we talked with other breeders, the more we discovered that we were not alone with this problem. Not all breeders would experience exactly the same symptoms, just as we would have differentiation in symptoms between two puppies within the same litter. However, the general pattern was quite similar and the results from post-mortems were identical.

Experience has shown that there is no one specific cause that could apply to all cases. Perhaps there is one cause for one case and another cause for another case, or perhaps a combination of factors is involved. To be honest, we never found the answer. We reached one basic conclusion, and that is: puppies that die within the first week of life as a result of fluid in the lungs are not normal puppies to begin with even though this may not be obvious from the beginning. We feel that the cause, whatever it might be, occurs during the puppy's prenatal life.

The first and perhaps most obvious cause could be the presence of a lethal hereditary factor. By and large we discarded this idea, although we will certainly concede the possibility does exist and could account for a percentage of the deaths. The main reason why we have discarded this idea is that puppy mortality resulting from artificial pneumonia is not confined to any one variety or any one bloodline (or any one breed, for that matter). It occurs in all varieties and in all bloodlines; it occurs in complete outcrosses as well as in close line breeding.

In 1960 an interesting article, written by two veterinarians, appeared in *The Saturday Evening Post*. It touched on the problems of puppy mortality (all causes) briefly. The sum and substance of the writers' explanation was that the puppy mortality was Nature's way of cutting down the overpopulation of a species. It is a proven fact that Nature does cut down the overpopulation of a species

of animals in the wild. This happens in ten year cycles even when the environment is ideal.

Another possibility worth mentioning is the presence of a low grade infection in the bitch. It is quite possible that the presence of such an infection would present no symptoms whatsoever; the bitch would act, look, and respond normally. The presence of such an infection could have a definite effect on the prenatal life of her puppies. With this in mind, it might be worth while to consult with your veterinarian about adding an antibiotic food supplement to the bitch's diet.

We do not know the specific cause of artificial pneumonia—much less the answer to the problem. However, if you have a similar problem or one entirely unrelated that is very discouraging to you, please do not give up if you are sincerely interested in breeding—tough it out. It's worth it.

A dog's size and shape are quite closely determined by inheritance. The general proportions are taken for granted. The causes for concern are the relatively small differences resulting in a specimen's being considered too tall, too short, overdeveloped, or lacking in development. It is probably safe to say that hereditary factors account for most of the major differences.

In comparing individual specimens, rather than groups, the greatest differences in body size and formation may arise through "internal environment" — chiefly glandular—which may be, in part or in whole, hereditary. The most striking examples, of course, are provided by comparisons between dogs and bitches. Here, two physically distinct groups of dogs are produced (generally) through overall developmental differences set in motion by the sex chromosome balances which cause the same inheritance to work in radically different ways.

Important differences, which may be in part genetic, have been found in the rate of growth and development in different animals. Thus, some dogs that grow faster in one period may grow less than average during another period. Also important is the fact that heights in different dogs are not achieved in the same way. Some genes affect body development uniformly, whereas others specialize with respect to certain segments such as length of legs, shoulder placement (which has an outward effect on the appearance of height), etc. A good example is the comparison of two dogs measuring the same height. One may look tall, even bordering on "oversize," whereas the other may actually look low with no appearance of "oversize."

It would be desirable to be able to predict ultimate growth with some reliability. In addition, it would be just as desirable to have a scale by which development could be charted along with growth. In other words, approximately how large or how small should any puppy be at any given age, and what would be a desirable weight to go with its size? This is necessarily complex because of the many factors involved. When it comes to weight, heaviness of bone must be taken into consideration. Also, there must be some consideration of type.

It would hardly seem possible that one scale could be set up for each breed that could be used widely and with reasonable accuracy by all. Such a scale or guide, however, could be set up by each individual breeder to apply to his own dogs, taking into account environmental differences, hereditary differences, and differences by which the data is viewed and recorded.

By recording accurately the weights and measurements of each puppy in every litter, a picture will begin to emerge for the breeder. The fewer the bloodlines involved, the easier the task. The more data collected, the greater the basis for comparison. The system of recording must be individual and consistent. In other words, measurements, for example, need not be official measurements so long as they are gathered and recorded in the same way each time. By way of illustration, data to be recorded could include records of puppy weights at various ages and records of puppy measurements at various ages. Measurements can be divided into different categories such as measurement of height (floor to withers, floor to elbow, elbow to withers) and measurements of length (withers to tailset).

Thus, when that important puppy comes along, the breeder can refer back to his records gathered on previous puppies from that bloodline and utilize what the data tells him. It should give him a reasonably good idea as to whether this current young hopeful is growing and developing as he should (compared to previous puppies) in order to bring out his ultimate potential.

The breeder should be able to come up with the answers to the following questions as they pertain to his own breeding stock:

1. Does size and weight of puppies at birth indicate size and weight at maturity?

2. What is the earliest possible age at which ultimate growth and/or development is predictable?

3. At what age is ultimate growth and/or development reached?

4. During what age period does the greatest rate of growth take place?

5. Is ultimate development correlated with ultimate growth, or is one attained before the other?

6. If diverse bloodlines are bred within the same kennel, what are the differences between them with respect to growth and development?

7. Is growth and/or development attained uniformly, or rather through sporadic leaps coupled with periods of quiescence?

8. Is growth and/or development attained at the same rate, or does one part grow and/or develop before another part?

It is quite possible that other interesting facts and ideas

will be brought to light as well. It is certainly true that by recording all of this data, the breeder will become more aware of what he is breeding. It is to his advantage to know and to understand all the various phases of growth and development his bloodlines entail rather than placing that promising puppy in the kennel without a second look until it has attained maturity.

STAGES OF DEVELOPMENT—HEREDITARY

The development of any puppy is a fascinating process to observe. No two develop in exactly the same way, yet there are definite similarities within the various bloodlines. This does not necessarily mean that all breeders engaged in breeding within a specific bloodline or combinations of that line will experience identical stages of development with respect to the growth of their puppies. It does mean, however, that certain similarities will exist, and the knowledge of these similarities will prove of great assistance to the individual breeder.

How any given puppy will look at maturity is predestined by its genetic heritage coupled with the environmental factors it experiences. Once the breeding has been made, the genetic heritage cannot be altered, although environmental factors can. However, the point of this discussion is how the puppy reaches maturity, disregarding (to the extent possible) both hereditary and environmental points of orgin.

For example, it is well known that most puppies go through what is commonly termed the "awkward stage." The onset of this phase can be as early as eight weeks of age and the phase can last until the puppy is eight months of age. Often breeders advise making selections when the puppies are eight weeks of age. This rule of thumb states that at this age puppies will show more indication of their adult potential than at any other age until they actually reach maturity.

This is well and good for puppies that actually follow the classic pattern mentioned above. However, not all puppies will fall into this category. There are many variations of the so-called awkward stage. The variations depend upon the different bloodlines involved and the individual differences within a bloodline which have been established through the process of individual selection. The latter will necessarily have a modifying effect on any specific bloodline, as will environmental influences, which will be dealt with later in this chapter.

Some puppies do not enter the awkward stage until they are three months old. Others wait until four months. Some

RECORD OF PUPPY WEIGHTS

SIRE _____ DAM_____

DATE WHELPED_____

| NAME | Birth | weeks | | | | | | | | | months | | | | | | | | 1 y |
		1	2	3	4	5	6	7	8	10	3	4	5	6	7	8	10	
Puppy A																			
Puppy B																			
Puppy C																			
Puppy D																			
Puppy E																			

RECORD OF INDIVIDUAL MEASUREMENTS

NAME_____DATE WHELPED_____

SIRE _____DAM_____

| TRAIT | weeks | | months | | | | | | | | 1 yr. |
	8	10	3	4	5	6	7	8	9	10	
HEIGHT											
Floor to Withers											
Floor to Elbow											
Elbow to Withers											
LENGTH											
Withers to Tailset											

Forms for recording puppies' growth.

emerge by six months and others by seven or more months. There are some fortunate puppies that never go through the awkward stage at all. These fortunate puppies are often dubbed "Flyers." They are outstanding at a very young age and continue to be so classified on through maturity. Their less fortunate brothers and sisters may very well emerge as equally outstanding in the final appraisal even though they (and their breeders) had to endure the awkward stage. In light of all this, selection at eight weeks is not necessarily the rigid criterion one should use arbitrarily in making one's selection. For the beginning breeder it may prove a useful rule, but as familiarity with development increases, it should be modified to meet the situation to which it is applicable.

Two primary conditions give rise to the awkward stage: one is the shedding of the baby teeth and the subsequent emergence of the adult teeth, and the other is a rapid rate of body growth. In some puppies the process of dentition creates a temporarily adverse effect upon head development. This is characterized by a cumulative "plaining out" period. Where the puppy once evidenced a deep stop, the foreface now appears to slide back into the skull like a ski slope. Most traces of chiseling disappear and the head becomes void of all embellishment. This is a trying period for any breeder but one which must be endured. Just as the puppy's head began to fade gradually, so it usually begins to improve gradually as the puppy approaches maturity. Generally, the improvement becomes noticeable at about six months of age and continues until the original head qualities have been restored.

In some cases the original head qualities are never quite regained. Although the stop and chiseling all but disappear during the plaining-out phase, the breeder can feel relatively assured that the head will revert to its original promise if it remains in balance during this period.

Plainness of head and awkwardness of body do not necessarily go together, although they may. Ungainliness of body in the growing puppy can be likened to the stage experienced by the teenager when he is all arms and legs and lacking in fine coordination. Another adage commonly applied to this phase of development states that all puppies that will eventually evidence good size will go through this period, and, conversely, that those puppies that are destined eventually to be small adults will grow in proportion and not evidence the awkward body characteristics. There necessarily are exceptions to this rule.

Awkward body characteristics can take many different forms. Some puppies go up on leg at a very early age and look as if they are walking around on stilts until their bodies begin to develop depth and breadth. Others will develop first through the body and will appear low and dumpy until they begin to get their leg growth. Sometimes

different parts of the dog's body will grow at different rates, giving rise to the up-in-the-rear, down-at-the-shoulder, long-in-the-body looks that were not apparent at an earlier age and will not be apparent at maturity.

Some of these developmental changes may not disappear—that is, some dogs upon maturity will lack body development, others may be low on the legs, some will lack the correct top line, and others will be irrevocably long backed. Of such things are faults made, of such things are disappointments born, and of such things do show prospects fade away. However, the appearance of these traits during the phase of body growth does not necessarily mean they will be evident upon maturity. Almost all body characteristics are subject to change. Some puppies have been known to develop heavy shoulders during the awkward stage, and subsequently the shoulders have smoothed out. Steep shoulders have been known to lay back, etc. It is almost impossible to state with assurance that a specific trait is not subject to change, for there will always be some breeder who has experienced that change in his stock.

The beginning breeder with his first young hopefuls will experience many periods of dejection and frustration as his puppies grow and develop (assuming that they are subject to any form of the awkward stage). By the time his second crop of hopefuls has arrived, he will be more assured in his own mind as to their eventual potential. And so it will continue until he can be fairly positive in his approach. Even experienced breeders are subjected to these periods of dejection and frustration. It is often during these periods that wrong decisions are made, the wrong puppy is sold for a pet, or the wrong puppy is retained as a show and/or breeding prospect.

Experienced breeders outcrossing into a new bloodline or obtaining new stock are also subject to this disquieting situation. All they have learned previously with regard to their own stock may be subject to complete revision as they incorporate the new.

It would be quite simple if it could be stated, for example, that all puppies from X bloodlines plain out in head at three months of age. Then breeders with puppies from X bloodlines would not become unduly dejected when their puppies entered this stage. This, of course, is not possible, for there are too many exceptions, individual differences, and environmental factors to be taken into account. It should be possible to say, however, that many puppies from X bloodlines do plain out in head about three months of age, and, therefore, should it happen, the breeder should not be unduly concerned, for the good characteristics will usually come back by, say, seven months of age. Armed thus, the breeder can bear this phase with patience and hope.

The same can apply to developmental stages of other body traits, and it therefore behooves breeders to take all of this into account. It is natural for a breeder to evaluate his own puppies in comparison with those of a fellow breeder, but in making such an evaluation a breeder is exposed to many pitfalls. At any given age, one breeder may feel his puppies are far superior to those of another breeder—a fact which may not hold true upon subsequent maturity of the puppies in question. It is unlikely that a breeder will be cognizant of the different developmental phases of another breeder's puppies, and therefore he may make his judgments on inapplicable criteria.

One further point should be mentioned in connection with the foregoing. It concerns the purchase or sale of a "show prospect" under four months of age. Common practice dictates that the younger the show prospect, the less the cost involved. Some of the reasons for this have been amply illustrated. Often the purchaser of a young show prospect becomes sadly disillusioned if the young hopeful begins to lose its original promise during the developmental stage. Purchasers of young show prospects should be prepared well in advance for this stage.

Unfortunately, it is not a rarity for the young show prospect not to live up to its original potential. The prospective buyer should realize or be made to realize that it is impossible for any breeder to predict ultimate development with absolute certainty. The majority of eight-week-old show prospects do not make the grade, and as each month passes, their ranks become thinner and thinner.

STAGES OF DEVELOPMENT—
ENVIRONMENTAL

Every year thousands of puppies are whelped in this country. Of these, hundreds are tagged as possible show prospects by their breeders. Of these hundreds, only a small percentage ever find their way into the show ring, to say nothing of the few that actually finish their championships.

What has happened to cause the others to fall by the wayside? Some of the answers are obvious. For example, as they grow, many puppies develop undesirable traits which were not discernible at an earlier age but which were, nevertheless, predestined by their genetic heritage. What about the others, those which do not evidence obvious faults but which, upon maturity, seem to be lacking that certain something? Unfortunately, some of the qualities necessary for the prospective show winner are hard to describe, especially those qualities that have little or nothing to do with conformation. Among them are health, condition, personality, and disposition. These qualities must be developed to their ultimate potential in order to bring out the best in any puppy.

In order for any young show specimen to fulfill its early promise, its environment must provide it with all the necessary conditions to ensure its ultimate growth and development, both physical and mental. The person responsible for providing such an environment is, of course, the breeder or the owner. The owner of a first show prospect or the novice breeder is often lacking in know-how. Often it is through initial mistakes that the realization sets in that there is more to raising a good puppy than providing food and medical care. In addition to this, conditions may arise over which the breeder or owner has little control—illness, for example.

In the very beginning, a puppy's first contact with the world can have an important effect upon its later life. Beautiful though they may be, some bitches are poor mothers. They do little to get their puppies off to a good start. Other factors, as well, may be responsible for getting a puppy off to a poor start. However, puppies which do not get off to a good start, through no fault of their own, will usually catch up with those which were more fortunate, providing they are normal and healthy. They may not grow as quickly, and their growing period will usually be longer, but by the time they reach maturity, there should be little difference in actual size.

The same premise usually holds true for the older puppy which has received a setback due to illness. Its growth may be halted temporarily during an illness, but such puppies have been known to make up that growth at a later date. Many breeders are tempted to discard puppies such as these—and many do, only to find out later that they made a mistake.

The quantity and quality of food a puppy receives is very important. Poor nutrition can result in a puppy's failure to live up to its potential. The limits of a puppy's eventual size, bone, and development have been predestined by heredity. Even though these limits have been predetermined, they can either be developed to their maximum or never reached because of poor nutrition.

Eating is often a habit, and the so-called "good doers" are one step ahead in developing their potential. Through his own lack of effort, the "poor doer" may be penalized regardless of nutritional opportunities provided. One of the most difficult tasks imaginable is to get the "poor doer" to develop properly. Any possible physical causes of lack of appetite, such as infected tonsils, worms, etc., should be investigated thoroughly. Unfortunately, there are some puppies that will never eat more than what is required for marginal sustenance.

The puppy that is a good eater will often be on the chubby, roly-poly side. Should it go through the awkward stage, its awkwardness will be more pronounced than that of its slimmer litter mates. The chubby puppy is the one which usually loads up in shoulder or which looks soft in back, sloppy, and cumbersome. The unknowing owner gives up on this specimen and discards it before a diet has had a chance to work wonders. Of course, one needs to be aware that extreme obesity can cause permanent structural faults. At the other extreme, the too-thin puppy, while retaining a semblance of its original promise, often indicates that it will never "body out" enough to amount to anything. This puppy will often appear unthrifty, for the actual lack of nutrition can easily have an adverse effect on physical well being. This puppy, too, is often discarded without the owner attempting to ascertain the causes of its lack of appetite.

Another factor that should be mentioned in connection with nutrition is the ability of the puppy to utilize that with which it is provided. Some puppies are limited by physical abnormalities in the utilization of the nutriments provided, appetite notwithstanding.

Obviously, condition and tone will mark the healthy puppy which has the advantage of proper nutrition and which utilizes it to the fullest capacity. Barring undesirable hereditary factors, its coat will be shiny and will develop commensurately with age. Cleanliness and frequent grooming are also important. Dirty, matted puppies may grow coat but will usually not retain it.

In breeds where an outgoing personality and good disposition are highly desirable, the breeder must be conscious of his responsibility in helping such a personality to grow. It has often been said that a show specimen must have something more than mere physical beauty. Some have called this additional, rather obscure factor "heart." Call it what one may, this extra "something" falls into the classification of personality and disposition.

The most perfect physical specimen is nothing but a shell without some spark of personality, something which makes the dog an individual in its own right. As for a bad disposition, nothing could be more of a detriment to a breed. Taking for granted that no inherited factors are involved, the responsibility for developing personality and disposition is just as important as providing food and medical care. The vast majority of shy, snapping, wetting puppies can usually trace their ills to environmental factors rather than to inherited ones.

Dogs which are shown must possess a certain sophistication not necessarily required by the more sheltered pets. New situations, strange people, and unusual noises must all be taken in stride and met with equanimity. The puppy which is kept like the proverbial hothouse flower and which has never encountered different situations, can hardly be expected to react in an unruffled manner when suddenly confronted with a new and different type of challenge. Some might react with panic and others may meet the situation by withdrawing.

Personality development should start at a very early age—in fact, the earlier the better. Just as human babies thrive on tender loving care, so do puppies. As wee babies they should be handled, petted, and loved. As they grow older, they will surely benefit from being played with, introduced to new situations, and offered the opportunity of human affection.

The manner in which a puppy is played with is very important. On the surface, the idea of playing with a puppy sounds like the simplest thing imaginable, but many breeders cringe inwardly while watching inexperienced people play with puppies. Some of the common pitfalls encountered are suddenly grabbing or lunging at a puppy, teasing, and even picking up the puppy in an improper way. The whole idea of playing with a puppy is to get across the idea to the puppy that it is doing something enjoyable and that this enjoyment is dependent upon the puppy's relationship with a human being—or with other puppies, as the case may be.

Introducing a puppy to new situations can take many forms. Rides in the car, trips to the shopping center, encounters with strange people, and often even with strange dogs, will certainly help to prepare the puppy for its first encounter with the world of dog shows. Far too many puppies are kept entirely within their own kennel walls—their only experience with the outside world limited to occasional visits to the veterinarian's office, where they are usually poked, prodded, and sometimes hurt. Certainly, those that have had nothing but this latter type of experience cannot be expected to develop the "savoir faire" necessary for the show dog.

Most puppies have the almost innate desire of wanting to please. By affording a puppy the opportunity of human affection, a person provides the puppy with the object to please. There are many important advantages in the breeder or owner becoming the object of the puppy's affection. A puppy that has the desire to please will respond to training more readily and sooner than the puppy that does not have that desire. This can make a big difference in training the puppy to go on a lead or to pose. Some puppies take to this form of training naturally and others do not. Those that do not often will respond positively merely because they want to please, if for no other reason. Human affection will also provide security for a puppy and the puppy will in turn respond to other people in an outgoing and friendly manner.

The finest genetic heritage is of no avail if it is not fully developed to take advantage of the ultimate inherent potential. Not only must the physical attributes of the animal be developed through proper nutrition and care, but also the mental traits evidenced by personality and temperament. The breeder or owner has no control over the limits imposed by Nature, but he does have positive control over a large percentage of the environmental factors which can either add to or detract from his dog's prospects.

Proper Care of Your Dog

A healthy dog is characterized by clear eyes, a coat that shines, skin that is clean, and one which has resilience and clean ears.

If your dog doesn't have those basic attributes, leave him home! No knowledgeable judge will put up a dog that is not at the top of his game. An unhealthy dog will not be a winning dog.

Healthy dogs have cool, moist, secretion-free noses. Although many believe that a dog's nose is the primary indicator of its health, this is untrue – the nose is only one of many factors used to evaluate a dog's overall health. A complete appraisal will also consider the dog's temperature, pulse, elimination, skin, coat, eyes, ears, mouth, weight, and behavior.

A healthy dog has a temperature of about 101.5° F, with one degree above or below considered normal. To take your dog's temperature, lubricate a rectal thermometer with Vaseline, lift the tail, and insert the thermometer an inch or two – depending on the size of the dog – into the anus. In roughly three minutes, remove the thermometer and take a reading.

A healthy heartbeat for a resting dog can vary from 50 to 130 beats per minute – depending on the age, weight, and physical condition of the dog. Therefore, it's a good idea to ascertain the dog's normal, healthy pulse to use as a basis for comparison for when your dog is ill. To take your dog's pulse, place your fingertips on the artery on the inside of one thigh, where the leg joins the dog's body, and count the number of beats for a full minute. Remember that your dog's normal pulse may change as he grows older, gains or loses weight, or experiences a change in physical condition.

Healthy dogs typically produce firm, brown stools once or twice a day, and also excrete clear, yellow urine. Normal stools will be neither foul-smelling nor excessively loose, and will be free of visible worms. The dog should not have to strain nor should the dog seem as though he's in pain when producing stools.

The skin of a healthy dog is smooth, supple, and free from parasites, scales, scabs, and bald patches. The skin may be either solid in color or spotted. The color of a dog's skin depends on its breed; this can range from the pink skin of the Bull Terrier to the bluish-gray skin of the Puli.

The dog's coat should be clean and free from mats; his eyes should be bright and shiny. The skin inside healthy ears is pink and clean – although a small amount of black, brown, or yellow wax is considered normal. The dog's gums should be firm, his teeth should be clean and white, and his breath should smell fresh rather than foul.

A healthy dog is neither obese or gaunt. You can weigh your dog by first weighing yourself on a bathroom scale, and then holding the dog and weighing yourself and the dog together. Then, subtract the first weight from the second to determine the dog's weight. For larger breeds, such as Wolfhounds and Mastiffs, you can arrange a weigh-in at your veterinarian's office.

An acceptable weight, however, does not necessarily mean good fitness. To check your dog's fitness level, gently pinch the skin on its underside near the lower ribs. If the animal has more than a very thin layer of fat, you may want to consider exercising your dog more frequently.

There are a number of noticeable symptoms a dog may exhibit when he is ill: vomiting, diarrhea, shivering, coughing, fever, and discharge from the eyes, ears, or nose are among the most common symptoms. Sometimes, however, the signs of illness may be more subtle, such as listlessness, a change in appetite, or a change in frequency or amount of excretion. Actually, you are the best judge of your dog's health because you will know your dog's habits and personality. Because any change in normal behavior or appearance may indicate illness in your dog, it is best to contact your veterinarian for a discussion and appraisal of your dog's current symptoms.

Keeping a dog healthy and happy requires constant effort. As the dog's owner, it is your responsibility to provide your dog with proper nutrition, kenneling, vaccinations, grooming, and large quantities of love.

Most high-quality commercial dog food, dry as well as canned varieties, will provide adequate nutrition for your dog. Normally, you need not supplement the food with vitamins, minerals, or food scraps. However, if your dog is underweight, deficient in a particular nutrient, lactating, or performing hard work (such as hunting or sledding), you may need to stimulate his appetite with vitamins or other supplements.

Feed the dog equal portions of dog food three times each day until he is five months old, then twice a day until one year old. After that, feed the dog once a day for the rest of his life.

Russel V. Brown, writing in the February 1987 issue of *The*

Basenji Magazine, recommends the following method of determining how much to feed your dog each day:

If the dog weighs more than 65 pounds, multiply his weight by 18 to determine the number of calories the animal should eat each per day. For example, if your dog weighs 80 pounds, he should be eating 18 x 80, or 1440, calories per day. Dry dog food usually contains about 1360 calories per pound, canned dog food usually contains 475 calories per pound. Therefore, an 80-pound dog should be eating just over one pound of dry food, or three pounds of canned food, each day.

If the dog weighs under 65 pounds, subtract one-quarter of his weight from 33, then multiply this result by the dog's weight to determine how many calories the dog should eat each day:

$$X(33 - X/4) = \text{calories per day.}$$

For example, if your dog weighs 20 pounds:

$$20(33 - 20/4) = 20(33 - 5) = 20(28) = 560$$
calories per day.

Therefore, (assuming, as before, dry dog food contains 1360 calories per pound and canned dog food contains 475 calories per pound) a 20-pound dog should eat just under one-half pound of dry food or just over one pound of canned food per day.

After calculating how many calories your dog should be eating each day, make the following adjustments based on age and activity:

Age adjustments
a. add 10% for dogs 9 to 15 months of age
b. add 30% for dogs 4 to 9 months of age
c. add 60% for dogs 1 to 4 months of age
d. for newborn puppies please refer to the table: "Recommended average caloric intake for puppies,"

Activity adjustments
a. add 25% for moderate activity
b. add 60% for heavy activity (hunting or coursing)
c. add 50% during cold weather for outdoor dogs

You will also need to adjust the diet of a pregnant or lactating bitch.

In addition to food, always provide clean, fresh water for your dog twice daily. Fresh water should be available to the dog at all times.

Dogs that stay mainly outdoors should be provided with a safe environment, space to run, and shelter from sun, wind, and rain or snow. If your backyard is not fenced, keep your dog on a long chain or in a large, fenced run. Also, remove all plants that may prove toxic to your dog. When applying chemical fertilizers, weed killers, or fungicides to plants or lawn, keep the animal away from the treated area until it is safe.

Every outdoor dog needs either a dog house or an entrance into a kennel building or other covered area. If you choose to build or purchase a dog house, provide one with the following features:
• a raised floor to prevent moisture from entering;
• a pitched roof to aid drainage;
• enough room for the dog to stand up, turn around, and lie down comfortably;
• a canvas flap over the doorway for insulation;
• a hinged or removable roof to facilitate cleaning the interior;
• surfaces painted with non-toxic paint.

If possible, place the dog house facing east or south in a high spot of the yard, and try to make sure that the chosen spot will be shaded in the summer.

Indoor dogs also benefit from having a special place where they can curl up and sleep. While many dogs feel comfortable and secure in their crates, others enjoy having their own pillows or blankets in the corner of a room.

If your show dogs spend time indoors, be certain to remove all dangerous indoor plants. At the top of this list is the popular dieffenbachia; the poison from its leaves can cause vomiting, diarrhea, and even death. If your dog is a chewer, rearrange furniture so that electrical cords are not exposed. Also, keep small objects that the dog could accidentally choke on out of reach.

Puppies need to receive their initial set of vaccinations at approximately six weeks of age. Usually, the breeder will see that the puppies receive their first shots. After that, it is your responsibility to have the dog immunized annually. Your veterinarian can supply a complete schedule of recommended vaccinations.

To maintain a lustrous coat, brush your dog at least three times a week, brushing all the way to the skin in order to stimulate circulation and remove dandruff. Mats, typically found behind the ears, may be combed out or clipped out. If you clip them out, first place a comb between the skin and the mat, gently pull the mat as far from the skin as possible, and then clip on the mat side of the comb. This will protect the dog's skin from getting nicked.

When showing your dog, bathe him just before each show, and when not showing, at least once a month. When you bathe your dog, use a gentle baby shampoo, or if the coat needs an enhancer use one of the advertised formulas, place cotton balls in the dog's ears, and place a couple of drops of mineral oil in his eyes. Next, wet the dog, work up a lather, and then thoroughly rinse the soap from the coat. Quickly wrap the dog in a large, absorbent towel before he has a chance to shake. On all but the warmest days, dry the animal completely before allowing him outside.

Once or twice a week, brush your dog's teeth with toothpaste using a child-sized toothbrush. This will help prevent plaque and tartar from accumulating on the dog's teeth and should also help keep its breath sweet. You need only brush the outside surfaces of the teeth, since the animal's tongue cleans the inside surfaces. If tartar builds up anyway, your veterinarian can remove it at the next check-up.

Once a month, clean the pink underside of your dog's ears with a cotton swab soaked in mineral oil. Clean only the parts of the ear canal that you can see; do not insert the swab too deeply into the ear canal. It is not necessary to remove every bit of ear wax; in fact, a little ear wax is normal and healthy.

Trim your dog's nails once a month using a special dog nail clipper, which can be purchased at a pet store. Be careful to cut the nail below the cuticle, removing only the part of the nail that curls down. If your dog's nails wear down naturally – for example, if the dog is walked regularly on pavement – you may not need to trim them. Most judges check out nails carefully, especially in sporting and hound breeds for they can hinder a dog's work in the field.

If your dog drags its rear on the ground or licks its anus, you may need to express its anal sacs. The anal sacs are located below the dog's tail, and slightly to either side of the anus. When the dog defecates, the anal sacs usually secrete a thick, odorous liquid to mark the dog's territory. However, sometimes this substance is not fully excreted and becomes impacted in the sacs. This is especially common in smaller dogs. To express the sacs, lift the dog's tail with one hand, hold a paper towel behind the dog's anus with your other hand, and place your thumb and forefinger underneath the dog's anal sacs. Press upward and pinch gently to expel the liquid from the impacted sacs. If the expelled material contains blood or pus, the anal sacs are probably infected and the dog should be seen by your veterinarian.

Every dog needs daily exercise; even outdoor dogs should be taken for one or two short walks each day. The taller the dog, the more distance the walk should cover. If your dog is not used to exercise, start out with a gentle, five-minute walk and slowly build up to 20 minutes. Watch your dog carefully for signs of fatigue, such as shortness of breath; and slow the pace if your dog appears tired.

Even though you may perform all of the above steps, your dog will thrive only if he is nurtured with love. Pet your dog often, and treat him with respect, patience, and affection. Remember, the love you give your canine companion will be fully reciprocated.

This dog understands everything you tell him.

Dog Behavior Analyzed

In order to understand why dogs behave as they do, we need to understand a little more about the history and evolution of the *canis familiaris* or domestic dog. In the book, *The Canine Clan, A New Look At Man's Best Friend*, by John E. McLoughlin, the author points out:

> The gradation between wild and domesticated canids is so smooth as occasionally to defy analysis. Certainly one may easily distinguish a wolf from, say, a pointer dog. But what of the husky, the malamute, and the Arctic wolves? A group of such canids (and they do associate – are encouraged, in fact to do so by human beings) presents a uniformly wolfish aspect indeed...

> Wolf pups are born to participate in organized social groups and human beings live in just such units....

> We may be reasonably certain that domestic dogs arose from various wolf subspecies. Originally present in the area where domestication took place, for instance, both the dogs of ancient Asia Minor and North Africa and those of the Dingo type seem to have arisen from the Arab and Southern Asia wolves, while larger Shepherd dogs may have derived from polar-type dogs descended from the northern wolf. There also may have been minor admixture of other species of genus canis for they have interbred easily.

> Wolves and domestic dogs share the same number of chromosomes...

> In tracing...the early progenitors of the dog and finally the occurrence of various wild canids, asocial and social, and at last the appearance of the domestic dog from wolf ancestors, we see the process of adaptive radiation as it results from natural selection. This is a slow process, extending in this case over many tens of millions of years, with the finding of a symbiosis between human beings and canids, however, a new form of evolution - one resulting from artificial selection - took its place. Within only 15,000 years or so of full domestication, the original wolf stocks have produced more than two hundred highly distinctive races of *canis familiaris....*

> The <u>very temperament</u> (emphasis added) and intelligence of dogs may also be manipulated through selective breeding; the ancient sight-hunting nervous gazehounds, for example, specialized to the chase in open country, share little in temperament with the wise and attentive shepherd dogs or the slavish spaniels and setters.

> Breeds of dogs originate as living tools for human use, and in order to survive, these tools must fit their applications precisely. As raw genetic material for the fabrication of such tools, the wolf was ideal. Of all canids, wolves are seemingly the most generalized in form, therefore the most adaptable within the context of their social-hunter nature. Their domestication may be envisioned as a process of sieving, during which certain complexes of genes were isolated by artificial back breeding to "fix" desirable forms....

> Withal, each breed of domestic dog originated as a useful subset of the possibilities of the original wolf, with a corresponding minimization of other wolf characteristics in accordance with the design at hand. That loving terrier, in other words, is a fraction of a wolf – delightful, but a fraction, nonetheless, of the old wolf potential.

Is it any wonder then that the dog as we know him today, sometimes displays the aggression, the shyness and the fright embodied in his wolf ancestors? Since we are directly responsible for creating a specific breed and its salient attributes, are we not also responsible for breed for those characteristics which will make the breed easier to live with – both for man and for dog.

According to Karen Overall, V.M.D., University of Pennsylvania's Behavior Clinic, speaking at the 43rd Annual Meeting of the Morris Animal Foundation in Denver in 1991: "We didn't totally domesticate dogs. Ours is a symbiotic relationship." Both dog and human benefit when the relationship goes well.

Dr. Overall points out behavioral problems are the leading cause of death in dogs. More dogs are taken to animal shelters and euthanized for bad behavior than for any other cause. An estimated 10 million pets are surrendered to shelters each year due to behavior problems.

Dog behavior problems range from noise phobias

and separation anxieties to outright aggression. Dr. Overall and her team learned when a pet is abused, often the children in the family are abused as well and are re-directing their anger at the pet.

"Any aggression can be dangerous," Dr. Overall cautioned. "It can be controlled, but not cured. These dogs are not normal, and will probably never be normal."

Factors that affect the success of a behavioral training program for problem dogs include owner compliance, the age at which the problem began and the length of time the dog has had the problem, and the predictability of the outbursts.

Much is known about animal behavior – from the early studies of the Fortunate Fields' German Shepherds in Australia to Clarence Pfaffenberger's work with guide dogs for the blind in California in the 1960s. Many writers, the author included, have, for many years, preached selective breeding. One who has caught the public's attention in recent years is Dr. Ian Dunbar. Dr. Dunbar, through his articles in the AKC *Gazette*, his series of behavior booklets and his video on puppy training, has driven home the point that breeding stock should be selected more carefully.

Writing in the AKC *Gazette* ("Nature vs. Nurture, Revisited," October 1990), Dr. Ian Dunbar points out:

Careful selection is obviously essential for the prevention of behavior, temperament and obedience problems. However, when dealing with behavior, genetic controls are not sufficient by themselves. Even the most well bred-dog may not necessarily grow up to be well-behaved, because behavior problems are caused in part (or at least exacerbated) by the environment (usually people). Consequently, the successful prevention and treatment of problems necessitates that people sufficiently socialize and train their dogs. To sit back and rely on the patency of selective breeding is downright dim-witted, fatuous, facile, short-sighted, silly and stupid.

It is important to realize that an individual domestic dog is not fully domesticated unless it has been fully socialized. Whereas some people feel that the necessity for human intervention to prevent or correct problems means that the animal is less than sound, in reality, all dogs require human assistance to determine the direction or refine the nature of their development. Human guidance is part and parcel of a dog's normal upbringing and development, and socialization and training should be the major ingredients of routine, modern-day canine husbandry, just as they were essential during the very earliest days of domestication.

Socialization and training can go a long way to prevent the majority of behavior problems in domestic dogs. If the pups were whelped and raised in a home environment and were given ample opportunity for enjoyable interaction with a wide variety of dogs and people, especially children, men and/or strangers, then as adults, the dogs would much rather socialize and play with dogs and people than hide, bite or fight.

One of the most fruitless speculations has always been why a dog barks. Most researchers have shrugged their shoulders and gone off to do more rewarding studies.

However, an article appeared in *Omni Magazine* (July 1991) that sheds some light on the problem:

A Cocker Spaniel under observation, barked 907 times in 10 minutes. Multiply that by 52 million, the number of dogs in the United States, and you have the potential for major noise. Hampshire College biologist, Raymond Cuppinger, who has spent 30 years studying dogs, teamed up with fellow linguist Mark Feinstein to figure out what's behind all that racket. Their conclusion: Dog barking is a pointless, energy wasting activity.

"When dogs bark, they are doing the same kind of thing they do when they chase balls or their own tails," Cuppinger and Feinstein report. "While these behaviors serve no real function, the dog is likely to repeat them over and over."

Barks can mean anything – "let me in," "let me out," "feed me," "pet me" – or nothing at all.

"Unlike other wild animal calls, the bark has no built-in biological meaning," Cuppinger says. Newborn pups make whimpering, tonal sounds that do have an innate meaning – take care of me. The snarls and growls of older dogs also convey a message: Get the hell out of here! The bark combines the tonal whines of a pup with the gnarly noises of an adult.

The result is gobbledegook, Cuppinger says, "It would be like a person saying 'comeheregoaway.' "

The explanation, they believe, lies in an evolutionary quirk that has left the domesticated dog in a state of permanent adolescence. Dogs bark for the same reason teenagers hang out in shopping malls: that's what adolescents do.

Have you ever watched wild animal babies at play? It can be fascinating, terrifying, most informative and can apply directly to puppies.

Robert Fagen, writing in the December 1983 issue of *Science Magazine*, observes:

Two lion cubs, tawny and spotted, tussle with seeming fury. One cub flees. Its pursuer bounds after it, swats at its legs, puts a forepaw on its shoulder and pulls it down. The attacking cub swarms over its victim, nipping its throat, tugging a leg. They spar, their mouths half open. The victim struggles free and lopes away a few steps, looks back, then rushes its partner, mauling the cub's flank with alarming determination. Unexpectedly, the cubs break off their combat, lie down close together and contentedly wash themselves.

It looks like fighting or panic flight, but it is not.

It might be described as gymnastics, perhaps even theater. Whatever, these scenes resemble, they are all play, a category of behavior in animals and a prime scientific puzzle. The endless examples of such seemingly useless activity have made play a difficult, even controversial, area of study. But recent research into the evolution of play suggests it is not just behavioral bauble. In play, animals cooperate to discover creatively their native skills and the world they live in.

So what is this thing called play? To look at a puppy romping with a stick, or a kitten springing on a leaf, it would seem that defining play is easy. Not so, say scientists. Play is impossible to define but inescapable in practices, states British ethologist Robert Hinde. We may all recognize play but just how we do so turns out to be surprisingly complex. Basically, play is a matter of means versus ends: Skilled actions such as leaping, catching and holding another animal...become goals in themselves.

Play is creative improvisation, as in jazz, interpretation of a familiar ballad, or a set of chord changes, certain basic themes are elaborated through repetition, interruption, exaggeration, and alteration of sequential order and context. And all this creative activity, it turns out, takes three basic forms, one of which is solo exercise. Partnerless and exuberant, playing solo involves vigorous locomotion and rotation of the whole body or of its parts. A colt will gallop, leaping vertically again and again, gamboling and capering, twisting its body and kicking out with its hind feet...these solo activities are non-threatening and can be further distinguished by the players loose body tone, by the repetition of movements, and the ease with which they are interrupted.

Another form of play, play-fighting, is social (quite prevalent in puppies) as the friendly pursuits and tussles of puppies suggest. Play-fighting is co-operative behavior-harmless chasing, wrestling, hitting and swatting. Unlike true conflicts, social play does not decide who wins a disputed resource. The play fights aren't injurious, nor do they lead to prolonged mutual avoidance by the players.

The third basic play form, known as object manipulation, is not too applicable to the domestic dog.

Researchers like Jane Goodall, George Schaller, Dian Fossey and Stuart Altmann, along with earlier naturalists and wildlife biologists have been instrumental in uncovering the significance and the score of play. In the past, it was frequently dismissed as simply practice of the physical skills a player needs to survive and reproduce. But field research - reveal that play's dimensions are richer. Young animals spend time and energy in play because out of those activities patterns of relationships emerge as well.

We have learned that building upon the very earliest puppy experiences can create a happy and outgoing dog. It just doesn't happen, we have to help it along. In the adult world, educational toys for children are big business. Why? Because parents have learned that as children play they learn to manipulate and understand their world. Jacqueline Fraser, a Staffordshire Terrier breeder, and former AKC columnist for the breed, wrote a simply wonderful explanatory article about puppy play titled "Games Puppies Play" in the AKC *Gazette* (September 1989). In it she points out that play conditioning works with very young puppies too.

Fraser states: "A young dog who previously showed with aplomb, could lose his confidence under a judge attired in a floppy sun hat or a rustling raincoat. If you condition your puppy to accept people who are wearing unfamiliar attire, this problem may never occur. Props include a wide-brimmed hat, glasses with shiny metal frames, an inexpensive plastic raincoat, big boots, an umbrella, a fake beard, possibly some Halloween masks." She suggests using only one prop at a time and to allow the puppy to watch you put it on before calling him over. Don't suddenly appear with flapping arms and a large cape, or you could crush his confidence forever.

Clamor around the house in everyday living is also good for the maturing pup. Children's raucous play and loud music are typical of what most households with kids are like.

I have definite concerns about the puppy raised as a kennel dog insofar as his internal fortitude or heart. I also am concerned that such dogs can never be truly joyous animals who can interact with people happily.

Yes, it is impossible to have all the dogs live indoors with you, but after they have been raised in the house as puppies and later put in the kennel, it is essential for their socialization and temperament to have a chance to come into the house at a minimum of once a week to play, to be fussed over and to feel they belong. Dogs treated in this fashion will be the ones who show heart in the show ring.

The most important factor in the development of a dog with good social skills and a good temperament is his early and continued good interaction with little and big people. As we have learned in domesticating the dog, he needs our nurture and guidance to become what we want him to be. The wolf is not that far away in his developmental history that we can ignore the inherent possibility of a behavior/temperament problem.

An excellent book to read about truly interacting with your dog properly is *How to be Your Dog's Best Friend*, written by the Monks of New Skete and published by Little, Brown & Co.

With all the concern about temperament in purebred dogs, you would expect that tests would be devised to evaluate litters of puppies for stability – and so they have. They range from very formal, rigid techniques to catch-as-catch-can methodology. Even the most structured are not truly validated and certainly it is most likely that the results of a one-time standardized test can offer only an approximation of the dog's behavior and temperament.

Citing Dr. Ian Dunbar once again, this time in an article in the February 1989 issue of the AKC *Gazette* titled "Puppy Aptitude Testing," he states: "A single test indicates how the pup fared on a certain day with a particular tester, under strictly monitored conditions. This may – or may not – tell us how the pup might fare on the same test with a different tester on the following day."

Contrast this with the situation described by Litzi Engel in an article in the *Akita World Magazine* (March/April, 1988) titled "Puppy Testing." She describes a trip with a friend to a site off in a canyon in a deep forest. The puppies were brought into a barn for testing. Engel had brought with her a large cardboard box full of puppy testing equipment – rags, papers, an umbrella, and atop it all a large turquoise-blue stuffed poodle.

The puppies had never been indoors before, so they were more stressed than might have been desirable, but still, the test showed their reactions and in a very new environment. Some were fearful, some were quite comfortable. Each puppy was brought in one at a time...put down on the floor, and after it had a few minutes to look around, the tester called to her and then asked it to follow her. She held it down on the floor on its back for thirty seconds, then let it up and petted it, then held it under its belly slightly above the floor for another thirty seconds. The puppy's reactions to these experiences establish its attraction to people, its confidence, its degree of submissiveness or dominance in relation to people, and its ability to forgive what it considers undesirable treatment. Scores were assigned from one to six. The next test consisted of throwing a wadded piece of paper and observing whether the puppy retrieved it, ran off with it, stood over it, or ignored it. Pfaffenberger says this is the best single test for determining a puppy's future as a guide dog and its willingness to work with people in general.

Next the puppy's touch sensitivity was checked by gently pinching the webbing between its front toes, and its sound sensitivity – someone banged a metal bowl against a post, unexpectedly. Prey drive was tested by dragging a rag on a string and seeing if the puppy attacks, avoids, or does something in between; this test is supposed to be useful not only in predicting how the dog will get along with your goats and chickens or its schutzhund potential...The final tests showed reaction to new and strange experiences; the puppy was presented with the turquoise-blue stuffed poodle, a person carrying the large cardboard box, and the umbrella being suddenly opened and set on the floor. A puppy that spooks at these things and does not recover quickly will be fearful and need careful handling.

Engel concludes by saying: "The tests are an invaluable aid in selecting and placing puppies. Perhaps they show no more than a breeder with a good eye, lots of experience, and plenty of time for observation already knows about a litter, but they have some clear cut advantages; they can be done by someone who doesn't know the litter and has only a couple of hours to watch it; they're standardized enough to counterbalance our sentimental and romantic predictions whether they be for the top dog or the loser; and they determine specific characteristics and abilities, such as obedience aptitude or tolerance for a noisy household."

For more detailed information about puppy testing read Melissa Bartlet's article on the subject in the March 1979 issue of the AKC *Gazette*.

Because of major concerns about stable personalities in dogs, the United States Temperament Testing Association (USTTA) was formed to further a proven scientific manner of determining how a dog can be expected to act under various social circumstances. This organization can be reached by writing to USTTA, Box 357, Sudbury, MA 01776.

The tests, with some modifications as introduced by the USTTA, have been used in much of the world for a number of years. They were introduced into the United States in 1975. Dogs that were successful in passing various tests are awarded the title "TT." All phases of the test must be passed with a score of 70 percent.

In view of the possibility of traumatizing puppies, it is recommended that dogs be at least 12 months of age.

The series of tests start with a dog being greeted by a friendly stranger who makes a fuss over the dog while ignoring the handler. The handler is then approached by a stranger who ignores the dog (who is on a leash). The dog is then exposed, in turn, to unusual noises, gunfire, a strange surface (a plastic bag and exercise-pen grating), an umbrella which suddenly snaps open near the dog, and finally, by a "hostile" stranger, who from a distance of 10 feet, threatens the dog and handler.

While the scoring is breed specific, any dog that shows no fear of the various stimuli, but reacts with healthy curiosity, will pass.

I will close this chapter by again citing Dr. Dunbar's article on puppy testing:

Human testing is the most important factor determining predictability. Tests with high validity only predict how the pup will probably develop if left to its own devices. However, it would be folly to assume that a dog's naturally good temperament will necessarily remain that way indefinitely. Similarly, it would be naive to expect a dog to cure its own faults. Behavior and temperament are in a state of flux, and without human guidance, faults generally tend to get worse rather than better. Nevertheless, there are some who would test a dog and upon discovering that it is overly fearful, rambunctious or aggressive, leave it to develop in this expected fashion. By staying in touch with owners of the pups she has bred and retesting a litter and observing its development, a breeder will learn a lot.

Eye Diseases in Dogs

Eye problems, such as progressive retinal atrophy and hereditary cataract, seem to be prevalent in many breeds today. Dr. Dan W. Lorimer, D.V.M., writing in *Pet Focus* (March 1991), stresses the following:

> To better understand hereditary eye disease one should first become familiar with basic terminology. Hereditary disease refers to a condition that is genetically transmissible from parents to their offspring. These defects may be observed at birth or develop later on in life.
>
> Congenital diseases refer to conditions that animals are born with. Although many congenital diseases are hereditary, if an animal is born with a condition it does not necessarily mean it is a heritable trait. For example, a pregnant female may have a uterine infection resulting in puppies with birth defects. These defects are congenital (because they are born with them) but not necessarily heritable.

CANINE EYE REGISTRATION FOUNDATION

Canine eye registration foundation (CERF) is an organization that exists for the sole purpose of eliminating hereditary eye diseases from purebred dogs. This organization is similar to Orthopedic Foundation of Animals (OFA) which helps to eliminate diseases like hip dysplasia from dogs.

Canine eye registry foundation (CERF) is a non-profit organization that screens and certifies purebred dogs' eyes as free of heritable ocular diseases. CERF is a cooperative program involving CERF, board-certified veterinary ophthalmologists, breed clubs, breeders, and dog owners. It also functions to collect data and document incidence about breed-associated diseases. It is through this certification program that abnormalities are identified and thus prevents genetic spread of ocular conditions within breeds. All information gained through this program is confidential; only the dog owner and the veterinary ophthalmologist have access to the records. The data accumulated by CERF is compiled by a computer to determine breed-associated risk of ocular disease.

Dogs certified free of ocular disease can be used in breeding programs. However, if they are known to carry genetic defects, they should not be used for breeding even if they are currently free of ocular disease.

It is recommended that dogs considered for breeding programs are screened and certified by CERF on a minimum of a yearly basis. People interested in acquiring puppies should request that the parents be evaluated to reduce the likelihood of heritable eye conditions.

For more information regarding CERF the reader is requested to write: Canine Eye Registration Foundation, SCC-A, Purdue University, West Lafayette IN 47907, 317-494-8179.

For information regarding location of board-certified ophthalmologists qualified to administer CERF, one should contact their local veterinary medical association.

When examining dogs for eye conditions the veterinary ophthalmologists use instruments that allow them to see structures at high magnification, sometimes at a cellular level. These instruments, including the slit lamp biomicroscope and the indirect ophthalmoscope, allow the ophthalmologist to identify and scrutinize ocular conditions. Often diseases may be observed at an early stage.

Following are a few conditions that are thought to have a hereditary basis in dogs.

CATARACTS

Cataracts are opacities or cloudy spots in the lens of the eye caused from trauma, infection and internal diseases like diabetes mellitus. But by far the greatest number of cataracts are caused because the dogs are genetically predisposed.

There is a long list of breeds that have a tendency to develop cataracts. These include congenital cataracts present at birth and developmental cataracts which occur as the dog ages.

Cataracts tend to affect each breed uniquely and can range from small opacities to complete mature cataract which cause total blindness. While many cataracts are associated with aging, a majority of cataracts are found in animals under five years of age.

TABLE 1. INHERITED CATARACTS IN THE DOG

BREED	APPROXIMATE AGE OF ONSET
Afghan Hound	6 months to 2 years
American Cocker Spaniel	Congenital
	6 months to 7 years
	4 months
Beagle	4 months
Boston Terrier	4 months
Chesapeake Bay Retriever	6 months to 2 years
German Shepherd	Congenital
Golden Retriever	Congenital to 3 years
Irish Setter	4 months to 3 years
Labrador Retriever	Congenital
Miniature and Toy Poodles	3 to 10 years
Miniature Schnauzer	Congenital
Old English Sheepdog	Congenital
Siberian Husky	6 months
Staffordshire Bull Terrier	4 months
Standard Poodle	1 to 2 years
West Highland White Terrier	1 to 2 years

TABLE 2. PROGRESSIVE RETINAL DISEASE IN DOGS

BREED	TYPE OF RETINAL DISEASE	AGE OF ONSET
Collie	rod-cone dysplasia	<1 year
Irish Setter	rod-cone dysplasia	<1 year
Cairn Terrier	rod-cone dysplasia	<1 year
ML Dachshund	rod-cone dysplasia	<1 year
Norwegian Elkhound	rod-cone dysplasia, cone degeneration	2 to 3 years
Samoyed	rod-cone degeneration	3 years
Cocker Spaniel	rod-cone degeneration	2 to 7 years
Miniature Poodle	rod-cone degeneration	3 to 6 years
Miniature Schnauzer	rod-cone degeneration	3 to 6 years
Akita	rod-cone degeneration	3 to 6 years
Schnauzer	rod-cone degeneration	>3 years
Golden Retriever	rod-cone degeneration	3 to 5 years
Labrador Retriever	rod-cone degeneration	3 to 6 years

As dogs tend to age the lens tends to compress and become cloudy. This condition is termed nuclear sclerosis and causes a grey-blue haze in the lens. This condition does not significantly affect vision and should not be confused with cataracts.

The only effective treatment of cataracts is surgical removal of the lens. There is no known medical treatment for cataracts despite many false claims. If a dog is noticed with cataracts it probably should be referred to a ophthalmologist so a detailed slit-lamp (biomicroscope) examination can be performed. This is especially important if the owner is planning to breed the dog or is considering cataract surgery to improve vision.

PROGRESSIVE RETINAL ATROPHY

Progressive retinal atrophy (PRA) refers to a broad category of inherited retinal diseases that result in the blindness of purebred dogs. Because of the insidious nature of the disease and in some breeds, the late onset, serial examinations may be required to detect affected individuals. Individuals affected should not be used in any breeding and pedigree studies are indicated to eliminate other potential carriers for these diseases.

Progressive retinal atrophy refers to a group of retinal diseases that cause blindness in dogs and cats by abnormal development or a slow progressive deterioration of the retinal tissue. The disease affects many breeds of dogs, each in a specific manner. In general the condition is thought to be inherited but each breed may have a special and individual mode of inheritance. Similarities in the outcome and the observed clinical signs are the basis for group classification. Specific breed variations include age of onset, rate of progression, condition, and other associated ocular signs.

As the name (progressive retinal atrophy) implies, an atrophy or a degeneration of retinal tissue occurs. In many animals a slowly progressive disease occurs and the early signs may be overlooked. The slow loss of light is similar to a dimmer switch to reduce light brightness in a room. If the light is ever so slowly reduced, our eyes adapt and the change is not noticed until total darkness occurs. A similar situation occurs in progressive retinal atrophy in animals; often the condition is significantly progressed. Unfortunately there are no cures available for progressive retinal atrophy. Identification of affected breeding animals is essential to prevent spread of the condition within the breed.

To better understand progressive retinal atrophy, one must have a basic understanding of the function of the retina. The retina is a highly specialized sheet of neurological tissue located in the back of the eye.

The retina is analogous to film in a camera; it is located in the back part of the eye and it is responsible for integrating light into vision. Interpretation by the brain and propagation of a signal by the retina is required for normal vision.

Within the general classification of progressive retinal atrophy are those that involve degeneration and those that involve dysplasia. Retinal dysplasia is defined as the abnormal development of the retinal tissue. Degeneration occurs when the tissue develops normally and then atrophies.

The early signs of retinal atrophy include night blindness in most cases which will frequently progress to day blindness. Because PRA can be difficult to identify, routine ophthalmic examination of all pets is recommended. This is especially important in animals that are being considered for breeding.

When the ophthalmologist views the retina with an instrument called an indirect ophthalmoscope, changes are frequently seen in the retinal blood vessel pattern, the optic nerve, and the tapetum. However, some breeds' characteristics have little or no early visible changes and may appear normal until the later stages of the disease. Some affected dogs show various rates of progression making generalization difficult.

Definitive diagnosis of PRA is supported by electroretinography. This non-invasive test involves use of sophisticated instrumentation to measure the electrical potential within the retina. It is similar to an electrocardiogram for the heart in that they both measure electrical impulses and produce characteristic recorded wave forms. This instrument is sensitive enough to diagnose affected dogs before they begin to demonstrate clinical signs.

Unfortunately, no effective therapy exists to prevent, treat or cure progressive retinal atrophy although a number of vitamin therapies have been suggested. As stated previously, affected animals should be identified as early as possible and eliminated from breeding programs.

The mode of inheritance of PRA in most breeds is not fully understood. Most breeds are thought to have autosomal recessive mode of inheritance. In animals with a recessive mode of inheritance, it is possible for animals to carry a trait for PRA or cataracts and yet be clinically normal an not express the trait. For dogs that do express the trait (diagnosed with PRA or cataracts) it is likely that both their parents carried that gene and passed it to their offspring. If an animal is diagnosed with heritable eye condition it is essential that the parents and siblings of the pet are contacted.

HEREDITARY EYELID DISORDERS

Each breed association selects conformation that they think is characteristic for the respective breed. Unfortunately sometimes the eyelid and face conformation leads to ocular condition that are not beneficial to the animal. In general eyelid conformation is not scrutinized as closely as conditions that might result in complete blindness of dogs.

Entropion is when the eyelids "roll in" toward the eye often causing corneal ulceration and scarring. Breeds commonly observed with entropion include the Chinese Shar-pei, Chow-chow, Golden Retriever and Rottweiler.

Ectropion refers to eyelids that are "rolled out" and often have the appearance of drooping. Breeds observed with ectropion include the Bloodhound, Springer Spaniel, and some retrievers.

INHERITED DISORDERS AFFECTING THE CORNEA

The cornea is normally clear and transparent. Some opacities (cloudiness) that occur may be due to hereditary eye conditions.

Corneal dystrophy refers to white opacities in the cornea usually consisting of fat or mineral deposits. They can also be a result of trauma or internal disease. Breeds most commonly seen with corneal dystrophy include the Shetland Sheepdog, Collie, Cocker Spaniels and many other breeds.

Pannus refers to a condition where pigment and blood vessels grow across the cornea appearing like a dark "film." This should not be confused with cataracts which affect the lens. The most common breed affected with pannus is the German Shepherd.

CONCLUSION

There are a large number of heritable ophthalmic conditions in dogs and other animals. The only way to reduce the incidence of the ocular disease in animals is to correctly diagnose each specific condition and prevent the affected animals from passing the traits on from generation to generation by eliminating them from further breeding programs. This is best achieved by early CERF exams by veterinary ophthalmologists. This requires communication between animal owners, dog breeders, breed associations, CERF, veterinarians and veterinary ophthalmologists and clearly the benefits are worth the effort.

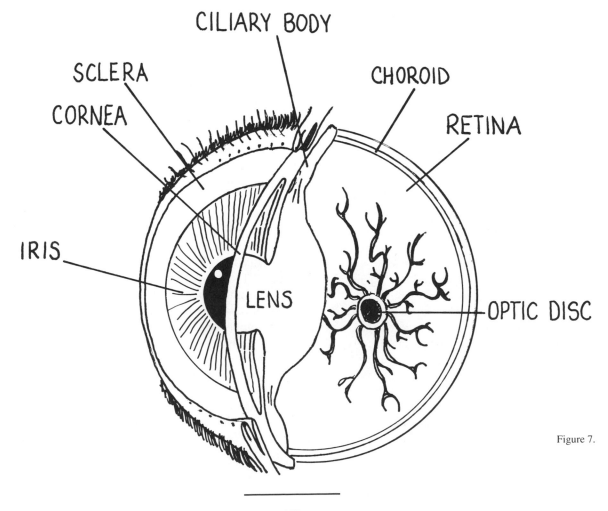

Figure 7.

The German Shepherd.

Hi-Boots Such Crust. Judge, Derek Payne. Owners-breeders, Marjorie and Alvin Grossman. Handler, Alvin Grossman.

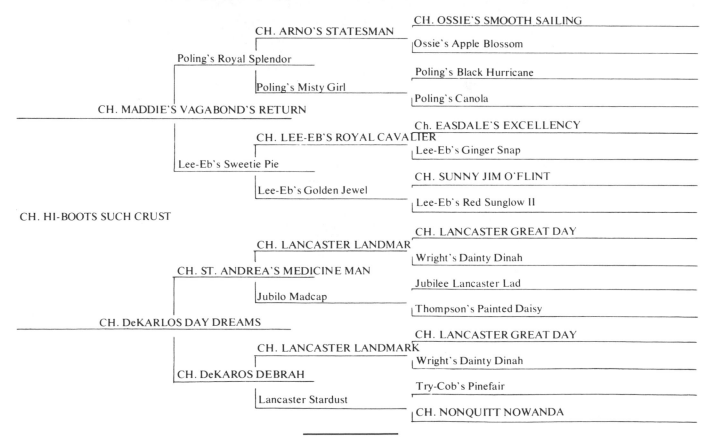

CH. HI-BOOTS SUCH CRUST

CH. MADDIE'S VAGABOND'S RETURN

Poling's Royal Splendor

CH. ARNO'S STATESMAN

CH. OSSIE'S SMOOTH SAILING

Ossie's Apple Blossom

Poling's Misty Girl

Poling's Black Hurricane

Poling's Canola

Lee-Eb's Sweetie Pie

CH. LEE-EB'S ROYAL CAVALIER

Ch. EASDALE'S EXCELLENCY

Lee-Eb's Ginger Snap

Lee-Eb's Golden Jewel

CH. SUNNY JIM O'FLINT

Lee-Eb's Red Sunglow II

CH. DeKARLOS DAY DREAMS

CH. ST. ANDREA'S MEDICINE MAN

CH. LANCASTER LANDMAR

CH. LANCASTER GREAT DAY

Wright's Dainty Dinah

Jubilo Madcap

Jubilee Lancaster Lad

Thompson's Painted Daisy

CH. DeKAROS DEBRAH

CH. LANCASTER LANDMARK

CH. LANCASTER GREAT DAY

Wright's Dainty Dinah

Lancaster Stardust

Try-Cob's Pinefair

CH. NONQUITT NOWANDA

The Meaning of a Pedigree

The pedigree of the dog is his family tree, the record of the names of his ancestors and of their relationship to one another and to him. The name of the breeder of the dog, the date of whelping, the AKC numbers of the dog and his parents, and other data about the animal are often included in the pedigree. These added data, however informative, are not properly a part of the pedigree.

Pedigrees are usually published as columns of names, which in each successive column from right to left are more widely spaced than in the succeeding column. This arrangement places the name of the parents in the first left hand column, the names of the parent's parents (the grandparents) in the second column, and so spaced that the name of the progeny appears midway vertically between the names of the parents. The pedigree may include as many generations of ancestors as its maker chooses to record or of which there is available data. (The usual number is five.)

A list of names in itself means little. A more meaningful pedigree would also list the colors of each ancestor and what numbers of quality progeny it had produced. I have even seen pictures of dogs in the first three generations included.

The pedigree may be in essence only a statement that all of the dog's ancestors for a certain number of generations are all of a stated variety. In fact, a great many pedigrees are little more than that, mazes of names of obscure dogs, perhaps here and there illuminated by the name of some more or less obscure champion. To the uninitiated, a pedigree is a pedigree. But such a limited pedigree has, in fact, little significance and no value.

No pedigree is of any worth if the dog whose lineage it records is sterile or is not to be bred from. The record of a dog's ancestry is only of use as a predictor of the kind of progeny he is likely (or liable) to beget. One is presumed to be able to evaluate the prospective generations ahead of the dog from the recorded generations behind him.

That this is possible is true only in part. A good pedigree confirms what a dog's type and his proved ability to produce good stock has already proclaimed. The proof of the dog or bitch is in the puppies. The role of the ancestors is but a prelude to what is contained in their chromosomes.

It is not to be denied that the son or daughter of two parents who are themselves of high quality and are recognized producers of stock of consistent excellence is likely, when mated adequately, to produce well.

As we have pointed out time after time, quality begets quality. An example close to home is the author's own Ch. Hi-Boots Such Brass, a black and tan Cocker Spaniel. The dog was a Best-in-Show winner and, as the sire of thirty-seven champions, among the all-time top twenty of his breed. His five-generation pedigree shows successive generations of top producing dogs and bitches. His pedigree, when correctly read, states that the dog should be a producer. While this is true, his two champion litter brothers were also of outstanding quality but neither sired anywhere near the quality sired by Such Brass.

Earlier we learned of the tendency of a breed to revert to a midpoint, or mediocrity. The work upon which this is founded was done by Frances Dalton, one of the great minds of the nineteenth century. His so-called "Law of Filial Regression," which declares, in effect, the tendency of races to revert to mediocrity, is what dog breeders mean when they use the term "The Drag of the Race."

Dalton reached his conclusions from statistical studies. He found that the adult children of very tall parents tended to be, while taller than the average of the population, not so tall as the mean height of the parents; the children of short parents, shorter than the average but of greater height than the mean height of the parents. His statistics reveal the tendency of exaggeration of type in the parents to be reduced or to disappear in the progeny.

Filial regression impresses upon us the imperative need of eternal vigilance and unremitting selection through the generations. The pedigree, intelligently read, indicates whether or not that selection has been exercised among the dog's progenitors.

The basic records of the breeder are his pedigrees. In his efforts to breed better dogs, he relies upon setting up superior lines of ancestors carrying superior genes. The outline of these lines of ancestors together with the data describing their qualities constitute the data which should be recorded in the pedigrees.

The ability to prepare an intelligible pedigree record and to read the value of a pedigree is one of the most precious gifts of a breeder. The facts are that most pedigree records are so incomplete as to render them entirely useless except as a record of the names and relationships of the different ancestors. To the great majority of breeders the meaning of a pedigree is as deeply concealed as though the writings were in Greek.

The pedigree provides a record of the matings made by the breeders of the past from which the animals of the present generation have resulted. Many of these matings were well made and in some instances are known to have resulted in suitable ancestors for the later generations. Many of the matings, including those even of the famous producers, were carelessly made and in no way showed an intelligent purpose of bringing the progeny closer to the accepted standards. Naturally the results of such matings were frequently bad. However, I have on a number of occasions seen a top-flight specimen produced from this "random choice" breeding. In most cases the breeder has been unable to duplicate the results. In certain cases great producers come about in this manner. However it is luck, not planning, that makes it happen.

We have seen that there are wide differences existing in the gene structure of dogs, even from the same litters, and that only a few of any breeding can be outstanding as producers. Thus, the existence of famous names in a pedigree is not enough. It is no assurance whatever that the pedigree is a good one.

Breeding for improvement must be a cumulative process, always in a fixed line of progression. Probably every noted producer has had sons or daughters which have proven worthless as breeders. Therefore, a pedigree showing a famous sire or dam or any number of them in the second, third, or earlier generations is relatively meaningless unless we can gauge accurately the producing power of the particular sons and daughters which bring these genes down to us.

The ancestors making up any pedigree have carried the direct lines of descent which will be passed on to the new puppies. Each of these ancestors has made its own

modification of these hereditary materials. Each has changed their composition somewhat. Some have improved them. Some have lowered their merits. Some have added to their purity for the desired qualities. Others have brought impurities into them in the nature of tendencies away from the ideal instead of toward it.

A good bloodline is one in which each of the ancestors has added to the purity of the gene structure for the qualities we want, and has improved it toward the development of those desired qualities. Obviously, therefore, a good pedigree is one recording such a line of ancestry in a form in which it can be recognized immediately as such. The existence of a recent ancestor known to be an inferior breeder or a producer of a serious fault may have turned an otherwise potent pedigree into a very poor one. Ancestors of unknown breeding potential turn a pedigree into one of undeterminable value unless these brackets are followed by ancestors known to have been superior producers. This is true irrespective of how many famous names appear in the pedigree.

That just certain of the ancestors were good is not enough. In their own generation they may have directed the tendencies of their line very definitely toward the ideal. The ones to which they were bred, however, may have entirely counteracted the good influences of these great producers and set up detrimental qualities or tendencies even in their direct offspring. Granting that their own offspring were as good producers on the average as we could ask for, the particular son or daughter shown

The Black Labrador.

106

by the pedigree to have carried the line down for another generation may easily have been a very poor producer. In such an instance all the beneficial influences of the noted ancestor may have been nullified.

To produce a superior line of genes, it is necessary to have an unbroken line of ancestors of superior breeding powers without any weak links in it. Any one ancestor whose individual producing ability is not known may have completely broken the continuity of the line of progressive breeding and nullified much or all of the improvement developed up to that time.

It is difficult to measure accurately the producing ability of a dog or bitch for many of the more intricate canine characteristics. We must, however, recognize the necessity of having an unbroken line of ancestors superior for producing each of the important qualities. We can draw entirely satisfactory proof of this principle from the production of qualities in other breeds of animals which can be measured accurately.

During the mid-1950s I lived in the state of Washington and it was my good fortune to make the acquaintance of Bob Bartos, the Kennel Manager of Carnation Farms. While visiting Carnation, I first became acquainted with the voluminous records kept by the dairy cattle industry. Painstaking care was shown in selecting herd sires and keeping track of the milk and butterfat production of their offspring. Today the records have been computerized and the ability to select proper specimens through computer analysis puts dog breeding to shame. Of course, the payoff in dollars is so great that this type of record keeping can be justified in the dairy cattle industry.

The purpose of a pedigree is to provide a record of the ancestry from which the nature of the hereditary qualities at the end of it may be determined. In the selection of prospective parents, a study of a pedigree is to determine the nature of those qualities which will be passed on to the puppies.

The best knowledge that can come from a study of a pedigree would be reached if one knew the exact nature of the heredity of both the sire and the dam. To rely upon more remote ancestors, and particularly upon famous ancestors scattered only occasionally through the different brackets of the pedigree, greatly increases the hazards.

A great producing sire or dam produces, as an average, much higher quality progeny than does the average of its sons or daughters. When the great producing sire and the great producing dam are mated together, the average quality of the progeny is brought to its highest level. Even in this extremely favorable mating, however, the sampling nature of Mendelian inheritance and the range of natural variations would ensure that some of the offspring would be above and some below the average of the parents in their own qualities and in their abilities to again transmit each of the qualities.

In this case the "drag of the race" would provide an entirely practical guarantee that the great majority of the offspring would be inferior, as producers, to their great producing parents. Only the occasional one would be the parents' superior or even their equal.

With the usual type of pedigree that contains little but names, the older, experienced breeder is at an advantage, for he has seen many of the specimens listed. To the novice, pedigrees are to a large extent a mystery, a genealogical puzzle. The experienced breeder fills in from his own knowledge such as he knows of the weighted average of individuality and known producing powers of each of the parents, the direct ancestors, and many of the collateral relatives. This is reading a pedigree, a gift of knowledge and insight which few breeders of any breed ever obtain. It has been my privilege to have lived and travelled all over this country in the past thirty years so that I have become intimately acquainted with a wide variety of dogs of my own original breed (Cocker Spaniels) but have also seen some of the great ones in many breeds. I saw and competed against Ch. Bang Away of Sirrah Crest (Boxer), Ch. Rock Falls Colonel (English Setter), Ch. Crookrise Denny of Muick (English Pointer), Ch. Gretchenhof Moonshine (German Shorthair Pointer), Ch. Waiterock Elmer Brown (English Springer Spaniel), and many others.

The case of the newcomer is not so hopeless as it may seem, however. Before the usual pedigree can even begin to become a reliable part of the basis of breeding, it is necessary to find out from other sources how superior or inferior as producers each of the different ancestors was, and for what qualities. The experienced breeder most frequently attempts to supply this information from memory—a system far superior to no method at all, but unreliable at best.

The most reliable methods and the shortest cuts to the most accurate and valuable knowledge available are progeny tests and records. We know from the chapters on breeding that each dog has two distinct beings, the phenotype, or what it actually looks like, and the genotype, or genes with which it will endow its progeny. It is like the proverbial iceberg—only one part shows on the surface. The phenotypes, or top of the iceberg, can be evaluated by sight, but the genotype can be accurately gauged only by a careful scrutiny of the progeny.

As was pointed out earlier, progeny from superior sires and dams are more likely to prove superior breeders than are the progeny of animals selected on the basis of individual merit and pedigree. However, vast numbers of breeders breed to the winner of the day and the genetic makeup of the dog is ignored. Perhaps that is why the average staying power of a breeder is only five years. Dog breeding is like the Las Vegas syndrome—hit it big now or forget it.

LITTER RECORD

Date of Birth:

Type of Birth:

Sire: Dam:

Number of Puppies: Alive: Stillborn:

Pedigree

Number   Sex   Color   Condition   Notes

This is a sample of the type of record card which provides space for complete information on an entire litter. "Type of Birth" would show whether puppies were born normally, by breech, etc. "Condition" would indicate whether a puppy appeared to be normal or was undershot, etc. Entries under "Notes" would show whether a puppy was sold, given away, etc. To be more complete, photographs should be kept of each puppy, with the dates. Further, a record of the show career should be attached for each winning offspring.

INDIVIDUAL PROGENY RECORD

Dog: Sex:

Dam: Sire:

Date of Birth:

AKC Registration Number:

Color:

Quality Score:

Temperament Score:

Health Record:

Date of Death: Cause of Death:

Health Score: Age at Death:

Number in Litter at Birth:

Number Surviving to 8 Weeks: M: F:

This is a sample of the type of record card that should be maintained for each individual dog and bitch owned by a breeder.

BREEDING RECORD—FEMALE

Dates of Heats	Dates Mated	Dog	Date Whelped	Litter Number

This shows the type of information to be entered on the back of the "Individual Progeny Record" card to provide a complete breeding record for a female.

BREEDING RECORD—MALE

Dates Mated	Bitch	Litter Number	Number of Puppies	Sex M F

This shows the type of information to be entered on the back of the "Individual Progeny Record" card to provide a complete breeding record for a male.

Progeny testing is invaluable since it reveals the true genetic makeup of the sires and dams. Successful breeders are those who select their prospective breeding stock from the best bloodlines rather than from the best individuals. It is the heredity concealed in the genes of an individual which determines its value in breeding. All methods of arriving at the true nature of this heredity are merely estimates or approximations, except the actual breeding test in which this true nature definitely is revealed in the progeny itself.

Pedigrees, when properly made, recording all the valuable information which might be included in them and coupled with a careful survey of the individuality of the parents, furnish a complete record of the parental generation. As a guide, however, to producing powers, they run afoul of every evil that may lie concealed in their chromosomes. The supplements necessary to bring them accurately up-to-date and render them reliably useful, are the progeny records. Progeny records show the averages and individualities of the offspring. The record books reproduced here illustrate a good method of keeping such records.

Progeny records show accurately the qualities of the progeny already produced, and, if extensive, establish definitely, within the limits of variation, what additional progeny from the same parents will be.

A study of pedigrees and bloodlines is very important but such records can never be brought to reflect the outcome of any mating with the accuracy often derived from a study of the progeny records. An individual may have the most wonderful pedigree imaginable, but it does not afford a reliable guarantee of his ability as a producer until the quality of his offspring can be seen and judged.

Any ancestry can merely fix the type center of its offspring. We have seen that because of natural variations, the degree of development of the different qualities will fluctuate about this type center with a great degree of regularity. Thus, even with the best lines of ancestry we will still have different degrees of merit in the different qualities and in the different individual dogs. The higher the average or type of these different qualities coming from any bloodlines or from any mating, the better are the chances of producing the superior specimens, the champions and Best-in-Show winners.

The most accurate index of the breeding worth of sires and dams is the average quality of their offspring as a whole. In the absence of an ability to gauge this average accurately, the index lies in a random sample of the offspring rather than the production of one super individual with the qualities of the others unknown. As a consequence, a bloodline or a single mating which is known to produce a higher average of good individuals must be considered to offer more substantial assurances that a champion will be forthcoming in the next litter than one which has produced one champion but a lower average quality in all the offspring.

Experience has shown us that the great mass of every breed fails to produce the required degree of excellence and is lost insofar as the perpetuation of the breed is concerned. The same principle applies, but of course in a lesser degree, to each line of ancestry, no matter how carefully the selections are made, and to the offspring of even the greatest sires and dams. It is common knowledge that the most prepotent sires of every breed have sired puppies which were inferior producers or even carried serious genetic faults. Thus we may say that the purity of the line, even in the best appearing pedigrees is no purity at all unless the progeny test can definitely be applied to each of the ancestors.

It is equally apparent that the mere appearance of famous individuals in a pedigree is not a sufficient guarantee that the line now retains any of their good qualities, which may have been dissipated in their own or any succeeding generation by one or more inferior breeders. To provide a reliable tool for the breeder bent on producing winners, the pedigree must show only lines of ancestors in which each is known to have a strong degree of purity for the sought-for qualities.

Decidedly more data is needed in most pedigrees. Until such data can be supplied, the short pedigree going directly to the known superior breeders is the best pedigree. Genetic theory shows that the greatest hereditary influence is exerted by the parents themselves, and that this influence decreases rapidly in each more remote generation. Until tested, the most desirable breeding animal is one directly descended from known superior breeders. Each intermediate generation of ancestors of undetermined or unknown breeding powers lessens the probabilities of producing superior puppies.

In conclusion let me state Grossman's Cardinal Principles of Breeding:

1. Breed only to a dog that is old enough to have a history of producing top-flight stock.

2. Stay close within your own bloodline.

3. Be sure the breeding stock you use has an unbroken producing line.

4. Do not breed to the current winner unless he meets the above-stated standards.

5. Remember the "drag of the race" theory and keep your expectations within reason.

6. A dog and bitch need *not* necessarily complement each other physically (have complementary phenotypes). If through progeny testing the sire throws what you are looking for, breed that bitch to him.

7. Demand pedigrees that provide more than a list of names. Color, number of champions produced, and a description of the first two generations are a big help in evaluating a bloodline.

The Lakeland Terrier.

The Relationship Between Structural Traits and Type

We have all heard a variety of references to soundness. It may be, "I don't care for so and so, but he is a 'sound' dog," or "Isn't so and so lovely, and so 'sound' too." Various words have been used to define "sound." Some of them are: (1) free from flaw, defect, or decay; undamaged or unimpaired; (2) healthy; not weak or diseased; robust of body and mind; (3) firm; strong; safe; also, figuratively, secure; trustworthy; (4) solid in structure; also, firm in texture; stable. Continuing, there are flawless, perfect, sturdy, dependable, reliable, etc. Are you beginning to get the picture?

Each breed has been bred for a purpose, and as such, is required to have the stamina and traits necessary to perform its function, coupled with the necessary instincts. Thus, soundness should mean that the animal is able to carry out the job for which it is intended. It should mean that the animal is free from flaw, healthy (both mentally and physically), capable of lasting endurance, and dependable. Theoretically, the basic purpose behind breeding dogs for the show ring is to produce specimens that most nearly approach this ideal.

It should be pointed out that a sound dog is not necessarily championship material, since the word "show" itself would denote that a little bit more is required. Thus type and style are also prerequisites for the title. However, type and style alone do not (and should not) make a champion. It is practically impossible to divorce soundness from type completely, for it might be said that soundness is the cause and type the effect.

Generally speaking, when a breeder describes a sound specimen, he means the dog is without major fault, using the Standard as his guide. However, even the best dogs have traits that should not be perpetuated *actively*. It is wrong to conclude that because a top specimen possesses an undesirable trait, that trait can suddenly become good and desirable.

Unfortunately, there are those who completely ignore and bypass the breed Standard in frenzied attempts to secure winners. Standards have been criticized as being vague, as being obsolete in sections, etc. However, it is one thing to read a Standard and quite another thing to discern what the Standard actually means.

It would be impossible for any one breeder or judge to render an interpretation of a breed Standard and say, "This is it!" However, there are certain traits actively sought after by breeders even though the Standard plainly says those traits are not desirable. There also are prevailing ideas held by the fancy that have no basis in fact in the Standard.

Dr. E. H. Barnes, writing in *National Dog,* pointed out that it is common at dog shows to hear the winners criticized for failure to meet the Standard. The critics, quite sincerely, insist that the angulation was not in accordance with the Standard's requirements, that the eye color was too light, that the ears did not break as required, etc. No mention is made of the ways in which the losing dogs fail to measure up to the specifications of the Standard. It is, of course, unlikely that any specimen meets the requirements of his Standard exactly. The judge merely has rendered an opinion that the merits of the winner are more important than his demerits. The judge has cast up a mental balance sheet and has concluded that the assets of one dog exceed his liabilities by the greatest margin. Although these critics stop short of actually asserting that ribbons should be withheld from any dog which deviates from the Standard in any respect, that really is the implication.

One also hears the "experts" criticize dogs with respect to fine points which are desirable in the breed but about which the breed Standard is either non-specific or silent. These experts also are found voicing their views in the breed columns of various publications. Theirs is a pontifical posture which regards the breed Standard as merely a primer for novices. They, the experts, know what an excellent specimen really should look like. Too often these "ideal" characteristics can be seen only in one of their own dogs.

These attitudes are unrealistic in opposite ways. One displays a blind and naive worship of the breed Standard. The other treats it in a cavalier fashion. Both err in being extremes, one falling into a ditch on one side of the road while the other goes off on the opposite side. One assumes that breed Standards are immutable and eternally correct. The other ignores the fact that all of the requirements for a breed about which there is a formal consensus are incorporated in the Standard. All other statements about the characteristics which a breed "ought" to display or "should not" display are not fact but opinions only. Such statements should be characterized clearly as such. Forming or voicing opinions on matters not covered by an AKC Standard is neither wrong nor undesirable. On the contrary, forming or voicing such opinions is a good, progressive thing to do.

There is objection, however, to those who would modify the Standards by personal fiat, those who attempt to use their authority or position to subvert the legislative process established for the creation of Standards. There is such a process, and it contains safeguards against errors and excesses. Breed Standards, by their very nature (and AKC attitude toward radical changes), tend toward the conservative. Radical changes seldom appear, so stability of breed type is promoted. Just read the proposed changes in breed Standards as they appear in the *American Kennel Gazette* to assure yourself of this fact. Although provision is made for evolution and improvement of breeds, revolution is prevented. A dog that is acceptable today most likely will be acceptable next year.

Breed Standards necessarily are retrospective. They can only describe the most desirable features of dogs that have previously existed. They cannot anticipate the development of features which may occur and which may be valued as improvements. That such changes have occurred in the past cannot be doubted by anyone who has seen the pictures of great dogs of the past and has compared them with the great winners of the present.

Contrary to popular opinion, improvements in the breeds have not been the result of breeders working toward the realization of an absolute vision of perfection described in the breed Standards. Efforts to breed to type have maintained the past improvements; they have been conservative rather than progressive. It has been the latitude permitted by the breed Standards, allowing the exhibition of specimens with minor deviations from the former ideal, which has resulted in the evolution of the breeds. If the breed Standards allowed no deviation from past ideals of perfection, no progress could be achieved.

Although it has been argued that many of the changes which have occurred should not be characterized as improvements, it is obvious that these changes could not have come about without the approval of the judges, the breeders, and the dog-owning public. However, it should be clear that it is the dog, not the Standard, which leads the evolutionary process. The Standard is the ratchet which keeps us from slipping backwards.

In interpreting the breed Standard, a breeder or judge must draw his first impressions in his evaluation of any individual specimen. However, to understand a written breed Standard completely, a true student of the breed must first have a clear picture of what he considers "ideal." This mental picture will vary from person to person, of course, and will change considerably as a breeder becomes more experienced.

The novice breeder of any breed, in order to set such goals, must have a clear understanding of the skeletal make-up of that breed, since it is this basic structure that he will attempt to manipulate in order to breed the *type* which he conceives as "ideal." Let us analyze the basic skeleton as our source of reference.

The skull is formed by a series of complex bones, the make and shape of which will constitute head type.

The neck consists of seven large cervical vertebrae. The first two, the *atlas* and *axis*, found immediately back of the occiput, differ in shape from the other five, and it is the manner in which they are joined that governs the arch of the neck. These vertebrae are joined to the forequarters by a very complex network of muscles, and therefore exert a certain influence on the front gait.

The Hindquarter Assembly

The hindquarter assembly begins with the three bones which form the *os coxie*, or pelvic section. These bones meet to form the *acetabulum*, or the socket into which the upper end of the *femur*, or upper thigh, fits. The *patella*, or kneecap, is held in place with strong tendons over the stifle joint, which is between the upper and lower thighs. The lower thigh is formed by the *tibia*, or shinbone, and the *fibula*. The *tarsal bones* form the hock. The most important of these seven bones is the *os calcis*, or tip of the hock. It is to this bone that the very powerful muscles of the lower thigh are attached by means of the easily felt *achilles tendon*. The remaining bones are similar in number and name to those of the pastern and front paw.

The minor deviations which form the varieties of *types* presently being bred are the result of differences in bone length and differences in joint angles.

The Forequarter Assembly

The forequarter assembly begins with the shoulder blade or *scapula*, a flat bone, roughly triangular, with an easily felt ridge of bone extending down the middle, which ends in the *acromium*, a hooklike formation of bone which forms part of the shoulder joint, limiting the forward movement of the upper arm. The bone of the upper arm, or *humerus*, is located between the shoulder joint and the elbow joint. The bones of the lower arm, more commonly called the foreleg, are the *radius* and *ulna*, the latter being slightly longer, extending above the elbow joint and behind the humerus to form the *olecranon process*, or tip of the elbow, and is so constructed as to permit only forward movement of the foreleg. The *carpal bones*, forming the pastern joint, are comprised of seven small bones arranged in two rows. The *pisiform carpal* is a short rod of bone projected slightly at the back of the joint. Five *metacarpal bones* form the pastern, and five *phalanges* form the toes or paw. The fifth, known as the dewclaw, may be removed.

The correctly constructed forequarter assembly shows the shoulder blades to be long, sloping, and well laid back over the rib cage, with the points of the blades fine and close at the withers. The *spinal column* forms the top line and tail. The first eight *thoracic vertebrae* form the withers, while the next four comprise the back. The seven bones of the *lumbar vertebrae* form the loin. Just above the croup assembly are the three fused bones of the *sacrum*. The remaining bones of the tail are known as the *cocygeal vertebrae*. The *thoracic cavity* is formed by thirteen pairs of *ribs,* twelve of which are connected to the breast bone or *sternum.*

Various points of the English Setter.

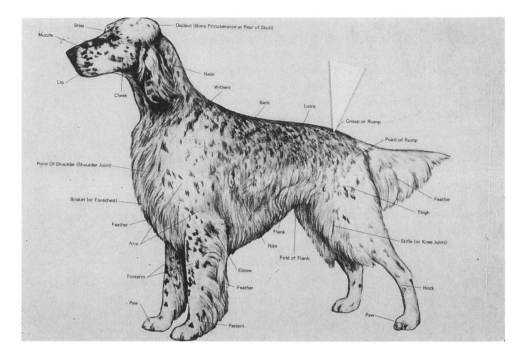

English Setter skeleton.

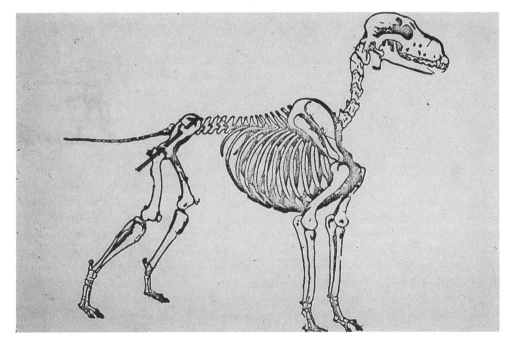

The Front Assembly

Placement of the scapula and the angle between it and the humerus create the major deviations in the front end assembly. Straight shoulders have plagued many breeds. There is good reason for this. In order to put the dog up on his legs and give him a more sporting look, the bones were spread, which resulted in rotating the shoulder forward at both the withers and elbow.

The other extreme is when the angle between the scapula and the humerus is less than "ideal." When the humerus is "laid back" too far, the specimen generally appears "low on leg," even though the bones of the forelegs may be equal in length to those of our "ideal." Differences in the length of the bones of the forelegs (radius and ulna), along with differences in the length and angle of the pasterns, add further type deviations.

The Rear Assembly

Prerequisite to good movement is balance between the front and rear assemblies. Most breeds begin their movement with rear quarter action, and if properly constructed in the shoulders and forelegs, a dog can reach forward without restriction in full stride to counterbalance the thrust from the rear.

The stifles should be well curved and turned neither in nor out. The hocks should be well bent and near the ground, and should be perfectly upright and parallel each with the other when viewed from behind. The dog should stand well up on the hocks.

It seems necessary to clarify a point concerning "well bent hocks." The reference is actually to the *joint* between the hock assembly and the bones of the lower thigh (*tibia* and *fibula*). The entire rear angulation requires this joint as well as the joint between the upper and lower thigh to be "well bent." There is a tendency to confuse "hindquarters" with the more restricted term "quarters." The latter term refers to the thigh muscle only and never to the lower part of the hind legs. One often hears the descriptive phrase, "powerful quarters," and this term may well be applicable, even though the overall hindquarters may be less than desirable in a variety of other ways.

Musculature has much to do with the overall quality and appearance of the hindquarters. Specimens with shorter lower thighs will generally have shorter, thicker muscles, which necessarily reduces the illusion of angulation. The over-angulated specimen will have longer, slighter muscles, and the illusion of angulation is therefore increased.

Generally, the degree of hindquarter angulation depends on how long the bones of the lower thigh are compared to the bone of the upper thigh. When these bones are nearly equal in length, the dog will appear to be very straight in stifle. The over-angulated specimen will have a much longer lower thigh.

Although the idea of the "well let down" or "close to the ground" hock is a bit vague, it seems that many authorities consider this as an overall part of "balance." The utilitarian value of the "well let down" hock is disputable, but there is little doubt that the longer hock, coupled with the shorter upper thigh bone and lower thigh, produces restricted, mincing rear action, lacking drive and covering little ground.

Viewed from behind, the "ideal" hind legs are straight, in that an imaginary line drawn vertically through the point of the buttocks, hock, pastern, and foot would center all four.

The most obvious faults to be considered when viewing the hindquarters from behind are cow hocks and open hocks.

After describing the various parts of the dog, it would be well to discuss what actually constitutes a "fault." To illustrate the obvious is easy—a bad mouth is a bad mouth and requires little or no discussion. To illustrate the subjective is more difficult in that there can be honest disagreement as to the proper shoulder lay back, the degree of angulation which constitutes proper angulation (both front and rear), etc. For this reason, many beginners become thoroughly confused when obtaining opinions from judges and breeders on any given dog. They often receive several conflicting, though honestly given, opinions on any one aspect of their dog's structure. Therefore, it is well to keep in mind that in most instances the only difference between a faulty trait and a desirable trait is the *degree* to which the trait is manifested. It is also conceivable that what is considered a fault in one specimen could be considered desirable in another. This is the key to the word "balance." A specimen may have a beautiful head when the head is viewed by itself—yet, when seen in relationship to the whole dog, the head may appear too large or too small; too refined or too coarse.

The blame for specific faults as well as credit for outstanding traits has been placed upon individual dogs and on entire bloodlines as well. It cannot be denied that prepotent individual dogs or bitches are certainly responsible for passing along their good and bad traits. However, it does seem unrealistic and prejudicial for any breeder to single out one bloodline and ascribe to it either credit or blame for generalized physical traits. A strain that is developed entirely within one specific kennel could have such influence, but to the outstanding studs of any bloodline are bred many bitches of diverse bloodlines and vice versa. Nevertheless, many prejudices are formed with respect to bloodlines and as a result many correct breedings have been bypassed and many improper ones have been made.

There appear to be specific characteristics that are both likely and unlikely to show up in certain types of dogs. It would almost seem that certain faults as well as certain desirable traits are linked more closely to type than to

The Samoyed.

The Welsh Corgi.

specific bloodlines within the breed. However, type could hardly be said to account for all faults and/or desirable traits which appear in a breed. Fronts provide many interesting illustrations, with a wide front, the pinched, narrow front, etc. As we have already noted, fronts cannot be divorced entirely from shoulders nor shoulders from neck, so certain mention of them must be made as well.

Faults associated with fronts appear to be linked closer to type than those concerned with any other aspect of the dog's structure.

Seldom, if ever, does one see a pinched, narrow front (with which one also associates shelliness and an extremely smooth blend of neck and shoulders) on a heavy boned, blocky type dog. Seldom, if ever, does one see the type front that one could "run a Mack truck through" (with which one also associates a loaded shoulder and thick, short neck) on a racy, streamlined type dog. It is not commonplace to see the blocky dog with a "Terrier" front nor the racy dog with an overabundance of set-back at the elbow.

Faults associated with rear quarters are not so closely linked with type. Nevertheless, some measure of proportion does exist, and it is conceivable that before many more generations pass, a definite linkage may be proven. Rear over-angulation on the blocky dog is not nearly so common as it is on the racy dog. Lack of angulation on the racy dog is not so common as it is on the blocky dog. The faulty top line that gives an appearance of a crouch is more often associated with the racy dog (as a result of over-angulation) than with the blocky dog. When angulation is not responsible for the faulty top line, the responsibility usually rests on pelvic rotation.

As we learned in an earlier chapter, the relationship between faults and/or desirable traits and type could be due mainly to "linkage." Linkage is a tendency of certain hereditary characters to appear together because the genes for such characters are located on the same chromosome. Sometimes the two or more characters which are linked together are both good—such as the black color in some breeds that is linked with heavy coat. Oftentimes one character is desirable whereas the other is not—as in the case of a long neck linked with a long body. It is easy to see why the faddist-type breeders can leave behind them a heritage which in the long run may prove debilitating to a breed. In their desire to obtain a certain trait quickly, they are likely to select a specimen which is outstanding in that trait but may have other undesirable traits. Constant line breeding and/or inbreeding to such a specimen may set up a pattern of linkage.

No one would deny that the first recorded specimens of any breed would bear little resemblance to our present-day specimens. In order to produce our modern-day dogs from the original ones, it was inevitable that certain sacrifices had to be made along the way. In any breeding program, the emergence of a desired trait usually results in some amount of loss in a pre-existing desired trait. The object, of course, is to keep that loss confined to a minimum and to the least important aspects of the dogs' body structure. The good can be utilized to advantage by the astute breeder, while the undesirable remain a challenge to the dedicated.

The Golden Retriever.

Gait

A typical Standard defines movement as follows: "Prerequisite to good movement is balance between the front and rear assemblies. He drives with his strong, powerful rear quarters and is properly constructed in the shoulders and forelegs so that he can reach forward without constriction in a full stride to counterbalance the driving force from the rear. Above all, his gait is coordinated, smooth and effortless. The dog must cover ground with his action and excessive animation should never be mistaken for proper gait."

To understand what this breed Standard means, one needs to understand that movement or action is the crucial test of conformation. The principal propulsive power is furnished by the hind legs, perfection of action being found in the specimen possessing long thighs and muscular second thighs well bent at the stifles, which allow a strong forward thrust of the hocks. Viewed from the front, the forelegs should form a continuation of the straight line of the front, the feet being the same distance apart as the elbows. One of the best word pictures of this action was given by Milo Vickey, writing in the *Cocker Spaniel Visitor*. He states:

"It's not easy to explain dog movement with words, but if one will visualize himself standing in the middle of a railroad track with a locomotive engine moving to and from him, then replace the engine with a dog, he'll get a pretty accurate idea of correct fore and aft gait. It will be apparent that when a dog is coming at you, nothing should be visible but his head, chest and front legs. The legs should reach forward at each stride, perfectly straight from the shoulders, with feet absolutely parallel to the legs, as though travelling on a single track. If either foot goes off the track inside or outside, or toes in or out, it's due to structural faults. If you get glimpses of its hind feet, side, rump, and tail, it's sidewinding or rolling, both due to structural faults.

"Going away, nothing should be visible but the back of the dog's head, the top of his back to buttocks and his hind legs, with feet traveling well apart and hocks staying absolutely perpendicular at each stride. If the feet go off the track inside or outside, or toe in or out, he has structural faults in his rear quarters. If you get glimpses of his front feet, side of head or shoulder, he's sidewinding or rolling."

The dog at rest or in a show pose appears entirely different from the dog in motion. When a dog is standing, his two front paws *should not* be pointing directly forward. Were they to do so, the dog would toe in when moving. At a stand, the front paws should be rotated *slightly* outward, and by slightly is meant that more of the inside of the paw is visible than the outside—not that the paw should actually turn out. This is nature's way of compensating for the fact that the dog cannot turn its front paw in the way a person can turn his hand by way of wrist action. Breeders who are not aware of this fact try to compensate for it by trimming the front feet so that they appear to be facing straight forward. Breeders who are aware of this fact, often do likewise in deference to judges who lack this knowledge.

Getting back to the dog in action, it is necessary to understand why a breed was bred to move as it does. To do so, one needs to know the purpose for which the dog was bred. As contrasted to the Terriers, which employ their front feet for digging, and the Hound breeds, many of which also employ their front feet for burrowing, and which are not required to have excessive speed, the Sporting breeds employ their front legs much as a rudder on a ship—that is, for navigational purposes.

There are many different means of locomotion. The three most commonly seen are: (1) the walk, (2) the trot, and (3) the pace. To gain a clearer understanding, all three will be described and discussed. It should be emphasized in the beginning that the trot is the basic gait and that the pace is incorrect.

In all types of locomotion, body support, to be efficient, must be under the center of gravity of the body. Visualize, then, an imaginary line drawn through the center of the dog's body from the tip of the nose to the end of the tail. It will be on this line that action will take place.

This may sound illogical, for the dog stands with its legs very nearly perpendicular to the ground. When the dog starts a slow walk, its legs remain pretty much in this same position. Because the eye can follow a slow walk but cannot follow fast movement, it is thought that perpendicular leg action applies to all gaits. But this is not possible when the body is supported by only one or two legs. Aside from the change in speed, the basic difference between the walk and the trot or the pace is that at the walk the dog's body is supported at three points, while at the trot or pace it is supported at two. The only exception in this is for a fraction of a second in the walk when the second foot is leaving the ground and the full support rests on a diagonal or lateral two-leg support. The time involved is not long enough to upset the dog's balance.

Figure 8.

Because it is the walk that can be observed by the naked eye, it is easy to see why it is assumed that this is the natural gait of the dog when moving. Based upon this popular misconception, structural faults, which in a true gait are easily discernible, are never truly identified by some because of their lack of awareness of the components of proper gait, which do not come into play in the walk.

The walk is a gait of convenience, not of efficiency. An airplane racing down a runway with its nose wheel down is employing this method of gathering speed until its nose wheel lifts off the ground and the plane is in a true flight attitude. So it is with a dog, as it gathers speed and shifts to its truly efficient, aerodynamically sound gait, the trot.

As in the Standard Bred Harness Racing Horse, the trot consists of placing the left front leg forward simultaneously with the right rear leg so that balance is maintained on one point on each side. As the dog follows through, the opposing two legs (right front and left rear) take over to propel it forward. The pattern of "single tracking" takes over at this point, which means moving forward on one line of progress with the least muscular waste. This is in contrast to "double tracking" with the perpendicular leg action of the slow walk.

In the trot, the dog must put its pads down under the center of gravity, in line with that of locomotion, and the back feet must move in the same line with the front feet, for both front and back feet are going to the same place. In order to do this, the front legs angle inward toward the mythical center line as the dog increases its speed. The angle inward toward the center should be at the joint of the upper arm and shoulder blade (the withers) and must continue to the heel pad with a straight column of bones with no inward or outward break. Back leg action should be on a straight column of bone support from the hip joint to the heel pad, and this, as in the front, also angles inward toward the center line.

Another type of gait often seen, while correct for the Standard Bred Pacer, is incorrect for the dog. This is the pacing gait. The pace is an artificial gait even for the Standard Bred Horse and must be taught. Some dogs use this form of locomotion as a solution for a structural defect which makes the trot uncomfortable for them. The pacing gait is best described as two legs on one side of the dog moving simultaneously (left front and left rear), forcing the center of gravity and support to their opposite members (right front and right rear). This results in a rocking or rolling motion even though effectively propelling the dog forward.

Since it has been established that the trot is the natural gait of the dog, the following discussion of deviations of proper movement will be made with reference to the trot.

In the trot, all dogs try to get their pads under the center of gravity whether their legs are constructed properly or not. Dogs with front legs that have an inward bend of pastern are inclined to move close. The dog with pasterns that bow outward will sometimes stand straight, but in motion the pasterns will bow outward from the force of concussion taking place in landing. A dog with a shoulder assembly that is carried mostly on the front of the rib cage (lacking lay back and set back), with shoulder points too close together and with elbows moving out from the body, will usually swing its front legs in an arc (to reach the center line) coming toward one.

A dog which stands correctly but which is cow hocked when in motion, is compensating for a structural fault that doesn't allow the dog to get its pads under the center of gravity naturally. The opposite of this is when the hocks bow outward, tending to turn in an outward arc. These deviations of proper gait lack the support of a straight column of bones, and an inferior mover is the result.

All dogs will overreach with their back legs unless they are extremely short-strided or long in the body for their height. This overreaching is called "crabbing" *only* when it results in taking the back action either to the right or to the left of the line of front action. In other words, when it creates two lines of progress which definitely could conflict with one another on turns and which are not efficiently coordinated. The main cause of crabbing is not the overreaching, which almost all dogs do, but, rather, the "timing" of front and back action. If the front action is timed sufficiently ahead of the rear, the dog will not need to side-step in his overreach, for the front pad will be out of the way and allow the back one to come in line with it.

When both rear pads go either to the right or to the left of the front action, the dog does not move in a straight line and the dog is called a "sidewinder." Sidewinding is a form of crabbing and is illustrated.

Sidewinding is quite common and when it occurs upon occasion, it might be the result of improper training or improper handling or both. It could also be due simply to the fact that the dog started off on the wrong foot, so to

The Bichon Frise.

The Wire Fox Terrier.

speak. A dog that sidewinds constantly, however, is something else.

Perhaps the rear pads do not both go to either the right or the left of the front action. Both rear pads might go to the outside (one going right and one going left) resulting in spraddled rear action. In this case, stilted rear action with lack of drive results, and the front, rather than steering, is pulling the back along.

Several different structural faults can cause the faulty timing of front and back action which results in crabbing. For example, straight, poorly angulated fronts ahead of normal, well-angulated rears cause faulty timing. The reach of the front leg is governed by the set of the shoulder blade. Therefore, straight shoulder blades result in a short, stilted stride that usually has trouble keeping out of the way of and fully coordinated with properly angulated rears. Shoulder blades of normal angulation also cannot keep the front out of the way of over-angulated, long striding rears.

The dog with a well-angulated front and a straight rear usually moves with a shorter rear stride and elevated rump. He does not crab or move out of line, for his hood front can stay out of the way quite easily. There is, however, no drive in the rear quarters that lack angulation, and the front is employed to pull the dog forward.

Unfortunately, breeders often encourage straight fronts and/or over-angulated rears in their desire to create an artificially extreme top line. This must necessarily result in a dog that moves poorly. The key to correct gait is the word *balance*. The front angulation must balance the rear angulation if the desired result is a good mover. Believe it or not, a dog with a straight front and a straight rear is a better moving dog than one with a well-angulated front and a straight rear or a straight front and a well-angulated rear. The reason the dog with the straight front and a straight rear is not desirable, even though the specimen may be a good mover, is because such a dog does not possess the endurance capacity of the specimen with good angulation in both front and rear.

Occasionally, a judge puts an extreme amount of emphasis on the dog's front and all but ignores the rear, whereas another judge will do just the opposite. Both are missing the point – *balance*. And, in asking that the dogs be gaited, such judges are merely going through the motions, for by their emphasis, or lack of emphasis, they have revealed their lack of knowledge. The foregoing should settle the point of any discussion as to what is more important – the front end of the dog or the rear end.

In addition to the proper and/or improper bone structure and construction, other factors have an effect on a dog's gait. One such factor is footing. Burrs in the grass, an uneven turf, or a slippery floor can all contribute to making a properly moving dog look faulty. A dog that is poorly trained or that is not feeling well and is fighting the lead will do many things that are not indicative of its true gait. There is also the aspect of illusion that is reflected in the viewer's eye as improper gait, but in reality is not. Two excellent examples of this are the leg markings on black and tan dogs, and uneven growth of coat in puppies, resulting in more coat on one side of the legs than the other. In addition, dogs with extremely heavy coats that fly in all directions and dogs that are improperly trimmed with too much or too little hair left in certain areas appear to have an improper gait.

Perhaps the best way to understand what is correct gait is to be aware of what is not. In *rope-walking*, the dog usually has a rather "pinched" front and therefore places one paw almost directly in front of the other. This faulty form of travel is also called *weaving* and *plaiting*, and the dog does look as if it could braid a rope in transit. These latter terms are usually used when the dog throws its paws more than in the ordinary *rope-walking* movement, and in exaggerated cases the paws actually seem to cross.

Rope-walking hind action is similar to that described above regarding front movement. Here the dog tends to "single track," placing one paw directly in the path of the other. Perhaps it might be wise to reaffirm the fact that the

The Saluki.

faster the trot, the greater the stride, and the greater the need for a dog to seek the center of gravity. A wise exhibitor will remember to keep the speed reasonable when moving his dog away from the judge, so that the dog will be given every opportunity to display correct movement.

One aspect of rear movement which is difficult to evaluate is just how far apart the hocks should be when the dog is moving and is viewed from the rear. Some dogs move very close, only one to two inches separating the hocks in action. Conversely, there are dogs with "more than enough air between the hocks," as some judges might describe it—and usually with admiration. If asked to evaluate two equally good specimens which vary greatly in this respect, what would be your decision—the dog with hocks that are parallel in action but with only two inches separating them when moving, or the dog with six inches between the hocks going away? This type of decision must be made by judges throughout the country at every show. Perhaps somewhere between lies the right answer.

It is understandable that no two individuals—whether they be breeders, judges, or spectators—observe the same animal in the same way. A head which appears pleasant to one individual may be perceived as unpleasant by another, and so it goes down the line of the other body traits. Does this hold true with respect to the gait of a dog as well, or does lack of basic knowledge cause breeders to condone deviations from correct gait? Experienced breeders have been known to exclaim with delight at ringside while watching a dog strut in the ring, throwing its front legs up, "hackney-style." Showy though this may be, it's not correct. Yet, many relish and applaud this type of movement!

There is also the dog that travels the proverbial "mile a minute," deluding most spectators (and some judges) into believing that it can really move, whereas, under that flying coat, its action is not true but faulty!

Unfortunately, too, upon occasion, there is that gorgeous, stacked specimen that can't or won't move, but that, nevertheless, gets the nod for winners.

It has often been said that a properly constructed dog moves correctly, that it cannot help but move correctly because its bone structure has been assembled correctly, and conversely, that an inferior or faulty specimen will not move correctly. Based upon the above premise, gait as a "trait" deserves optimum consideration and top priority.

In writing about gait, the problems of terminology become apparent. Obviously, there is no set of standardized terms describing the deviations involved. One breeder describes a certain action by one term whereas another breeder describes the same action by another term. This leads to confusion and should be taken into account.

In this chapter an attempt has been made to show the link between characteristics of gait and conformation, and to ascribe faulty gait to faulty body construction. However, it is not structure alone that makes a winner. If it were, picking winners at the race track would be an easy thing, once we understood conformation completely. Thoroughbreds and Greyhounds may have "their day," only to be "out of the money" the next time. Their conformation has not changed. Perhaps their condition was not quite at its peak. But more than likely, failure was due to their "state of mind"—a quality the best judge would find difficult to anticipate. Therefore, show dogs must be judged "on the day."

A final word regarding balance in action seems appropriate. Oftentimes one hears the expression "all of a piece," which really sums it up, in that the dog described is well balanced both in stance and in action.

Ch. Tagalong's Winter Frost.

THE END

The Cairn Terrier.

Glossary

Afghan Hound	Descended from the Persian Greyhounds of antiquity. Hunts by sight. A member of the Hound Group.
Afterbirth	The placenta attached to the sac in which puppy is born.
American Kennel Club (AKC)	The governing and registration body along with the United Kennel Club for purebred dogs.
AKC Field Representative	AKC's official representative on site at dog shows. Interprets and monitors adherence to rules. Evaluates judges, administers judge's tests and answers exhibiter's questions.
AKC Gazette	A monthly publication of the AKC containing articles, statistics about shows and registrations and official and proposed actions of the AKC.
All-Breed Club	A club devoted to the showing and breeding of purebred dogs. Membership is open to breeders and exhibiters of all breeds. Holds championship shows.
All-Breed Show	An AKC-approved show in which all AKC-approved breeds can be exhibited.
American Water Spaniel	Ancestry is clouded but suggests Irish Water Spaniel and Curly Coated Retriever. A good little hunter. A member of the Sporting Group.
Aqueous humor	The watery fluid present in the anterior chamber of the eye.
Arbiters	Dog-show judges.
Artificial Insemination	Impregnating a bitch with frozen or extended sperm.
Awkward Phase	Rapid-growth period for a puppy usually associated with plaining out of the head features. Occurs from three to eight months.
Back	That portion of the topline starting just behind the withers and ending where the croup and loin join.
Backcrossing	To cross a first generation hybrid with one of the parents.
Baiting	Keeping a dog alert in the ring through the use of food or a favorite toy.
Balance	Overall fitting of the various parts of the dog to give a picture of symmetry and correct interaction.
Basenji	An African barkless dog. A member of the Hound Group.
Best In Show	Top award in an all-breed show.
Best Of Breed	Best of that breed in an all-breed or specialty show. In the all-breed show it goes on to compete for higher awards.
Best Of Variety	Top award for breeds that are divided by variety based on coat, color or size.
Best Of Winners	Defeats other sex winner. Captures that sex's points if greater than its own on that day.
Bitch	A female dog.

Bite	Position of upper and lower teeth in relation to each other. Various breed standards call for different kinds of bite often based on function.
Bloodline	A specific strain or type within a breed.
Bottle Feeding	Using a doll bottle to feed formula to a newborn puppy.
Breaking Point	Limit to what the dog can endure.
Breech Presentation	Puppy born feet first rather than head first. Can cause whelping difficulties as puppy may get turned sideways in the birth canal.
Breed Ring	Exhibition area where dogs are judged by breed.
Brittany	A leggy, close-coupled dog that is an excellent combination hunter, pointer and retriever. A member of the Sporting Group.
Brucellosis	A sexually transmitted disease or infection.
Brussels Griffon	Many small dogs went into the creation of this breed. His popularity grows. A member of the Toy Group.
Bulbus Glandis	A portion of the penis closest to the testicles that fills with blood to three times its size during the sexual act. It serves to "tie" the male and female together while the male ejaculates sperm.
Caesarean Section	Removing puppies from the womb surgically.
Cairn Terrier	Feisty little terrier with a great love of people. His breeding is handed down from the old working terriers on the British Isle of Skye. A member of the Terrier Group.
Campaigning A Dog	Seriously exhibiting a champion to compete for top honors in his breed, group and top 10 all-breed honors.
Canine Herpes Virus	An infection in puppies caused by an infected dam. A leading cause of puppy mortality.
Canine Parvovirus	Myocardial forms attack only puppies. Severe, often fatal reaction. Cardial form attacks older dogs.
Cataract	A cloudiness or opacity of the lens.
Caveat emptor	Latin for "let the buyer beware."
CERF	Canine Eye Registry Foundation
Championship	A title earned by winning 15 points under AKC rules, including two major awards of 3, 4 or 5 points under two different judges.
Championship Points	Awarded on the basis of the number of dogs competing by sex and breed. Each part of the country has a different point rating based upon previous year's entries. Maximum number of points per show is 5. Fifteen are needed for a championship, with two major awards among them.
Cheetah	The fastest land animal for short distances.
Choroid	The part of the uvea that nourishes the retina with blood.
Chromosome	Cell nucleus of all multicell organisms that contain DNA. Comprising the genes of that species.

Ciliary body	The part of the uvea that produces the aqueous humor.
Collie	A medium-sized dog (rough-coated and smooth-coated varieties) that was developed to herd sheep. A member of the Herding Group.
Colostrum	A part of the bitch's milk which provides puppies immunity from many viral and bacterial diseases.
Cocker Spaniel	Smallest member of the Sporting Group. Bred to flush and retrieve upland game.
Congenital	Present at birth.
Conjunctiva	The tissue lining the eyelids which is continuous with the eyeball.
Contour	Silhouette or profile, form or shape.
Conformation	The form and structure of the various parts to fit a standard.
Corgi (Welsh)	Two varieties are Cardigan and Pembroke. A small, hardy dog used to herd cattle. A member of the Herding Group.
Cornea	The clear membrane covering the front of the eyeball.
Corneal dystrophy	White opacities in the cornea.
Crabbing	Moving with body at an angle with the line of travel like a land crab. Also called sidewinding.
Crapshoot Theory	Author's definition of anything can happen at any time in purebred dogs.
Crate	A metal, plastic or wood kennel (in various sizes). Dogs may sleep and travel in them.
Cropped	Trimming the ears to fit a breed pattern.
Cryptorchid	A male dog with neither testicle descended. Ineligible to compete at AKC shows.
Dachshund	A small, longish dog bred to go to ground after game. A member of the Hound Group.
Dalmatian	The black and white spotted dog. A member of the Non-Sporting Group.
Dam	Mother of a litter of puppies.
Degeneration	Used in reference to inbreeding. After primary generations, stock shows reduction in size, bone and vigor.
Dehydration	Loss of body fluids - may lead to death.
Developmental Phases	Stages through which puppies grow.
Dew Claws	Hardy nails above pastern. Most breeds have them removed. In many breeds they are not present.
DNA	Deoxyribonucleic acid - genes are made up of DNA. They are regarded as the building blocks of life.
Doberman	A working dog originally bred in Germany. A quick and strong animal. A member of the Working Group.

Docking	The clipping off of the tail to a prescribed length to meet a breed standard.
Dominant	Color or characteristic that covers up all others which are recessive to it.
Dropper-feeding	Feeding formula to newborn puppies through the use of a small medicine dropper.
Eclampsia	An attack of convulsions during and after pregnancy.
Ectropian	Rolling out of the eyelid.
Egg	A female reproductive cell.
Electroretinography	Measure of the electrical impulses within the retina.
Entropian	Rolling in of the eyelid.
Estrus	Period of bitch's heat cycle when she is ready to breed.
Exhibiters	People who show their dogs.
Expression	Facial aspect or countenance.
Eye For A Dog	An old dog-game expression meaning the ability to select a good dog without a lot of effort.
Fading Puppy Syndrome	A malnourished puppy due to loss of electrolytes. May lead to death.
Fallopian Tubes	Conduits for eggs from ovary to uterus.
Fetus	The growing puppy within the womb.
Filial Regression	The tendency of offspring to regress toward mediocrity if controlled breeding is not carried out.
Finishable	A dog capable of completing its championship.
Fluid Pressure	Pressure caused by pumping action of the heart as the blood flows through the veins and arteries.
Forechest	The point of the thorax that protrudes beyond the point of the shoulder.
Foreface	That part of the muzzle from just below the forehead to the nose.
First Call Dog	Handler selects one of his dogs to show at group level if he has more than one breed winner in that group. Same applies to handler who wins two or more groups when selecting dog for Best In Show. Usually selected by client or dog's seniority or additional money paid for that honor.
Gaiting	Walking or trotting a dog to discern proper movement.
Gene	The smallest unit of hereditary information.
Genetics	The study of the science of heredity.
Genotype	Genetic term meaning the unseen genetic makeup of the dog.
Gestation	The organic development of the puppy within the uterus.
German Shepherd	A versatile working dog. Originally bred in Germany to guard and herd. A member of the Herding Group.

German Shorthaired Pointer	A continental gun dog. Bred for game. A member of the Sporting Group.
German Wirehaired Pointer	A Hunter-Pointer-Retriever breed with a harsh, wiry coat. A member of the Sporting Group.
Glaucoma	An elevation of the pressure within the eye.
Golden Retriever	A mid-size, heavy-coated dog used for both water and upland game. A member of the Sporting Group.
Gordon Setter	A black and tan hunting dog. Heavier than the English and Irish Setters. A member of the Sporting Group.
Gravity	The pull of the earth upon a body.
Great Dane	A very large dog whose history shows it to have been used to hunt wild boar and as a war dog. A member of the Working Group.
Greyhound	The oldest pure breed in existence. He hunts by sight. A member of the Hound Group.
Groom	To comb, clip and brush a dog.
Grooming Table	A specially designed (often foldable) table with matting for grooming and training dogs.
Handler	Person showing the dog.
Handler's Apprentice	A person learning the handler's trade.
Handler's Assistant	Usually a person who has graduated to the next rung on the career ladder.
Handlers Guild	An association of professional handlers stressing professionalism.
Heat	A bitch coming into season so she can be bred. Usually twice a year.
Heredity	The sum of what a dog inherits from preceding generations.
Heritable	A trait capable of being genetically transferred to offspring.
Hetrozygous	Non-dominant for a trait or color. Carries both dominant and recessive genes for a variety of traits.
Homozygous	Dominant for a trait or color. Carries no recessive for that characteristic.
Hybrid	Dogs who have gene pairs – non-dominant.
Hybrid Vigor	The extra vigor or development exhibited by offspring of an outcross.
Hyperthermia	A chilling of the puppies which is liable to cause death.
Idling Speed	Energy consumed when body is not in kinetic motion.
Inbreeding	Very close familial breeding, i.e., brother X sister, father X daughter or son X mother.
Inguinal Ring	Muscles of the abdominal cavity (groin) that prevent adult testes from going back up into abdominal cavity and, which can prevent their proper descent in puppies.
Intraocular pressure	The pressure inside the eye.

Irish Setter	A tall, mahogany-red dog of striking style. A hunting dog of the Sporting Group.
Irish Water Spaniel	An exuberant, red, curly-coated hunting dog with a monkey-like tail. An excellent hunter and a member of the Sporting Group.
Irish Wolfhound	This is a massive dog. Bred to chase and kill wolves he is now a gentle pet. A member of the Hound Group.
Judge	A person approved by AKC or UKC to judge various breeds.
Kinetic Energy	Relating to the motion of bodies and the forces and energy associated therewith.
Komondor	An Hungarian sheep and cattle dog. Excellent as a guardian of the flock or herd. A member of the Working Group.
Labor	The act of attempting to whelp puppies.
Labrador Retriever	A wonderful water retriever. His otter tail is unique. A member of the Sporting Group.
Lakeland Terrier	A dog of English origin bred to kill fox that hound pack had run to ground in rocky den. A member of the Terrier Group.
Lead	A strap or cord fastened around dog's neck to guide him. Also called leash.
Lead Training	Teaching the dog to walk and trot properly so as to best exhibit his conformation. May also be used for control.
Lens	The crystalline structure in the eye located behind the iris.
Levers	Angles to improve multiplication of force.
Line Breeding	Breeding closely within a family of dogs, i.e., grandfather to granddaughter.
Match Show	A practice show that serves as a training ground for young dogs, prospective judges and members of the dog club holding the show.
Malnutrition	Lacking the proper nourishment to provide normal healthy growth.
Gregor Mendel	A monk in 19th Century Czechoslovakia who discovered the mathematical formulas for the inheritance of color and size in sweet peas and launched the science of genetics.
Metritis	A uterine infection in the dam that can transmit bacterial infection to an entire litter.
Monorchid	A male dog with only one testicle descended. Ineligible to compete in AKC shows.
Monstrosities	Severe, often lethal deviations from expected structure, usually brought out through inbreeding.
Nasal Aspirator	A suction device for sucking mucous from infant puppies' nasal passages.
Nasolacrimal apparatus	The tear duct system which runs from the eyes to the nose.
Natural Selection	Charles Darwin's theory of how species evolve.
Neonatal	New born.
Neonatal Septecemia	An infection in newborn puppies picked up by staphylococcus germs in the dam's vaginal tract.

Non-Dominant	An animal with characteristics that are mostly recessive.
Nuclear sclerosis	Scarring of the lens with age.
Nucleus	The center of a cell. Contains chromosomes and is essential to all cell functions, such as cell division for reproduction.
Otter Hound	A Standard-Poodle-sized dog originally bred in England to hunt otters. A member of the Hound Group.
Outcrossing	Matings of animals that are somewhat inbred to unrelated animals to reinstate vigor and substance.
Ovulation	The female process of creating eggs for reproduction.
Ovum	An egg ready for sperm to fertilize it.
Pannus	Layer of pigment and blood vessels growing across the cornea.
Parasites	Infestations of lice, ticks or fleas as well as internal infestation of various worms.
Pastern	The body's shock absorber. Located at the juncture where the paw meets foreleg.
Pedigree	Hierarchical listing of ancestors. Best used when combined with photos and anecdotal data.
PHA	Professional Handlers Association. A group stressing ethics and training.
Pharaoh Hound	One of the oldest domesticated dogs in written history. Images of this type of dog are found on ancient Egyptian paintings. A member of the Hound Group.
Phenotype	The actual outward appearance as can be seen–opposite of genotype.
Placenta	A vascular organ that links the fetus to the dam's uterus. Nourishes and mediates fetal change. Also known as an afterbirth.
Plaining Out	Usually occurs as head changes because of the loss of puppy teeth.
Pointer	A breed of dog used for pointing birds. The modern dog comes from England by way of Spain. A member of the Sporting Group.
Poodle	This popular breed comes in three sizes, Standard, Miniature and Toy. The Standard and Miniature are to be found in the Non-Sporting Group with their diminutive cousin in the Toy Group.
Portuguese Water Dog	An ancient working dog who was bred to help herd fish into nets and act as a courier between ships. A member of the Working Group.
Postpartum	After birth.
Pounding	Results when front stride is shorter than rear. Hindquarter thrust forces front feet to strike the ground before they are fully prepared to absorb shock.
Pregnant	Term used for bitch carrying puppies.
Producing Power	The ability to stamp one's get with positive features of championship caliber.
Proestrus	First part of heat cycle.

Professional Handler	A person paid to show and train dogs.
Profile	Outline or silhouette.
Progressive Retinal Atrophy (PRA)	Atrophy or degeneration of the retina.
Proportion	Relationship, ratio of one body part to another.
Proven Sire	Male dog that has enough offspring to judge his potency.
Puli	An Hungarian shepherd dog. His name means driver. A member of the Herding Group.
Puppy Septicemia	Bacterial infection caused by a mastitis infection in the dam. Often fatal if not treated immediately.
Purebred	A dog whose sire and dam are of the same breed and whose lineage is unmixed with any other breed.
Quarantine	A period in which a dog is isolated from other animals while being observed for communicable diseases.
Recessive	Color or trait which is not dominant and must link up with another recessive for expression.
Reserve Winners	Dog or bitch that is runner up to the winner. May gain points if winner is ineligible or is disqualified.
Retina	The pigmented layer lining the back of the eye.
Ribs	The thorasic vertebrae that surround the heart and lungs.
Rin Tin Tin	A German Shepherd Dog who was a star in the early days of the film industry.
Ringside Pickup	When a handler takes on a dog on the day of the show rather than having him in his traveling string of dogs.
Ring Stewards	Persons assisting the judge by assembling classes, giving out armbands, arranging ribbons, and in general, being an assistant for the judge.
Russian Wolfhound	Officially known as the Borzoi. Hunts by sight. A member of the Hound Group.
Sac	Membrane housing puppy within uterus.
Saluki	A tall, sleek dog that hunts by sight. A member of the Hound Group.
Sclera	The white of the eye.
Scrotum	Housing for male dogs testicles.
Sheltie	Known as the Shetland Sheepdog. A working Collie in miniature. A member of the Herding Group.
Show Pose	Setting a dog in a position to exhibit its conformation. Also called stacking.
Showmanship	The bravura exhibition of a dog.
Show Superintendent	A person (organization) hired by club giving show to manage and run the show.

Sidewinding	See Crabbing.
Sire	Father of a litter.
Special	A champion dog or bitch competing for Best of Breed or Best of Variety award. A class for champions only.
Specialty Club	A club devoted to fanciers of one specific breed of dog.
Specialty Show	An AKC-approved show for members of a single breed only.
Spermatozoa	Motile sperm from male dog.
Spoon-Feeding	Slowly feeding milk formula to baby puppy using a small spoon.
Springer (Spaniel)	Two different breeds included in this appellation. English Springer and Welsh Springer. Both members of the Sporting Group.
Stacking	See Show Pose.
Standard	An official description of the breed developed by that breed's parent club and approved by AKC.
Structural Design	The blueprint from which the originators of a breed sought to create a dog for the task at hand.
Subcutaneous Muscle	That type of muscle which lies directly under the skin.
Symmetry	A pleasing balance of all parts.
Tardive	Appearing at some time after birth.
Test Breeding	A mating usually of a parent of unknown genotype and one of a known genotype to reveal what characteristics the unknown one will throw.
Tie	The locking together of the dog and bitch during mating caused by the swelling of the bulbis glandis just behind the penis bone.
Topline	That portion of the dog's outline from the withers to the set on of the tail.
Toxic Milk Syndrome	Toxic bacteria in dam's milk having a toxic effect on nursing puppies.
Tube-Feeding	Inserting a tube down the esophagus into the puppy's stomach to release milk formula slowly.
Type	Characteristics distinguishing a breed.
Unbroken Line	A pedigree line of continuous producers down to the current sire or dam.
Umbilical cord	A cord that connects the fetus with the placenta attaching at the puppy's navel.
Uvea	A blood vessel rich layer consisting of the iris, ciliary body, and choroid.
Vaccinations	Shots administered to ward off certain diseases.
Vizsla	A continental gun dog from Hungary bred for hunting, pointing and retrieving. A member of the Sporting Group.
Vulva	External parts (lips) of bitch's genital organs.
Wean	Gradually changing puppies to solid food away from mother's milk.

Weimaraner	A grey hunting dog from Germany who points his game. A member of the Sporting Group.
Whelping Box	Where you wish to have the litter born (and the bitch doesn't). Used later for nursing bitch and her puppies.
Winners (Dog & Bitch)	Best from all the competing classes. Wins points toward championship.
Withers	Highest point on the shoulder blades.
WYSIWYG	What you see is what you get. A desktop publishing term. Here applied to a dominant animal who throws the characteristics you see.

Bibliography

Articles:

Allen, Michael (ed.), *American Cocker Magazine*, numerous articles from several issues.

Ardnt, T. K., "Breeders Forum," *Akita World*, December 1985.

Asseltyne, Claire, "Form Follows Function," *The Great Dane Reporter*, May/June, July/August, Sept/Oct, 1980.

Beaver, Sandra, "This is a Test," *Dog Week*, June 20, 1988, pgs 35-36.

Beckman, D.V.M., Samuel, "Cesarean Section," *Focus Magazine*, Vol 2 No 2 1990.

Bierman, Ann, "Feeding Your Puppy," *The Golden Retriever Review*, March 1987.

Brown, Russell V., "Nutrition and Feeding of the Basenji," *The Basenji*, Feb. 1987.

Burnham, Patricia Gail, "Breeding, Litter Size and Gender," *American Cocker Review*, 1981.

Clothier, Suzanne, "Selecting for Vigor," AKC *Gazette*, June 1987, pgs 46-57.

Companion Animal News, publication of Morris Animal Foundation, Spring 1990, "Genetic Study Seeks Answers for Dogs."

Companion Animal News, publication of Morris Animal Foundation, Summer 1990, "Saving Dogs Through Better Behavior."

Consumer Reports, "The Telltale Gene," July 1990, pgs 483-487.

Donnely, Mary, "Cesarean Section...The Home Care," *Min Pin Monthly*, March 1987.

Dunbar, Ian, "Nature vs. Nurture," AKC *Gazette*, October 1990, pgs 30-31.

Dunbar, Ian, "Puppy Aptitude Testing," AKC *Gazette*, February 1989, pgs 24-26.

Engel, Litzi, "Puppy Testing," *Akita World*, March/April 1988, pgs 84-86.

Fagen, Robert, "Horseplay & Monkey Shines," *Science*, December 1989, pgs 71-76.

Faser, Jacqueline, "Games Puppies Play," AKC *Gazette*, September 1989, pgs 18-20.

Furumoto, Howard H., "Frozen and Extended Semen," *The Ilio*, Hawaii's Dog News, Oct. & Nov., 1986.

Golden Retriever World, Summer 1991, "Overview of Breeding Services - International Canine Genetics, Inc.," pgs 6-7.

Grossman, Alvin, "The Basis of Heredity," *American Kennel Club Gazette*, April 1980.

Grossman, Alvin, "Color Inheritance," *The American Cocker Review*, March, April, May & June, 1974.

Grossman, Alvin, "Faults and Double Faults," *The American Cocker Review*, March 1980.

Grossman, Alvin, "Form Follows Function," *Akita World*, July/August 1986, pgs 64-68.

Grossman, Marge, "Evolution of the Cocker Head," *The American Cocker Review*, June 1961.

Grossman, Marge, "To the Victors," *The American Cocker Review*, August 1966.

Hane, Curtis B., "Training Your Dog, A Consumers Guide," *The Great Dane Reporter*, March/April 1987.

Harris, Kristy Reed, "Observations on Temperament," *Dog Week*, January 25, 1988, pgs 26-27.

Lawson, Deborah, "Heads & Tails," *Dog News*, 1990.

Lorimer, D.V.M., Dan W., "CERF and Hereditary Disease in Dogs," *Pet Focus*, Vol 3 No 1, pgs 3-6.

Madl, Janet, "A.I. with Extended Live Semen," AKC *Gazette*, March 1991, pgs 94-96.

Meritt, Jim, "Design of Life," *Modern Maturity*, June/July 1989, pgs 43-47.

Mohrman, R.K., "Supplementation — May be Hazardous to Your Pet's Health," *The Great Dane Reporter*, April 1980.

Schaeffer, Ruth C., "The View From Here, A Breeder's Report on Collecting Frozen Sperm," *American Kennel Club Gazette*, November 1982.

Spalding, Jane Cochran, "Building Attitude for the Show Ring," *Dog Week*, March 28, 1988, pg 44.

Sullivan, Diann, "Improving Conception Rates in Dogs Using Artificial Insemination," *Labrador Quarterly*, Fall 1991, pgs 8-27.

Wittels, Bruce R., "Nutrition of the Newly Born and Growing Individuals," *The Great Dane Reporter*, Jan/Feb 1985

Newspapers:

Marvin, Rub, "From Twisted Chains of DNA, Scientists Unravel the Genetic Codes for All Life, *The Oregonian*, 4/11/91.

Petit, Charles, "Gene Splicers to Try New Animals," *San Francisco Chronicle*, 5/26/87.

Thompson, Larry, "New Theory Suggests that Darwin had it Backward," *Science & Medicine*, editorial, *San Jose Mercury News*, May 24, 1984.

Books:

Benjamin, Carol L. *Mother Knows Best, The Natural Way to Train Your Dog*. New York:Howell Book House, 253 pgs., 1987.

Burnham, Patricia G., *Play Training Your Dog*. New York:St. Martin's Press, 1980.

Burns, Marsh A. & Fraser, Margaret N., *The Genetics of the Dog*. Farnham Royal Eng.:Commonwealth Agricultural Bureau, 1952.

Carlson, D.V.M., Delbert G., and Griffin, MD, James M., *Dog Owners Home Veterinary Handbook*, Howell Book House, Inc., 1980.

Collins, Donald R., D.V.M., *The Collins Guide to Dog Nutrition*. New York:Howell Book House, Inc., 1973.

Connett, Eugene V., *American Sporting Dogs*. D. Van Nostrand Co., Inc.

Craig, Ralph, *Elementary Spaniel Field Training*. New York:American Spaniel Club, 21 pgs., 1947.

Creager, Joan, Paul G. Jantzen & James L., *Mariner Biology*, MacMillan Publishing Co. New York, 1981, 961 pgs.

Daniels, Julie, *Enjoying Dog Agility - From Backyard to Competition*, Doral Publishing, Wilsonville, OR, 1991, 310 pgs.

Evans, Job M., *The Evans Guide for Counseling Dog Owners*, New York:Howell Book House, Inc., 1985.

Fox, Michael W., *The Behavior of Wolves, Dogs, & Related Canids*, New York, Harper & Row, 1970.

Fox, Michael W., *Understanding Your Dog*. New York:Coward, McCann & Geoghegan, 1972.

Gaines Dog Research Center, *Training the Hunting Dog*. General Foods Corporation, 15 pgs., 1973.

Greer, Frances, Editor, *A Century of Spaniels; Vols. I & II*. Amherst, Massachusetts:American Spaniel Club, 1980.

Grossman, Alvin, *The American Cocker Spaniel*, Doral Publishing, San Jose, CA 1989, 682 pgs.

Grossman, Alvin & Beverly Grossman, *Winning with Purebred Dogs - Design for Success*, Doral Publishing, Wilsonville, OR, 1991, 288 pgs.

Grossman, Alvin, *Breeding Better Cocker Spaniels*, Denlinger, Fairfax, VA, 1977, 144 pgs.

Holst, Phyllis A., *Canine Reproduction—A Breeder's Guide*. Loveland, Colorado:Alpine Publications, 1985.

Hutt, Fredrick, B., *Genetics for Dog Breeders*.San Francisco:W.H. Freeman & Co., 245 pgs., 1979.

International Canine Genetics, 271 Great Valley Parkway, Malvern PA 19355.

Little, C.C., *The Inheritance of Coat Color in Dogs*. New York:Howell Book House, Inc., 194 pgs., 1973.

McAuliffe, Sharon & McAuliffe, Kathleen, *Life for Sale*. New York:Coward, McCann & Geoghegan, 243 pgs., 1981.

Moffit, Ella B., *The Cocker Spaniel: Companion, Shooting Dog and Show Dog*. New York:Orange Judd Publishing Co., 335 pgs., 1949.

Monks of New Skete, *How to be Your Dog's Best Friend*, Little, Brown & Co., Boston, 1978, 202 pgs.

Onstott, Kyle, revised by Phillip Onstott, *The New Art of Breeding Better Dogs*, Howell Book House, Inc., 1962.

Paffenbenberger, Clarence, *The New Knowledge of Dog Behavior*, New York, Howell, 1963.

Sabella, Frank & Kalstone, Shirlee, *The Art of Handling Show Dogs*. Hollywood:B&E Publications, 140 pgs., 1980.

Scott, John Paul, *Animal Behavior*, University of Chicago Press, Chicago, 1958.

Smith, Anthony, *The Human Pedigree*. Philadelphia: J.B. Lippincott Co., 308 pgs., 1975.

Tayton, Mark (revised and updated by Silk, Sheila T.), *Successful Kennel Management, Fourth Edition*. Taylors, South Carolina: Beech Tree Publishing Co., 248 pgs., 1984.

Whitney, Leon F., D.V.M., *How to Breed Dogs*. New York:Orange Judd Co., 1947.

Whitney, Leon F., D.V.M., *This is the Cocker Spaniel*. New York:Orange Judd Co., 1947.

Winge, Dr. Ojvind, *Inheritance in Dogs*. Ithaca New York:Comstock Publishing Co., 1950.

Wolters, Richard A., *Game Dog*. New York:E.P. Dutton & Co., 201 pgs., 1983.

Wolters, Richard A., *Gun Dog*. New York: E.P. Dutton & Co., 150 pgs., 1961.

Index